SRI LANKA IN CHANGE AND CRISIS

Sri Lanka
In Change and Crisis

Edited by James Manor

ST. MARTIN'S PRESS
New York

© 1984 James Manor
All rights reserved. For information, write:
St. Martin's Press, Inc., 175 Fifth Avenue, New York, NY 10010
First published in the United States of America in 1984

Library of Congress Cataloging in Publication Data
    Main entry under title:

    Sri Lanka in change and crisis

    Includes index.
    1. Sri Lanka – Politics and government – 1978-
I. Manor, James.
DS489.84.S69 1984   954.9'303   84-15921

ISBN 0-312-75452-3

Printed in Great Britain

CONTENTS

ABBREVIATIONS

CP	Communist Party
CRM	Civil Rights Movement
CWC	Ceylon Workers Congress
JSS	Jatika Sevaka Sangamaya
JVP	Janatha Vimukthi Peramuna
LSSP	Lanka Sama Samaja Party
MEP	Mahajana Eksath Peramuna
NSSP	Nava Sama Samaja Party
SLFP	Sri Lanka Freedom Party
TC	Tamil Congress
TULF	Tamil United Liberation Front
UNP	United National Party

For
R.St.L.P. Deraniyagala
and
S. Nadesan, QC

Modern Sri Lanka: Provincial Divisions and Principal Towns

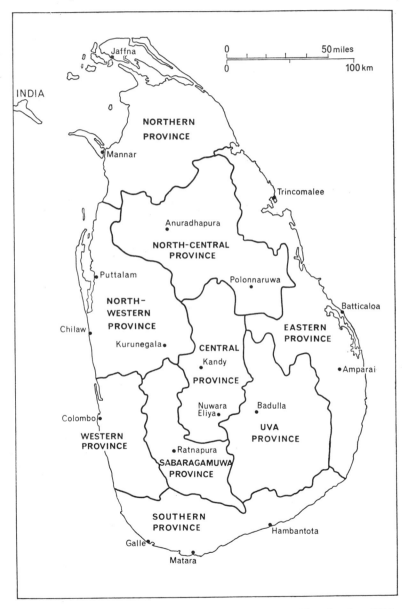

Source: A.J. Wilson, *Politics in Sri Lanka 1947–1973* (Macmillan, London, 1974).

1 INTRODUCTION

James Manor

In the year from August 1982 to August 1983, momentous changes occurred in Sri Lanka.[1] They unfolded in two phases. The first of these, which extended over the last five months of 1982, witnessed the first popular election of a powerful executive President under the Gaullist Constitution of 1978 and the subsequent decision by the ruling party not to hold the parliamentary election which was due by mid-1983. Instead the Constitution was amended to prolong the life of the existing Parliament, which was elected in 1977, until 1989. A referendum was held in December 1982 at which 54.66 per cent of those voting approved this course of action. This was certainly the most dramatic change in political practice in Sri Lanka since Independence in 1948. Many observers regard it, and the lawlessness and draconian treatment of the opposition which in their view attended it, as grave threats to democracy and to an open political order capable of arranging accommodation between antagonistic social groups, of which there is no shortage in Sri Lanka. Others argue that these measures were necessary, given the need to safeguard economic development and the existence of what they describe as a plot to overthrow the government. Both of these views are aired in this volume.

The second phase, during July and August of 1983, witnessed a gravely serious outbreak of violence which consisted almost entirely of attacks by members of the Sinhalese majority (71.0 per cent of the population) upon the Tamil minority (21.6 per cent). This was almost certainly the most severe spate of communal rioting in the island's history, surpassing similar episodes in 1958, 1977 and 1981. There are disputes about both its causes and its implications. Some believe that elements within the ruling party actively promoted violence, partly to destabilise their own government in order to enhance their position in a factional struggle for control, and partly to embitter relations between Sinhalese and Tamils in order to promote Sinhalese hegemony. The government maintains, however, that the riots were caused by violent separatist elements within the Tamil minority and by Marxists seeking to overthrow the regime and to

1

promote a general conflagration. Both of these views will be discussed in the second part of this book, which deals with the violence of mid-1983. The overriding purpose of this volume is to examine these two sets of events and to assess their implications for the survival of both a democratic political order and minimal social cohesion in Sri Lanka.

Sri Lanka is a comparatively small island nation, with a population of just over 15 million. But it has long aroused the interest of observers far beyond its shores because it has been the scene of a number of important political, social and economic experiments and problems. The first important experiment, which was the result of an historical accident[2] while Sri Lanka was a British colony, involved the people of the island in elections on the basis of universal suffrage a full twenty years before any other Asian or African colony/nation in the British Empire/Commonwealth experienced them. Legislatures were chosen by that means in 1931, 1936 and 1947.[3] After Independence in 1948, Sri Lanka developed a highly competitive, Westminster-style multi-party democracy with two major parties — the centre-right United National Party (UNP) and the centre-left Sri Lanka Freedom Party (SLFP) — alternating in power at six successive parliamentary elections between 1956 and 1977.[4] Over that period, the political system survived attempts at a military coup in 1962[5] and an insurrection by youthful leftists in 1971.

The second experiment was the provision, from the mid-1940s onwards, of a broad array of welfarist programmes. These included free education, extensive health care schemes and state subsidies on food, transport and other items. These initiatives contributed to achievements in areas such as literacy, infant mortality and life expectancy (see Table 1.1[6]) which greatly exceeded those of most developing nations and which compared very respectably with some countries in Europe, despite Sri Lanka's limited resources and the low level of *per capita* incomes.

Alongside these experiments and achievements, there existed two major problems which eventually gave rise to two further experiments under the present government which was elected in 1977. The first problem involved relations between the island's two main linguistic groups, the majority Sinhalese[7] and the minority Tamils. As we shall see presently, this is actually a complex *set* of problems since both linguistic groups can be subdivided on regional, religious and cultural grounds. But at this point, it is sufficient to say that in the

Table 1.1:   Vital Statistics and Literacy Rates

	Life expectancy 1960	1981	Infant mortalities within one year per 1,000 1960	1981	Adult literacy (%) 1960	1980
Sri Lanka	62	69	71	43	75	85
India	43	52	165	121	28	36
China	41	67	165	71	43	69
Brazil	55	64	118	75	61	76
Saudi Arabia	43	55	185	111	3	25
Portugal	63	72	82	26	63	78
Italy	69	74	44	14	91	98
Romania	65	71	77	29	89	98

mid-1950s a Sinhalese revivalist movement which had developed over several decades emerged forcefully onto the political stage. It had begun as a protest against Westernisation and the use in public institutions of the English language which was spoken by only a small elite minority of Sinhalese, and — since the Sinhalese are overwhelmingly Buddhists — about the advantageous position of Christians and Christian institutions and the neglect of Buddhism. Many of these anti-Western, pro-vernacular sentiments were shared by the predominantly Hindu Tamil minority. But during 1955 and 1956, the Sinhalese movement grew increasingly chauvinistic and acquired an anti-Tamil colouring which has remained its central feature ever since.

At the watershed general election of 1956, the centre-left SLFP defeated the UNP which had held power since Independence, mainly on the strength of the Sinhalese revival. In the intervening years, Sinhalese chauvinism has intermittently proved a major threat to social cohesion and national integrity, sparking major outbursts of anti-Tamil violence in 1958, 1977, 1981 and, most savagely, in 1983. The chauvinistic view of the Sinhalese majority as a 'nation', indeed as *the* nation, stands in clear contradiction to the concept of Sri Lanka as a modern, pluralistic nation-state. Politicians of both parties, when in office since 1956, have sought to minimise its impact by making concessions to the Sinhalese language and people and to Buddhism, while seeking to maintain open political institutions in an effort to find a *modus vivendi* within the Tamil minority. But many Sinhalese politicians in opposition — most of whom sought accommodation with the minority when in power — have seen Sinhalese chauvinism as a major political resource and have encouraged it as a means of regaining office. It has, therefore, not withered away over time as many had hoped. The Tamils, who have suffered increasingly as a result, have gradually become deeply alienated. Since the late 1970s, the main Tamil party, the Tamil United Liberation Front (TULF), has sought an autonomous Tamil state in the northern and eastern portions of the island where they form the largest social group. And violent acts carried out by a small but resilient force of Tamil separatist guerrillas have had a powerful impact on national politics. Since the ghastly anti-Tamil violence of mid-1983 — which was triggered by a guerrilla ambush in late July of 13 Sinhalese soldiers, all of whom died — the problem of national unity is more daunting than ever.

The second problem is the difficulty, amid conditions of scarcity, of keeping pace with the material needs and expectations of a rapidly growing population, particularly the young. This problem is in large part a product of the achievements of the welfarist programmes of successive governments. The impressively high life expectancy and low infant mortality rates, which were the result of successful health and education schemes and of subsidies on food, contributed to the doubling of the island's population between 1948 and 1981. The widespread provision of free education enabled many people of humble background to become literate and study at secondary and even tertiary levels. In the process they naturally developed high aspirations, often to white collar work, which the state and the economy were unable to satisfy. This came as a painful irony to those who had come of age in the immediate post-1956 period, when politicians often spoke glowingly of opportunities for the common man. With such a large portion of the island's scarce economic resources committed to welfarist measures and with governments between the 1950s and 1977 pursuing an economic strategy that involved hefty doses of state control and protectionism, the economy in that period achieved low growth rates. This further curtailed the resources available to meet popular aspirations. The dangers which this situation entailed were vividly demonstrated in 1971 when radicalised Sinhalese youths drawn largely from humble backgrounds mounted an insurrection against the centre-left government of Mrs Sirimavo Bandaranaike, which nearly succeeded.[8]

These two problems — maintaining national unity amid intense suspicion between Sinhalese and Tamils, and responding to the material needs and aspirations of a literate and rapidly growing population despite limited resources and economic stagnation —

gave rise to two major interrelated experiments by the government of J.R. Jayewardene after its election in 1977. The first was a substantial restructuring of the political system along Gaullist lines. The second was the radical liberalisation of the economy. Both experiments deserve extensive discussion, since they provide the immediate backdrop to the events of 1982 and 1983 which are the principal concern of this book. But before we turn to them, we need to look briefly at several topics which are fundamental to an understanding of these experiments and of recent events in Sri Lanka.

To comprehend some of what follows, readers need a brief introduction to the social groups that matter in Sri Lanka, and to the parts of the island that they inhabit. In providing these, we will for the sake of clarity simplify somewhat this very complex situation.[9] Let us begin with the main minority group, the Tamils, who account for 21.6 per cent of the island's population and who number over three million. They are subdivided, in the first instance, into 'estate Tamils' and 'Sri Lanka Tamils'. Estate Tamils reside overwhelmingly in the high hill country at the centre of the island (sometimes called the Kandyan areas), mostly in the Central Province (see Map 3.1, p. 61) where the tea estates on which most of them work as labourers are mainly located. They number 1.6 million and trace their origins to the mainly low caste people recruited from India to work the estates in the late nineteenth and early twentieth centuries. As Eric Meyer and Gananath Obeyesekere explain more fully in their articles in this book, the estate Tamils are separated by caste, culture, occupation, time of arrival and place of residence from the Sri Lanka Tamils most of whom live in the low coastal belt which rings the hill country. Many estate Tamils are either Indian citizens or stateless persons, in spite of the fact that over 400,000 of them have obtained Sri Lankan citizenship since the 1950s. This also tends to set them apart from Sri Lanka Tamils who are called that because, after several centuries of residence on the island, they are citizens of it. And, as C.R. de Silva's essay explains, estate Tamils also support a political party which is distinct from the Tamil United Liberation Front (TULF) to which many Sri Lanka Tamils give their loyalty.

Sri Lanka Tamils number around 1.65 million and can be found throughout the island, but they are concentrated in three areas: the Northern Province where they form an overwhelming majority, the Eastern Province where they are predominant in some areas (although the population of the entire province is divided roughly equally among Sri Lanka Tamils, Muslims and Sinhalese), and greater Colombo where over half a million of them comprise about one-sixth of the population. The last of these three groups and their fellows in other areas where the Sinhalese majority predominates are obviously more vulnerable than those in the north and east. They also tend to be less sympathetic to Tamil separatism and to the TULF.

The Sinhalese majority predominates everywhere except the Northern and Eastern Provinces, but, like the population as a whole, they are most densely concentrated along the western coastal belt from above Negombo down to Galle and particularly in the Western Province round greater Colombo. The Sinhalese are divided by a caste system, but since caste does not figure very prominently in this volume, it can be left to individual authors to explain its relevance to the events of 1982 and 1983.[10] Two other divisions within the Sinhalese community are worth discussing, however. The first is that between Low Country and Kandyan Sinhalese. These terms refer to the part of the island from which one's family originates. Low Country Sinhalese are from the lowland coastal belt around the entire island, but this usually means the strip along the western or southwestern coast. The island's coastal areas were ruled by the Portuguese, Dutch and British for over three centuries and, in the process, the Low Country Sinhalese became far more Westernised than residents of the hilly Kandyan areas at the centre of the island which remained autonomous until the British conquest in 1815. The lines and the differences between these two groups have become rather blurred over the last few decades, but the different images of the two still have some substance. The Kandyan Sinhalese are seen to be less urbanised, less at ease using English, more traditionalist and more solidly Buddhist since Christian conversions made less of an impact in the Kandyan region and since the headquarters of the two most important orders of Buddhist monks are located there. Many Kandyan Sinhalese have faced greater economic hardship than those in the Low Country because the development of tea estates in the hill country has left the Kandyan peasantry facing a severe shortage of land. There are roughly 6.3 million Low Country Sinhalese and 4.3 million Kandyan Sinhalese.

This brings us to the other division within the Sinhalese ranks and, at the same time, to another important minority group in Sri Lanka, the Christians. The Sinhalese and indeed the Tamils are divided between a large majority who follow the traditional faith — Buddhism for the Sinhalese and Hinduism for the Tamils — and a Christian minority. In his essay in this book, R.L. Stirrat deals at length with the Roman Catholics who form the overwhelming majority of Christians. So, at this point, it is sufficient to note that roughly four-fifths of the island's one million Christians are Sinhalese and one-fifth are Tamils. But since very few estate Tamils are Christian, Christians comprise a larger and more important minority among Sri Lanka Tamils than among the Sinhalese.

Two other minorities merit brief mention here. Sri Lanka has a small but significant Muslim population. They number just over a million and can be found in urban areas across most of the island, particularly in the four largest cities — Colombo, Kandy, Jaffna and Galle. But there is also a large Muslim population in the rural areas of the Eastern Province where they comprise one-third of the total population. A tiny minority among them, called 'Malays', live mainly in Colombo and the southern town of Hambantota and speak Malay or English. Most of the rest of the Muslims, who are called 'Moors', speak Tamil but are considered to be a community distinct from the 'Tamils'. Muslims who live in the Western and Southern Provinces, however, tend to speak Sinhalese.[11].

To clarify matters, Table 1.2 offers a breakdown[12] of the island's population.

Table 1.2: The Composition of Society

Social groups	% of total population	Approx. number
Sinhalese	71.0	10,650,000
Low Country Sinhalese	42.2	6,330,000
Kandyan Sinhalese	28.8	4,320,000
Tamils	21.6	3,240,000
Sri Lanka Tamils	11.0	1,650,000
Estate Tamils	10.6	1,590,000
Muslims	6.7	1,005,000
Others	0.7	105,000
Total	100.0	15,000,000

If we are to understand how relations between the Sinhalese majority and the Tamil minority have developed — some would say deteriorated — over the last three decades or so, it is necessary to look briefly at the world view or ideology of Sinhalese nationalists or chauvinists. This is dealt with more extensively elsewhere in this collection by Gananath Obeyesekere, R.L. Stirrat and Jonathan Spencer, but a few preliminary comments are essential here.[13] Central to this ideology is the belief that the Buddha selected Sri Lanka to be a citadel of Buddhism in its purest form, to be what is described elsewhere in this book as a *dhamma dipa*, island of the doctrine or the Buddhist *dharma*. The Sinhalese people were charged with the task of seeing that Sri Lanka becomes and remains such a citadel. Given this view, it is not surprising that non-Buddhists and (since almost all of the island's Buddhists are Sinhalese) non-Sinhalese are viewed by some people as polluting aliens who have no legitimate place in Sri Lanka. This ideology also makes much of the stories of ancient Sinhalese rulers who struggled against the Tamils, who have also resided on the island for centuries. Indeed, several politicians in recent decades have at times sought to cast themselves in that mould and to appear to promote what one scholar calls the 'reconquest' of the island from the Tamils.[14]

We have until now spoken of the Sinhalese 'people', but this word is insufficiently emphatic since in this ideology the Sinhalese are conceived of as a 'race' — a term and a concept which appears to have been borrowed from British rulers of the island in quite recent history. As we shall see in Obeyesekere's paper in this volume, there is a good deal of evidence to suggest that the Sinhalese are a far more heterogeneous group than the word 'race' implies. The ancestors of large numbers of people who now consider themselves to be Sinhalese clearly migrated from South India — a fact which casts doubt upon the notion that this 'race' is 'Aryan' (or North Indian) in origin. Many families living near the margins of Sinhalese- and Tamil-majority areas in Sri Lanka who now mainly speak Sinhalese, and who are therefore seen as members of this 'race', were mainly Tamil speakers only a generation ago.[15] And many Sinhalese leaders who speak often of their 'race' acknowledge non-Sinhalese forebears. The Bandaranaikes, for example, list a Tamil and a European in their family tree and President J.R. Jayewardene has spoken to this writer of his Muslim ancestors.[16] But despite all of this, the idea of the Sinhalese as a 'race' lives on and lends an assertive, abrasive quality to their dealings with minorities.

This idea also tends to take precedence over notions such as caste, class or region in the self-conception of most Sinhalese. In every region of South Asia, the term '*jati*' (or some variant of it) is used by people to mean 'our kind' or 'our ilk'. In India, *jati* usually refers mainly to one's caste or, more often, sub-caste. Among the Sinhalese, *jati* can refer to caste, but in most cases it refers principally to the Sinhalese linguistic group, conceived of as a 'race'. And although the Sinhalese are clearly a substantial majority on the island, they tend to see themselves as an endangered minority within the South Asian region, and their culture as threatened by hundreds of millions of Indians to the north. Sinhalese revivalists emphasise that while Hinduism and Tamil are sure to flourish in South India, Sinhalese is spoken and their brand of Buddhism is practised only in Sri Lanka. Therefore, in their view, the government has a responsibility to promote Buddhism and Sinhalese at the expense of minority religions and languages.

In the years since the late 1950s, the Sinhalese ideology has stood as a potent counter-ideology to the more cosmopolitan, secularist conception of Sri Lanka as a heterogeneous civil society. For a time, from the early 1960s to the early 1970s, it appeared that the latter view might prevail as the Sinhalese became preoccupied with economic issues,[17] and as their dominance of the political system made them feel less insecure than before 1956.[18] But this change did not take place. Mrs Bandaranaike's SLFP-led government between 1970 and 1977 responded to and in turn catalysed Sinhalese chauvinism by pursuing a number of policies which were patently discriminatory against Tamils, particularly in the field of education.

When Tamils in the north reacted angrily, her government — which, after the abortive insurrection of Sinhalese youths in 1971, turned increasingly to the use of force — sent substantial contingents of security forces into the north with orders to crack down. Since a state of emergency existed for several years after 1971, they had no difficulty in taking draconian action. The security forces were overwhelmingly Sinhalese and soon came to be perceived by the Tamils as a heavy-handed army of occupation. As a result the main Tamil party, the Federal Party, felt compelled to demand a Tamil state or *Eelam* and to change its name to the Tamil United Liberation Front (TULF). In the same period, groups of more radical young Tamils took arms, formed themselves into a separatist guerrilla organisation called the Tamil Liberation Tigers and indulged in violent attacks on the security forces. This was the perilous situation which greeted the UNP government of J.R. Jayewardene after its defeat of Mrs Bandaranaike's SLFP at the general election of 1977.

The first of the two experiments which Jayewardene's government undertook after 1977 in response to the problems of economic stagnation and communal discord was a major restructuring of the political system. This was achieved through the Constitution of 1978, modelled on that of the Fifth French Republic. It was the island's third since Independence, which replaced that enacted by Mrs Bandaranaike's government in 1972. At the time, it appeared to seek to balance libertarian and democratic provisions against the need for more forceful, authoritative leadership.[19] People concerned about civil liberties took heart from the fact that for the first time, several fundamental rights were entrenched in the Constitution and made justiciable before the Supreme Court. Certain changes, such as the prolongation of the lifetime of Parliament, could only be made if approved at a referendum. Tamil was made a 'national' language, and although Sinhalese remained the only 'official' language, provisions were made for the official use of Tamil in Tamil-majority areas. And stateless persons (estate Tamils in the main) were granted many (though not all) of the civil rights enjoyed by citizens. Its more illiberal provisions included making certain fundamental rights subject to restriction in the interests of the economy (particularly trade union rights) and national security. Parliament was empowered to pass retrospective legislation providing retrospective punishments against persons found guilty by a Presidential Commission of Enquiry.

The other two main innovations were (i) the creation of a strong executive presidency to which J.R. Jayewardene was soon elected by Parliament (although future Presidents would be popularly elected), and (ii) the introduction of proportional representation for parliamentary and local elections. At first sight this second provision appeared to be an attempt to make the Constitution safe from major changes and to signal a desire by the new government to put an end to the manipulation of the Constitution for partisan advantage, which they alleged to be a favourite ploy of Mrs Bandaranaike's pre-1977 government. This seemed to be the case because under proportional representation, it would be virtually impossible at future elections for any party to obtain a majority of more than 60 per cent in Parliament, and to amend the Constitution, a two-thirds majority was required.

It was not long, however, before doubts about the government's desire to be evenhanded arose in the minds of some observers. The very manner in which the Constitution was passed caused concern. In early 1978, Mrs Bandaranaike was persuaded to join a Parliamentary Select Committee to 'revise' the 1972 Constitution. It was not until May of that year that it was announced that the Committee's purpose was to draw up an entirely new Constitution, a course of action of which she disapproved. She felt duped and heatedly resigned from the Committee.[20] This manoeuvre by the ruling party seemed to many an attempt to insult Mrs Bandaranaike and this undermined bipartisan trust in the new Constitution. In that same period, heckling from the government benches sometimes prevented Mrs Bandaranaike from speaking in Parliament and, in 1980, after being found guilty of 'abuse of power' during her premiership by a Presidential Commission with retrospective powers, she was stripped of her civic rights for a period of seven years. In order to accomplish that, the government had used its greater-than-two-thirds majority in Parliament to pass an Amendment to the Constitution overruling a court decision that the Presidential Commission's Enquiry was *ultra vires*. This appeared to intrude upon the independence of the judiciary and — along with a second Amendment that seemed prompted by the desire of two MPs to defect to the ruling party — gave some people the impression that the Jayewardene government was prepared to turn the Constitution into a partisan instrument. As several essays in the first half of this book suggest, subsequent Amendments, and above all the Fourth Amendment in 1982 prolonging the life of the first Parliament by six years, reinforced this view in many minds. This impression gained further credence from the widespread allegations that some MPs of the ruling party were indulging in extremely aggressive and even lawless behaviour — for which Jayewardene had bitterly criticised Mrs Bandaranaike's followers when they held power before 1977.

It is important to emphasise that some features of the new Constitution of 1978 and certain other government initiatives clearly amounted to an overture to the Tamil minority. This contained three basic elements, one of which — the entrenchment of certain fundamental rights and the constitutional recognition of Tamil — has already been noted. The second element was contained in the Constitution's new electoral rules which were intended to make Tamil votes actually *count* in national elections. Until 1978, Tamils in the areas[21] where they form the majority had chosen a handful of MPs who played a distinctly marginal role in a Parliament dominated by one of the two major Sinhalese parties.

By basing parliamentary elections on proportional representation (see the essays in this volume by C.R. de Silva and, especially, by Robert Oberst), the 1978 Constitution ensured that the major parties could not enjoy the overwhelming numerical predominance in Parliament which had accrued to them under the old first-past-the-post system. This appeared to raise the possibility that Tamil MPs might on occasion hold the balance of power — although Robert Oberst's calculations in this book raise doubts about that. More crucially, the new Constitution decreed that the great prize in the political system — the powerful presidency — would go to the person who obtained a majority of votes from the *entire* electorate. Since Tamil votes might prove crucial in this, indeed since a candidate with support from most Tamils and a minority of Sinhalese might defeat an opponent backed by the majority of Sinhalese, the new system offered Sinhalese politicians of both major parties clear-cut incentives to refrain from their customary Tamil-bashing.

The third main element of the Jayewardene government's overture to the Tamils was not contained in the Constitution. This was the promise that Development Councils would be created in every district (county) on the island. Councils would have substantial powers, and most of their members would be popularly elected. This proposal went some way towards conceding the demand of the Tamil-majority areas for greater autonomy. (It might also be argued that the radical liberalisation of the economy after 1977 was a further concession to the Tamils, since it implied free competition in the market and a decline in state power — power which had often been used to aid Sinhalese at Tamils' expense.)

By late 1982, however, many observers — especially Tamils — had concluded that in practice these three initiatives came to very little. Sinhalese chauvinists in the government and the ruling party had thwarted attempts to enlarge dramatically the official use of Tamil. They had also seen to it that District Development Councils had far less autonomy from the central government than Tamils had hoped. Tamils were further embittered by the harsh and undisciplined behaviour of the overwhelmingly Sinhalese security forces in Tamil areas, particularly in Jaffna District. This not infrequently took the form of rioting, murder or lawless acts which were designed to insult the Tamils. In 1981, after a scuffle at a fairground in Jaffna involving off-duty policemen, police rioted and killed several Tamils. In 1981, security forces again rioted in reaction to violent attacks by Tamil Tigers and burned the Jaffna Public Library, which contained manuscripts precious to the Tamil community. Very reliable allegations of the torture and rape of Tamils by the security forces in the Northen Province persisted through 1982 and early 1983, as did further incidents such as the destruction in 1983 of a statue of a Tamil hero in Jaffna by an unidentified gang (widely suspected of being off-duty policemen). The main Tamil party, alienated by such incidents, decided to boycott the presidential election in October 1982. This meant that one of the changes in the electoral rules, which was intended to draw Tamils more fully into the political process, had little impact. When the Jayewardene government then decided to prolong the life of the existing Parliament by six years, the other change which was in part intended as a concession to Tamils — proportional representation in parliamentary elections — was nullified.

Government spokesmen stress that they were forced to move slowly and cautiously in bestowing powers on District Councils and in enlarging the scope for the use of Tamil by the need to proceed with care and deliberation in making major political changes and by the practicalities of politics in Sri Lanka — most especially the strong reservations among many Sinhalese about concessions to Tamils. They also argue, as does Lalith Athulathmudali's essay in this volume, that there were compelling reasons for prolonging the life of the sitting Parliament by six years. None the less, many Tamils concluded that the government's first major experiment since 1977 — the restructuring of the political system — had not succeeded in easing their alienation from the Sinhalese majority and from the prevailing political order.

The second major experiment after 1977 was the Jayewardene government's radically changed economic strategy. It is often equated with that pursued earlier by Singapore, but that is a somewhat misleading oversimplification. It is true that the Sri Lankan economy was opened up to tourism and to foreign imports and investments, and that an Industrial Promotion Zone (sometimes called an Export Promotion Zone or Free Trade Zone) with huge incentives to industrialists was created in the hope that industries might spring up using cheap Sri Lankan labour to produce goods for export. A major devaluation of the rupee and substantial cuts in state subsidies were designed to assist in this process. But this side of the government's strategy was considerably less important than the main thrust which was to seek a revival of agriculture in order to reduce or eliminate very costly imports of food, especially rice. It was argued that if the island could become fully or nearly self-sufficient in food, then earnings from industrial exports, tourism, remittances from Sri Lankans working abroad (mainly in the Middle East) and traditional exports — particularly tea — would place it on a sound economic footing. It is somewhat ironic that the two things which made advisers from conservative agencies like the International Monetary Fund optimistic about the prospects for a revival of agriculture were the high literacy among rural dwellers, which was the result of decades of welfarism, and the relatively equitable distribution of land which was the result of the land reforms of Mrs Bandaranaike's centre-left government between 1970 and 1977. These pre-conditions plus realistic market prices for produce and the massive river projects which were eventually to provide cheap hydro-electric power and, crucially, irrigation for 750,000 acres of dry land were intended to raise food production dramatically. The hydro-electric power would also help to reduce oil imports which in 1980 represented nearly 22 per cent of import values.[22]

The story of the Sri Lankan economy since 1977 and of the impact of these changes upon society is far too complex to be dealt with exhaustively here, but several things are worth noting briefly. They add up to a rather mixed record. On the positive side, it should first be said that considerable progress has been made in food production, despite the fact that a substantial portion of the improvements in irrigation from the river valley schemes were still to materialise. Agricultural incomes rose in many areas, although producers of chillies and onions in the mainly Tamil Northern Province suffered from foreign competition. The food import bill — particularly for rice — has been considerably reduced and agriculture, which had been nearly stagnant, has undergone something of a revival.

It is also true that between 1978 and 1983, tourism was booming. This provided major earnings of foreign currency and many badly-needed jobs. As C.R. de Silva has noted in his contribution to this book, around 60,000 Sri Lankans found jobs in the Middle East which further eased the serious unemployment problem and brought a large volume of remittances back to the island. Firms both in the Industrial Promotion Zone and outside made headway and the growth of real Gross Domestic Product accelerated dramatically to 8.2 per cent in 1978 and 6.3 per cent in 1979.[23] In early 1980, the government raised taxes and the controlled prices of certain essential commodities and cut public investment in an effort to reduce public deficits at a time when world prices for Sri Lanka's exports were unfavourable.[24] In the period thereafter several factors — the fear of inflation (which at its height in 1979—80 was running at 40 per cent or higher), pressure from the IMF and a determination not to let the economy become overextended in the manner of 1978—9 — have combined to impose greater restraint on the government. As a result, the real growth of GDP slipped to 5.8 per cent per year in 1980 and 1981, since when it has remained at these more modest but still impressive levels — when compared to the figure of around 3 per cent per year between 1960 and 1977.[25]

On the debit side, the Industrial Promotion Zone proved to be something of a disappointment: it turned out to be exceedingly difficult to attract major foreign firms, for several reasons. The basic infrastructure (facilities and services) in the Zone was seen by some firms as inadequate. Sri Lanka also faced competition from free trade zones in more autocratic Third World countries where future elections were unlikely to occur. As a result, trade union assertiveness seemed less likely in those countries and there was little danger of an election bringing a more left-leaning regime to power. On both counts, multinationals preferred Sri Lanka's competitors. It is also arguable that by the late 1970s and early 1980s, it was too late to 'do a Singapore' — that is, to achieve an economic breakthrough on the basis of cheap labour — because of technological change. Major international firms were now less interested in labour-consuming industries than in robotics and machine-based factories. Thus, despite a decision by Motorola to build a large semiconductor plant in Sri Lanka's Industrial Promotion Zone, industries such as small-scale garment manufacturers were the norm in the Zone. And given the recession in the industrialised nations, such firms encountered crippling tariff barriers in the Western countries which were their biggest potential markets.

Nor is there any doubt that poorer people, especially in or near urban areas, suffered as a result of cuts in state subsidies and the inflation which was particularly serious in 1979 and 1980. Officials in private non-profit agencies that existed to promote self-help programmes among the poor found that there was considerable desperation and near-starvation among disadvantaged urban dwellers. As a result, the agencies were forced in some cases to forego self-help schemes and provide hand-outs merely to sustain people.[26] Nor was it only the poor who suffered.

The large salaried middle classes — particularly, but not exclusively those employed by the state — faced severe hardship in this period as inflation outstripped pay increases. At least as serious was the disruption that overtook the urban status hierarchy within which white collar employees of the state and state-owned enterprises lived their lives.

One of the most striking things about twentieth-century Sri Lanka is the intense preoccupation of many of its people — particularly urbanised Sinhalese — with status. They surpass even their counterparts in India in this regard, partly as a result of the nature of the Sinhalese caste system.[27] In the period up to 1977, many Sinhalese families made great sacrifices to ensure that their children obtained positions in the salaried middle classes, particularly in government jobs, since this offered both security and status. In those years, the status hierarchy in the urban sector — though rather muddled — never underwent sudden or radical change. However, the new economic policies after 1977 changed that. In a very short time, menial workers in booming sectors like tourism found themselves better off than leading groups in the old status hierarchy. A watchman outside a leading hotel earned more than the Inspector-General of Police, and a waiter in its restaurant earned more than a leading civil servant in a government department. The salaried middle classes soon felt themselves to be shorn of much of their former status, and this made their economic distress as a result of inflation all the more painful to bear. The extreme reactions of urban Sinhalese facing less serious status problems have been ably documented.[28] It is arguable that this disruption of the status hierarchy plus the economic difficulties which — as Gananath Obeyesekere shows in his essay in this book — drove urban lumpen elements into organised law-breaking that created an atmosphere of disorder and decay in urban areas, contributed to an atmosphere that abetted the anti-Tamil violence of mid-1983.

The liberalising of the economy also contributed to suspicions (or perhaps the word is fantasies) in the minds of some Sinhalese about minorities — notably the Tamils, the Muslims and expatriate Indians. Under the new free market system, it was far less possible for the government to intervene on behalf of Sinhalese than it had been before 1977 when the state controlled so much of economic life. Many Sinhalese prospered under the post-1977 liberalisation, but this was often overlooked by Sinhalese chauvinists who were preoccupied with the success that some Tamils, Muslims and Indians enjoyed. Despite the fact that many Sinhalese found employment in the Middle East, the notion that Muslims were the main beneficiaries of opportunities there appears to have fuelled serious

Sinhalese – Muslim clashes in Batticaloa and Galle — the first such incidents since 1915.

The new economic strategy also generated resentment among more traditionalist and puritanical Sinhalese who were offended by the influx of foreign films, music and consumer goods, some of which were seen to be risqué, and by what they regarded as the decadent aspects of the tourist trade. These things seemed all the more offensive in the light of the Jayewardene government's widely-advertised promise to create a *dharmista* (righteous, virtuous) society. These traditionalists were by no means all Sinhalese chauvinists. But their exasperation added to the general sense of unease in urban society and in some cases their resentments found an irrational outlet in the anti-Tamil violence of mid-1983, which in turn did serious damage to the economy. At least 70 factories were destroyed in greater Colombo alone,[29] putting tens of thousands at least temporarily out of work, and confidence overseas was gravely undermined with potentially dire implications for foreign investment and tourism.

This brings us to the events which are our central concern here. This book is divided into two parts, the first dealing with the presidential election and referendum of late 1982, and the second with the violence of mid-1983.[30] A brief survey of each should help to identify the major themes, issues and disagreements which emerge in this collection.

C.R. de Silva opens Part One by providing a general overview of events from the adoption of the Third Amendment to the Constitution in August 1982 which permitted the President to seek early re-election, to the presidential election on 20 October and the referendum on 22 December on the Fourth Amendment which prolonged the life of the Parliament elected in 1977 until 1989. In his view, the presidential election was conducted in a reasonably fair manner, although he notes that the most prominent opposition leader, Mrs Bandaranaike, was unable to stand or participate because she had been deprived of her civic rights until 1987 and that the press (most of which has been state-controlled since before the present government took office) was heavily biased in favour of the incumbent. He argues that the government's economic strategy was the crucial issue in the election, although he believes that Jayewardene also profited from divisions within the opposition, the advantages of incumbency and his own forceful personality. This is followed by an assessment of the impact of the result upon the opposition and upon politics in general.

De Silva then turns to the decision to abandon parliamentary elections and to hold the referendum. In his view, this was mainly the result of the desire òf the ruling party to maintain their five-sixths majority in Parliament which enabled them to alter the Constitution at will. He is sceptical of the government's claim that this was necessary to deal with a plot by leftists to assassinate the President and others, for which little evidence was advanced, then or since.[31] He is somewhat critical of the conduct of the referendum, but he stops well short of the scorching indictment which 'Priya Samarakone' mounts later in Part One. De Silva reports the detention of various opposition organisers for various periods during the referendum campaign, the sealing of some opposition presses and the use of force in some areas to intimidate the opposition. But he argues that the unity which the opposition achieved and the re-issuing of some long defunct opposition newspapers partly compensated for these things.

His principal concern is with the implications rather than the conduct of the referendum. He sets out the objections of those who see it as an inadequate substitute for a parliamentary general election. He then notes the dangers inherent in excluding radical elements from Parliament which was one result of the 'yes' vote at the referendum. He sees three things — the use of force during the campaign, the ruling party's tendency to modify the Constitution for short-term partisan advantage (which is made possible over a further six years by the referendum result) and the immense power which President Jayewardene appeared to possess at the end of 1982 — as elements of a trend that arouses anxiety about the survival of the substance and not merely the forms of democracy in Sri Lanka.

M.P. Moore's essay analyses changes in voting behaviour in Sri Lanka between the 1977 parliamentary elections, the 1982 presidential election and the referendum in the same year. In his view, the evidence strongly suggests that ethnic group identification was the main cause of the shifts in the voting over these three elections. His specific contention — which has major implications for the discussion of communal violence in Part Two of this volume — is that President Jayewardene and the ruling UNP 'suffered a relative *loss* of support from Sinhalese Buddhists' between 1977 and the presidential election of 1982 'and became more dependent on the support of the ethnic minorities'. This is to say that despite Jayewardene's inability to deliver fully on the three initiatives to overcome Tamil alienation which were outlined earlier, many minority voters took heart from his efforts and when they saw leaders in the opposition SLFP show sympathy to Sinhalese chauvinist demands during the presidential campaign, they turned to Jayewardene as a more reliable guardian of their interests.

The one minority group which did not conform to this pattern was the Sri Lanka Tamils of the Northern Province where the government's security forces had been in abrasive conflict with Tamil separatists, especially since mid-1979. This indicates that polarisation had developed between Sri Lanka Tamils in the north and their fellows elsewhere in the island. Moore's findings suggest a painful, indeed a deeply tragic irony if some commentators (like Gananath Obeyesekere in Part Two) are correct in arguing that certain elements within the ruling UNP were responsible for some of the attacks on Tamils during the violence of mid-1983. It means that members of the UNP made organised attacks on their party's own supporters, people who had backed the UNP mainly because it seemed to offer *protection*.

Rather surprisingly, Moore found as much variation in voting patterns between the two 1982 elections as between 1977 and the presidential election of 1982. In another essay in this book, 'Priya Samarakone' argues that the change between October and December 1982 was the result of large-scale intimidation of opposition voters and impersonation by government supporters at the referendum. Moore offers a rather different view, although their two interpretations are not necessarily inconsistent with one another. He points to strong correlations (i) between gains by the ruling party and areas in which the centre-left SLFP has traditionally been strong, and (ii) between losses by the ruling party and areas in which the parties of the Marxist left have traditionally flourished. It is possible that both explanations are correct since any attempts at intimidation might make greater headway against the relatively 'soft' SLFP organisation than against the 'hard' structure of the Marxist parties.[32] It should also be stressed that both authors' conclusions emerge logically from the nature of their sources — Moore's being aggregate election data and Samarakone's being case studies of events in many specific electorates.

Lalith Athulathmudali defends the record of the government in which he has played prominent role since 1977 and the decision to prolong the life of the existing Parliament by six years. He stresses the importance of economic liberalisation which, he argues, achieved great popularity by creating jobs, providing new wealth to many and making consumer goods widely available. He sees this and the personal popularity of President Jayewardene as responsible for the victory at the presidential election.

The government preferred a referendum on the extension of the life of the sitting Parliament to a full-scale parliamentary election because of 'a pervasive fear of an anti-democratic "Naxalite" type of movement' and because 'fruitless delays and expenditure would be extremely harmful' to the drive for economic growth. The referendum also made it possible to avoid 'a crisis in the country as well as in the Constitution' which would have arisen if 'the President was of one party and the Parliament of another'. Athulathmudali also shows how often other nations have used referendums to consult the electorate. He stresses that Sri Lanka's voters were given an opportunity to pass judgement on the six-year extension of the life of this Parliament, whereas the decision of Mrs Bandaranaike's government in 1972 to extend the previous Parliament's term by two years was not put to the people. He argues that the referendum conformed fully to the principles and methods of democratic elections so that, for example, the ban preventing the former premier, Mrs Bandaranaike, from participating in elections did not extend to referendum campaigns and she took to the hustings. Athulathmudali argues that people had 'the same freedom and secrecy laws, the same rights to campaign' as are normally available in any democratic election anywhere.

'Priya Samarakone' takes a radically different view of the referendum. The need to protect a stable democracy from leftist subversions was used to justify a diminution of the democratic process, and in the author's view, this was outrageous. Matters were made worse by the government's failure to produce solid evidence of a plot by assassins and/or insurrectionaries. Samarakone's main attack, however, is on the conduct of rather than the justifications for the referendum. Among the actions which come in for criticism are the continuation of the state of emergency through the campaign and polling day, a massive effort to display pictures of the 'lamp' — the symbol on the ballot indicating a 'yes' vote at the referendum — which was illegal, and the harassment and in many cases the detention of key opposition personnel. On this last issue, this essay stands in clear contradiction to the one wich precedes it. Samarakone also advances evidence of the seizure by police raid of vital documents in the main opposition party's headquarters, police denials of permits for opposition rallies, attacks by toughs on meetings that were attempted, the sealing of opposition presses, the heavy bias of the state-controlled newspapers, radio, television and film units, and the hounding of civil servants who had been evenhanded during the presidential campaign.

The main thrust of this essay is its argument that opposition voters, organisers and polling station observers were threatened, physically intimidated, robbed or jailed on false complaints both during the canvassing and on polling day. Samarakone also writes that widespread impersonation occurred, either after opposition voters were robbed of polling cards or with the co-operation — often achieved under duress — of officials at polling booths. The author then examines the curious swings in pro-government votes between the presidential election and the referendum, and suggests (as we noted in our comments on Moore's essay) that intimidation and impersonation were responsible for many of them. Samarakone then asks whether the 'yes' vote in the referendum was a genuine expression of the popular will and whether there is some connection between the use of thuggery during the referendum campaign and the anti-Tamil violence of mid-1983.

Robert Oberst completes Part One of this book with an analysis of the logic and implications of the new system of proportional representation for parliamentary elections. This may at first glance appear to be a pointlessly hypothetical exercise, but despite the abandonment of parliamentary elections in 1982, the system remains in force for future occasions. More crucially, the implications of the new system of proportional representation probably figured very prominently in the government's decision to seek to avoid its use and to prolong the life of the sitting Parliament. Oberst concludes that although this particular system of proportional representation will be more equitable in distributing seats than the old Westminster-type system, it is not as equitable as more commonly used systems of proportional representation. It would tend to create a two-party system in the Sinhalese areas, and smaller parties of the left like the Communist Party or the Lanka Sama Samaja Party would probably never be a force unless they formally *united* with the large centre-left Sri Lanka Freedom Party. Since the chronic divisions on the left make such a union under a single label exceedingly unlikely, the leftists (including the newly emergent Janatha Vimukthi Peramuna) have much to lose under the new system.

But Oberst's most startling conclusion is that unless such a formal union occurred, Mrs Bandaranaike's Sri Lanka Freedom Party would itself have little hope of winning power. In other words, the new system of proportional representation comes close to ensuring that Jayewardene's United National Party will — on past performance — remain permanently in power. It is virtually certain that if a parliamentary election had been held in late 1982 the ruling party would have been returned to power, given the serious divisions among opposition parties, but with a reduced majority. This implies that the decision to prolong the life of the 1977 Parliament until 1989 was intended to preserve both the hegemony of the ruling party and, more specifically, their greater-than-two-thirds majority which enabled them to alter the Constitution at will.

Part Two deals with the violence of July and August 1983, in which at least several hundred people[33] — almost all of whom were Tamils — were killed, many tens of thousands driven into hiding or to refugee camps and a vast number of Tamil homes and businesses were looted and burned. In several areas, members and even units of the security forces led or abetted the rioting and much of the violence (particularly in greater Colombo) seemed more carefully organised than on earlier occasions. A large number of killings were performed in particularly gruesome, sadistic fashion and corpses were often mutilated or burned. On successive days, 35 and then 17 Tamil prisoners in the Welikada Jail were massacred by Sinhalese inmates and, according to some accounts, by prison staff as well.[34] For the first time, Tamils of the commercial and professional classes of Colombo — an important source of Tamil moderates — were attacked, quite systematically. Many observers fear that the violence of 1983, coming after similar eruptions in 1958, 1977 and 1981, has dashed any hope that ways can be found to sustain a minimally workable plural society in Sri Lanka.

The first of the contributors to Part Two — all of whom were present on the island during the troubles — is Eric Meyer who provides a general introduction to the violence. He begins with a review of the first half of 1983 in which lawlessness, that in his view followed logically upon trickery and violence during the referendum campaign, increased and in which Sinhalese – Tamil tensions rose.[35] He then carries us through the attack by Tamil guerrillas on a Sinhalese army patrol and the days of anti-Tamil rioting which followed. He pays particular attention to the surprising three-day delay during the first intense phase of the rioting before the President and his ministers addressed the nation, and to the pro-Sinhalese tenor of their remarks when they did speak. This stands in stark contrast to the President's early speech during the violence of 1977, when he reminded the nation that some of his own relatives are Tamils. Meyer then considers the two main theories about how the violence occurred: the government's argument that three leftist parties were responsible and the claim of other commentators that a section of the ruling party itself organised attacks. He finds much of the government's theory implausible, but does not rule it out entirely. He regards the second hypothesis as more persuasive, particularly the idea — which is not shared by several contributors to Part One — that President Jayewardene was a good deal less powerful than he appeared to be since he could not control chauvinistic forces in his own party. Meyer then turns to the demoralised and ill-disciplined armed forces. He believes that their role in the crisis was decisive and that their adventurism may present serious problems in the future. The latter half of his essay analyses the roots both of Tamil extremism and of Sinhalese chauvinism. After an assessment of the impact of the new economic liberalism upon communal relations, he surveys the prospects for rebuilding consensus and understanding.

Gananath Obeyesekere presents an extended discussion of the historical, cultural and religious origins of the inter-communal conflict. He then examines the increase in and the institutionalisation of political violence under both major parties since the 1960s, but particularly under the present government. He voices special concern about politicians' use of thugs, their manipulation of the police and the development of a trade union under the auspices of the ruling party in recent years which in his view rendered these practices systematic. He then discusses a recent reworking of the Sinhalese chauvinist ideology by a member of the present government who has close ties with this trade union. Obeyesekere reviews a number of incidents from recent years in which the government or its supporters engaged in lawless or intimidatory action. In his view, the most serious of these was the government's flouting of Supreme Court decisions, a development which suggests that the very structure of the state is being altered by the forces of chauvinism. He offers a scathing critique of the government's explanation for the violence of 1983 and ends with a pessimistic assessment of the general outlook for Sri Lanka and of President Jayewardene's capacity to reverse the process of deterioration.

Elizabeth Nissan reports the reactions of Sinhalese people in the city of Anuradhapura to news of the rioting and then considers these alongside the justifications for the violence which were offered in speeches by leading government figures during the troubles. These justifications were anchored in a Sinhalese identity that asserts the majority's 'natural' right to ascendancy in the island. Since Tamils were seen to have challenged this right, they were held responsible for the suffering which they themselves underwent as a result of Sinhalese attacks.[36] Government ministers stressed the forbearance shown by many Sinhalese in the face of the Tamil threat to national unity, and tended to emphasise the difficulties which Sinhalese experienced as a result of the disorders, often without acknowledgement of the Tamils' plight. The troubles were also depicted as the outcome of a plot by Tamils and Marxist extremists to bring down not only the Sinhalese 'race', but the existing political order and open economy too. And yet by assuring the nation that the government would protect the Sinhalese, ministers appealed to the same chauvinism which they accused Marxists of manipulating. Nissan then argues that the official explanation of events leads logically on to more extreme conclusions: that any Tamil might be a terrorist; that therefore Tamils should be seen as threats to the state and the majority 'race'; and eventually that people who dissented from the government's outlook should also be seen in that way. Nissan fears that the tendency to see dissent or any opposition activity as inherently anti-state and anti-Sinhalese may prepare the ground for increasing political repression.

Here and in Obeyesekere's concern that Sinhalese chauvinism may be altering the character of the state, we see possible links between the crisis of the liberal political order and the problem of communal conflict in Sri Lanka. 'Priya Samarakone' argued in Part One that the lawbreaking and use of intimidation by the ruling party during the referendum may have opened the way to anti-Tamil violence in mid-1983. Now Nissan and Obeyesekere are suggesting that the violence in turn produced a further erosion of democratic norms. Taken together, their findings imply that the two things feed off of one another and interact to produce a rising spiral of lawlessness and bigotry.

Jonathan Spencer presents a chilling examination of the mood of Sinhalese people before the troubles erupted and their perceptions of it once it began. He writes from the perspective of a rather remote village on the southern edge of the central highlands where he had lived for over a year. He argues that the most horrific incidents of 1983, the various massacres of Tamils, can only be understood against the background of the popular fears that prevailed among ordinary Sinhalese in the months prior to the violence. He shows that slanted reports in the Sinhalese press led villagers to conclude that Sinhalese attacks on Tamils in Trincomalee during March 1982 were the work of Tamil terrorists. But he is quick to add that these misconceptions may be less the result of newspaper stories than of stereotypes and the rumours that made the rounds in rural areas. People tended to perceive Tamils as 'inherently violent and dangerous', prone to acts of savagery. Thus when reports of rioting began to come in, villagers quickly assumed that Tamils were the main perpetrators and that at least half of the people in refugee camps were Sinhalese. Tamils came to be regarded, especially after the emergence of the separatist Tigers, as 'blessed with superhuman cunning'. People tended to see Tigers everywhere and to conclude that Tamils who struggled during the riots to defend their property were — by reason of their aggressive behaviour — terrorists. It was in these circumstances that several massacres took place. This reached its insanely logical conclusion when the struggle of a Sinhalese man in a Colombo market to prevent his watch being stolen was taken as proof that he was a Tamil terrorist, so that he was murdered. Spencer believes that the claims by apologists for the violence that most of those killed were terrorists have generated new and more dangerous myths which can be drawn upon for more extreme action against the minority the next time round. This could be seen as further evidence of the upward spiral of which we just spoke.

The last two contributions weigh the implications of the violence for two minority groups and find that Tamil – Sinhalese distrust is a more desperate problem than ever. R.L. Stirrat considers the Roman Catholic community which is especially interesting since it contains within its ranks large numbers of Sinhalese and Tamils. He finds that over the last century, ethnicity has replaced religion as the main division in the island's society, to the point where in 1983, Sinhalese Catholics attacked their Tamil co-religionists. He gives special attention to the years since 1956, the period in which Sinhalese – Tamil conflict has quickened and in which the Church has sought to indigenise itself after Vatican II. This latter change has led to quarrels between Tamil and Sinhalese Catholics over the language of worship in mixed churches. And, as Sinhalese Catholics have sought to accommodate themselves to the Buddhists and successive governments — both of which have tended towards Sinhalese chauvinism — Tamil Catholics have become exasperated. Things had deteriorated so much during the 1970s that some priests in the north, imbibing 'liberation theology', showed sympathy for Tamil guerrillas which of course led to further polarisation. During the riots of 1983, some churches used by Tamils were attacked, Catholic agencies that assisted Tamils came under pressure from Sinhalese and a nun who was assaulted by a crowd looking for Tamil priests later died. And yet because Sinhalese Catholics feared that they might be the next target of rioters, some of their formal statements tended to soft-pedal criticism of anti-Tamil violence. This has caused profound alienation between Catholics of the two linguistic groups, so that the Church which might have provided a bridge has instead come to indicate the depths of the divisions in the island's society.

The final essay by R.P. Slater looks at Tamils in the mainly Sinhalese hill country in the wake of the violence. Despite the outward appearance of normality, he finds these people deeply traumatised and much changed in their relations to the Sinhalese around them. Many small shopkeepers whose businesses were wrecked have taken their insurance money and departed. Those who remain appear to be operating normally but have moved their families and liquid assets out. They buy in one day's stock at a time and maintain only a very tenuous link with their locality. In both cases, Sinhalese rivals are taking advantage of the situation. Larger businessmen are reopening, but are taking the precaution of finding Sinhalese partners. Tamil public employees have largely returned to their posts but feel insecure. They are demoralised and lonely without the support of evacuated families. Tamil estate labourers are seeking transfers to safer places higher in the hills or to jobs in the Tamil north or abroad. The appearance of a rapid return to normality is distinctly misleading, for most Tamils believe that the violence of 1983 changed things fundamentally, probably irreversibly.

It should be clear by now that our aim in this collection is not to achieve unanimity, but to approach recent events in Sri Lanka from a diversity of viewpoints. Some of these essays are critical of the present government in Sri Lanka, but there are marked variations in the degree and nature of those criticisms and one paper offers a straightforward defence of the government. There are also disagreements on several other matters. It is hardly appropriate at this point for the editor to impose his own interpretation[37] upon this material. Instead, let us draw together several of the strands of the story by posing three interrelated sets of questions that may help to focus the discussion which follows.

First, it is probably obvious that Sri Lanka — now more than ever — needs political structures that are durable, democratic, broadly accepted and capable of arranging accommodations between conflicting social groups. But we might ask whether recent constitutional changes, the elections of 1982 and the violence of 1983 have helped or hindered that process. Some of the provisions in the 1978 Constitution were clearly intended to reverse certain trends towards illiberal and partisan rule which had developed under the pre-1977 government. But did those liberal provisions become the paramount elements in the new Constitution? And did the people who sought to promote them become the predominant force in the ruling party?

The second set of questions concerns the economy and will not be fully answerable until more time passes and solid, detailed data become available. But they are still worth keeping in mind. Some of the architects of the government's economic strategy after 1977 regarded it both as a way to generate the wealth needed to sustain some part of the expensive welfarist provisions which had served the needs of common people remarkably well and as a means of defusing Sinhalese – Tamil tensions. Liberalisation was intended to serve this latter purpose partly by giving minorities greater opportunities to better themselves and partly by turning the attention of potential Sinhalese chauvinists away from 'race' relations towards economic issues.[38] The new strategy has enabled many Sri Lankans to prosper but, at least in the short run, it has imposed serious hardships on others. What will the fate of these latter groups be? And since Lalith Athulathmudali and Gananath Obeyesekere — from very different perspectives — have both referred to the new socioeconomic groups which have arisen in recent years, we might also ask what sort of forces economic liberalisation has generated. Athulathmudali writes of newly prosperous elements throwing off the cynicism inspired by economic stagnation under previous governments. In his view, these people will grow in number and will provide democratic institutions with a reliable bedrock of support. Obeyesekere voices concern over lumpen elements in urban and semi-urban areas who are disoriented by uncertainty about their social status and economic survival, and drawn (or in some cases forced) into a trade union which serves as something akin to a private army for the most virulently anti-Tamil and anti-democratic leaders in the government. Will the government's economic strategy — particularly after the damage suffered during the 1983 violence — forge a new basis for a rational democratic order, or will it rend and deracinate society and open the way to an autocracy of narrow purpose?

Finally, in trying to determine how the ghastly violence of 1983 happened and how some of the damage might be repaired, one further question needs to be asked. How powerful has President Jayewardene actually been in recent years? The general view which is shared by several of our contributors is that his position is well nigh unassailable. But Meyer and Obeyesekere and others[39] — recalling the President's difficulty in delivering on promises to the Tamils because of opposition within his own party and Cabinet, and his timid reponse during the 1983 violence — suspect that he is far less strong than he appears. This question is important because all of those who venture an opinion on the subject in this book — including severe critics — agree that Jayewardene is not a Sinhalese bigot. And as this collection was being prepared, this point was strongly reiterated to the editor by two impeccable and highly authoritative sources, one an Indian and the other a Sri Lanka Tamil. If the President is to reconstruct some sort of minimal understanding with the Tamils, as he has apparently sought to do in the months since the violence,[40] he will need not only to offer major concessions but to deliver on them as well. This will have to be accomplished in the teeth of opposition from Sinhalese extremists, both within and beyond the ruling party, who thwarted the fulfilment of earlier commitments. The outcome of this test of strength will hinge upon the power which the 77-year-old President possesses in the wake of the trauma of 1983. A great deal probably rides on the result. For if anti-Tamil fervour and the trend towards more repressive government actually nourish one another, as some of our contributors argue, the survival not only of the island's social fabric but of its democratic traditions is at stake.

Notes

1. Sri Lanka was officially known as Ceylon until 1972, but for clarity, the latter name will be used throughout this book.
2. A Commission from Britain happened to be sent to Sri Lanka at a time when an unusually progressive government held power, and it contained particularly progressive members. The result, the Donoughmore Constitution, awarded universal suffrage to the island.
3. The earliest elections elsewhere by universal suffrage were in independent India in 1952 and in British Gold Coast, later Ghana, in 1954.
4. The results of these were as follows:

		% of votes		% of seats		
		UNP	SLFP	UNP	SLFP	Turnout
	1952	44.08	15.52	44.2	9.5	70.7
	1956	27.44	39.96	56.8	53.7	69.0
March	1960	29.62	21.12	8.4	30.5	77.6
July	1960	37.57	33.59	33.1	49.7	75.9
	1965	38.93	30.24	19.9	27.2	82.1
	1970	37.92	36.63	43.7	60.0	85.2
	1977	51.2	29.8	84.3	4.8	86.3

For further reading on Sri Lanka politics, see: W.H. Wriggins, *Ceylon: Dilemmas of a New Nation* (Princeton, 1960); R.N. Kearney, *The Politics of Ceylon (Sri Lanka)* (Ithaca and London, 1973); A.J. Wilson, *Politics in Sri Lanka 1947–1979* (London, 1979); and J. Jupp, *Sri Lanka: Third World Democracy* (London, 1978).
5. D.L. Horowitz, *Coup Theories and Officers' Motives: Sri Lanka in Comparative Perspective* (Princeton, 1980).
6. *World Bank Development Report 1983* (New York, 1983) pp. 192–3, 196–7.
7. The strictly proper rendering of the language spoken by the majority in Sri Lanka is *Sinhala*, not Sinhalese. And some scholars use the term 'Sinhala people' to describe the linguistic group. But for the convenience of readers new to the topic, the term 'Sinhalese' shall be used throughout this book to refer both to the language and the people who speak it.
8. See for example, A.C. Alles, *Insurgency 1971* (Colombo, 1976).
9. More thorough treatments of this can be found in Jupp, *Sri Lanka: Third World Democracy* and R.N. Kearney, *Communalism and Language in the Politics of Ceylon* (Durham, NC, 1967).
10. For further material on caste, see B. Ryan, *Caste in Modern Ceylon* (New Brunswick, 1953) and J. Jiggins, *Caste and Family in the Politics of the Sinhalese, 1947–1976* (Cambridge, 1979).
11. Jupp, *Sri Lanka: Third World Democracy*, pp. 32–3.
12. These figures are extrapolated from ibid., p. 30. The population of Sri Lanka now exceeds 15 million, but since a precise figure is not available, we use this figure for the sake of clarity.
13. For further reading, see M. Roberts, 'Variations on the Theme of Resistance Movements . . .', *Ceylon Studies Seminar* (1970–2), pp. 18–31; and his 'Foundations of Sinhala and Tamil Nationalisms and Some Implications', *Ceylon Studies Seminar* (1973), pp. 1–5; Kearney, *Communalism*; and R.A.L.H. Gunawardena, 'The People of the Lion', *Sri Lanka Journal of the Humanities*, v, 1–2 (1979).
14. D.E. Smith, 'Religion, Politics and the Myth of Reconquest' in R.N. Kearney and T. Fernando (eds.), *Modern Sri Lanka: A Society in Transition* (Syracuse, 1978), pp. 83–100.

15. Jupp, *Sri Lanka: Third World Democracy*, p. 30. R.L. Stirrat's research confirms this.
16. Interview with J.R. Jayewardene, Colombo, 11 September 1978.
17. See, in this vein, D.E. Smith, 'The Dialectic of Religion and Politics in Sri Lanka', *Ceylon Journal of Historical and Social Studies*, new series, iv, 1–2 (January–December 1974), pp. 111–18.
18. This view, or rather this hope, was put to the author by a distinguished Tamil scholar in Sri Lanka in 1978.
19. For a fuller discussion of the Constitution see J. Manor, 'A New Political Order for Sri Lanka', *The World Today* (September 1979) and, in greater detail, A.J. Wilson, *The Gaullist System in Asia* (London, 1980).
20. *Report of the Select Committee on the Revision of the Constitution*, parliamentary series no. 14 (Colombo, 1978), p. 169.
21. We are referring here mainly to Sri Lanka Tamils. Estate Tamils were largely disenfranchised soon after World War II.
22. W.H. Wriggins, 'Institutional Innovation and the Constraints of the 1980s' in P. Lyon and J. Manor (eds.), *Transfer and Transformation: Political Institutions in the New Commonwealth* (Leicester and Salem, NH, 1983).
23. Arjuna Kannangara, 'Sri Lanka: An Economic Overview', typescript 1983.
24. Ibid., and Wriggins, 'Institutional Innovation', p. 243.
25. Ibid.
26. This is based on interviews in Colombo in September 1980 and on subsequent correspondence.
27. This is far too complex a topic to be dealt with adequately here, but it will be discussed at length in J. Manor, *Utopia and the Main Chance: Bandaranaike and Ceylon*, forthcoming.
28. See for example, G. Obeyesekere, 'Social Change and the Deities', *Man*, xii (1977), pp. 377–96.
29. This figure comes from a statement by the Minister of Labour, reported in *The Hindu* (Madras), 16 August 1983.
30. See, on these two topics, W.A. Wiswa Warnapala and L. Dias Hewagama, *Recent Politics in Sri Lanka* (New Delhi, 1983) and T.D.S.A. Dissanayake, *The Agony of Sri Lanka* (Colombo, 1983).
31. This is apparent even from the official investigation into the alleged plot. *Report of the Investigation . . . into the Alleged Conspiracy to Assassinate His Excellency the President . . .*, Sessional Paper III (1983).
32. Note that Samarakone stresses the intimidation of *SLFP* activists, but note as well the higher turnout in SLFP than in Marxist strongholds.
33. The government estimate was just under 400 deaths, but this is clearly an underestimate, on the basis of evidence from eyewitnesses and press reports. The World Council of Churches figure was 1,000 and some Tamils use 2,000, probably an overestimate. Further evidence is needed to resolve this issue firmly.
34. *Amnesty International Statement Updating its Human Rights Concerns in Sri Lanka, July–September 1983* (London, 1983), p. 3. One who was injured on the second day died of his wounds soon afterward.
35. Those months were marked by highly plausible charges of arbitrary arrests, torture, incommunicado detention of prisoners, all against Tamils. Army men rioted in May in Jaffna and Vavuniya and, in May and June, attacks on Tamils occurred in many places. In Trincomalee where armed forces again rioted, 214 houses, 24 shops and eight Hindu temples were burnt, and 19 Tamils were killed. A law was passed allowing the disposal of corpses without inquests. Sources: *Amnesty International Statement* and a typescript on the background to the violence of mid-1983 by Satchi Ponnambalam.
36. This goes some way towards explaining the following phenomenon

encountered by an established Sri Lanka specialist in the aftermath of the violence:

The most appalling thing is the complete lack of compassion for the victims among the younger (under 40) Sinhalese I met. Some were gleeful, some matter of fact, a few expressed regret that people died. But no one wondered what the Tamils were going to do or even seemed to understand that the situation had changed. It was just another riot, and they have grown accustomed to them.

37. See J. Manor, 'Sir Lanka: Explaining the Disaster', *The World Today* (November 1983).

38. It should be noted that some scholars think the communal conflict quickens in prosperous times. They cite the low level of trouble between 1960 and 1976, when the economy was rather depressed.

39. Manor, 'Sri Lanka: Explaining'.

40. In late 1983, Jayewardene put a package of proposals to the TULF and summoned a ten-party round table conference for January 1984 to consider it. (The conference did not include two left-wing parties, the JVP and the NSSP, because they had been banned and many of their leaders had been jailed since the mid-1983 violence.) The proposals included the establishment of a high court in each region of the island, regional public services, regional police services reflecting the ethnic balance in the area, and the appointment by the President of the Chief Minister in each region who will be drawn from the party with the largest number of members in the province's Regional Council. These proposals will generate vigorous opposition from Sinhalese chauvinists.

PART ONE
SRI LANKA IN CHANGE — LATE 1982

2 PLEBISCITARY DEMOCRACY OR CREEPING AUTHORITARIANISM? THE PRESIDENTIAL ELECTION AND REFERENDUM OF 1982

C.R. de Silva

This paper has two purposes. The first is to analyse the factors that led to the victory of J.R. Jayewardene in the 1982 presidential election and the 'yes' vote in the referendum on the constitutional amendment to prolong the life of the existing Parliament by six years. The second is to assess the implications of these developments both for Sri Lanka's politics in late 1982 and for the prospects for democratic structures over the longer term.

Since Sri Lanka's Parliament was elected for a six-year term in July 1977 while the President had begun his six-year term of office in February 1978, it seemed inevitable in mid-1982 that parliamentary elections would be held well before a presidential election. The decision to change the Constitution to allow the election of a President to occur before a parliamentary election stemmed directly from political calculations within the ruling United National Party (UNP). It was generally agreed that 1983-4 would be a difficult period for Sri Lanka in terms of economic development. The world-wide recession showed little signs of abating and this severely affected Sri Lanka's search for export markets. From 1981 private foreign investment showed signs of tapering off in anticipation of an election and the possible return of a government less hospitable to multinationals. Moreover, the large multi-purpose river valley projects undertaken by the Jayewardene regime were due to yield substantial economic returns only in and after 1983. Thus there was growing feeling in UNP circles that an election in 1982 would be much easier to win than one in 1983. This impression was reinforced by a relatively strong showing of the ruling party in the Development Councils Election of 1981.[1] Then in the same year came the demonstration of the 'Mitterand effect', when the new President of France who was elected in May 1981 promptly dissolved Parliament and won a decisive majority for his party. Virtually all political observers agreed that President Jayewardene was personally more popular than his party. So, not surprisingly, several UNP strategists advocated that the President stand for election before the end of his six-year term and before the government encountered the problems which 1983 would bring in the hope that the momentum of his victory would enable the UNP to gain a clear parliamentary majority even under proportional representation.

The introduction of the Third Amendment to the Constitution in 1982 suggested that this strategy had gained acceptance. The amendment empowered a first-term President[2] to submit himself for re-election after four years in office. Although the opposition realised the political advantages that this yielded to the UNP, they could hardly publicly oppose a law which permitted the advancement of the date of the presidential election. The amendment was thus approved by Parliament by a vote of 138 to 1 in August 1982.[3] President Jayewardene made immediate use of the opportunity, and 20 October was fixed as election day.

Jayewardene went to the polls with several advantages. In the first place, his most formidable opponent, the former Prime Minister Mrs Bandaranaike, had been debarred from the contest. There is little doubt that her plight aroused considerable sympathy, but the efforts of her Sri Lanka Freedom Party (SLFP) to stage demonstrations in protest failed due partly to its ineffective organisation and partly to the impact of the hearings of the much publicised Presidential Commission which had disqualified her. Jayewardene's second advantage was the divisions within the SLFP. This was partly due to the effective elimination of Mrs Bandaranaike from political life till 1987. She remained leader of the SLFP, but had done little since 1977 to revitalise her party. A struggle for the succession began which eventually resolved itself into competition between the 'moderates' and the 'radicals'. The 'moderate' wing was led by deputy leader Maithripala Senanayake and Mrs Bandaranaike's son Anura. The 'radicals' were spearheaded by Party Secretary R. Wickramanayake, former minister T.B. Ilangaratne and Mrs Bandaranaike's son-in-law, Vijaya Kumaranatunga. When the 'moderate' Senanayake suggested that Mrs Bandaranaike should temporarily step down from the party leadership, she saw this as a threat to her position and joined the 'radicals', eventually to defeat Senanayake's proposal. Relations between the two groups steadily worsened until an open split occurred in November 1981. The reconciliation of Anura Bandaranaike with his mother in March 1982 weakened the Senanayake faction but introduced new discord within Mrs Bandaranaike's group because of the continuing rift between Anura Bandaranaike and the 'radicals' led by his brother-in-law Kumaranatunga.[4]

Jayewardene also benefited from dissension among the left-wing parties and the lack of co-operation between them and the SLFP. All of these parties saw the need for a common anti-UNP candidate with a common programme, but agreement on both matters proved difficult. Three of the old left-wing parties, the Lanka Sama Samaja Party (LSSP), the Communist Party (CP), and the Mahajana Eksath Peramuna (MEP) seemed to have a minimum programme which both SLFP factions could support. This included the provisos that the victorious candidate should immediately restore civic rights to Mrs Bandaranaike, immediately dissolve Parliament and have fresh elections and secure a return to the Constitution of 1972.[5] The Janatha Vimukthi Peramuna (JVP), successor to the organisation that mounted the insurrection of 1971, whose leaders had been incarcerated by Mrs Bandaranaike under the 1972 Constitution, was noticeably less enthusiastic about this. Its leadership also had visions of replacing the SLFP as the major opposition party.[6]

Agreement on a common candidate proved more difficult to secure than agreement on policy. As early as July 1982, Maithripala Senanayake's SLFP — hereafter the SLFP(M) — put his name forward as a common opposition candidate,[7] but this was not acceptable to Mrs Bandaranaike. The LSSP then suggested its leader, Dr Colvin R. de Silva, as a compromise candidate. This prospect was, however, quickly extinguished by developments within Mrs Bandaranaike's SLFP — hereafter SLFP(S). Since the return of Anura Bandaranaike to the group he had been considered a leading contender for the party nomination. However, in early August 1982 the 'radicals' who were opposed to him united to nominate his uncle and former Minister of Agriculture and Lands, Hector Kobbekaduwa. He also received the support of the CP and the MEP.[8]

His hopes of becoming the sole anti-UNP candidate, however, were soon dashed. Colvin R. de Silva refused to yield and pressed on with an increasingly forlorn campaign, casting doubts on the legality of Kobbekaduwa's nomination on the grounds that the SLFP(S) was led by a politician without civic rights.[9] However, he was deserted by a faction of his own party led by two former ministers who formed a rival LSSP to support Kobbekaduwa.[10] In this situation the extreme

Nava Sama Samaja Party (NSSP) also decided to put forward its leader Vasudeva Nanayakkara as a presidential candidate.[11] Far more significant was the nomination of Rohana Wijeweera as the candidate of the JVP. The JVP, as a relatively new party, could attack the ruling UNP, the SLFP and the LSSP as jaded old forces which had failed the people. It attracted vociferous support among the youth, especially in the south-west coastal areas.[12]

Thus the opposition campaign was fragmented and slow to get off the ground. However, the SLFP(S) campaign made a significant gain just nine days before nomination day. Both factions of the SLFP had applied to the Commissioner of Elections for the award of the coveted 'Hand' symbol. The Commissioner after an inquiry decided to award it to the SLFP(S) group.[13] The SLFP(M), which was already badly shaken by signs of faltering support, capitulated almost immediately. Maithripala Senanayake withdrew and pledged to support Kobbekaduwa.[14] At long last the SLFP seemed to be united. However, before long some prominent members of the SLFP(M), including a former minister and a current SLFP MP, announced their support of President Jayewardene.[15]

Jayewardene also had two other advantages. The more important of these was the steadfast support given by the Ceylon Workers Congress (CWC) led by S. Thondaman.[16] The CWC had formed part of the government since 1977 and was the major political group among the Tamil plantation labourers, some 400,000 of whom had obtained citizenship since 1949. The other advantage — a somewhat debatable one — arose from the decision of the Tamil United Liberation Front (TULF) to adopt a policy of non-participation in the presidential election. The TULF held that they had had a mandate for a separate state and argued that an election in Sri Lanka thus had no relevance to the Tamil areas in the north and the east. Given all of this, it was expected that President Jayewardene would outpoll his opponents in Tamil areas in view of the safeguards introduced for Tamil minority interests in the Constitution of 1978.[17] In any case it was anticipated that the lower poll in the north and the east would reduce the absolute total required by him for a majority on the first count.

Some of these calculations were upset by the entry into the campaign of Kumar Ponnambalam, leader of the Tamil Congress. For years he had been advocating equal status for Tamils *within* Sri Lanka, with minimal impact on Tamil politics. He challenged the TULF to nominate a Tamil candidate in order to obtain a clear mandate for a separate state. When the TULF failed to respond, Ponnambalam presented himself as a candidate and requested all Tamils supporting separation to vote for him. Despite TULF efforts to blunt this campaign, he attracted some support even among TULF voters, especially in the Eastern Province.[18]

The election was fought largely on the post-1977 economic policies of the Jayewardene government. Jayewardene had turned his back on the protectionist 'home-oriented' growth strategy of all governments in the last two decades and had opened up Sri Lanka's economy in emulation of Singapore and Taiwan, as has been explained in the introduction to this volume. There were also two significant parallel developments. First, there was a massive investment in the multi-purpose Mahaweli (River) Development Scheme which was designed to increase food production, provide hydro-electric power and alleviate land hunger. There was also a significant reduction in food subsidies. The free weekly ration of rice available to virtually all was replaced by food stamps allotted according to a 'means and needs test' available only to about half of the population.

The aim of these changes was to jolt the economy out of stagnation, increase investment in export-oriented industries, reduce the import bill in food and, most important, reduce unemployment. They were undertaken when international conditions were far from propitious. Recession in industrialised countries made the search for new markets difficult. Exports rose by 40 per cent in value in the period 1977–82, but imports rose by a massive 150 per cent. Meanwhile, deficit financing by the state and large inflows of investments led to a steep rise in inflation which peaked at around 40 per cent in 1980. Despite financial restraints, it remained at about 25 per cent in 1981.

On the other hand, there was unquestioned expansion in the domestic economy. GNP rose in real terms at an annual rate of over 6 per cent between 1977 and 1982 as against 3.5 per cent seen in the period between 1970 and 1977. Real *per capita* income thus rose by over 4 per cent between 1978 and 1982 as compared to less than half that rate in the previous period.[19] More important, the 'open economy' eliminated the irksome shortages and queues and made available hitherto scarce consumer goods. For instance, during the three years 1974–7 only 1,000 bicycles were imported into the country. In 1978 alone 12,000 were imported; in 1979, 33,000; and in 1981 a record 98,000. As the wages of semi-skilled and unskilled workers kept up with inflation, a widening group began to appreciate the benefits of the new economic policy.[20] It made a visible dent in unemployment, which had been steadily growing since the 1950s and had become a major problem. The new economic climate fostered business confidence. The expansion in trade and the service sector provided many new jobs. The opening up of the Mahaweli lands and the construction of dams, irrigation canals and roads created a new demand for labour, while the Industrial Promotion Zone (IPZ) north of Colombo had by late 1982 directly provided 25,000 opportunities for industrial workers. Opportunities for employment in the oil states absorbed at least another 60,000 persons and also provided additional avenues of upward mobility.[21]

Government spokesmen also made much of Prime Minister Premadasa's fulfilment of the promise of building 100,000 houses within six years. Many of these houses were low-cost units built in villages all over the island and given to the homeless. They proved to be a highly visible and effective campaign argument in favour of the ruling party. The government also made political capital out of its schemes in distributing land to the landless and in providing scholarships for university education.[22]

The government, of course, used its incumbency to good advantage. In the run-up to the election, the controlled maximum price of sugar was reduced by .50 cts, the police were awarded a salary rise and pensions were raised to keep up with inflation. A long drawn out strike at a chemical works was settled on terms favourable to the workers and fishermen were offered incentives.[23]

The opposition naturally concentrated on inflation and the reduction of the food subsidy. They also promised to aid 40,000 public employees (clerical and manual) who had gone on strike in defiance of the government in June 1980 and had consequently lost seniority, pay and in some cases even employment.[24] The SLFP promised to ban the import of subsidiary crops like onions and chillies to provide better prices for local farmers,[25] and to replace food stamps with the old free rice ration. Their economic arguments proved largely ineffective, however, as the UNP stressed that incomes had risen with inflation and that the SLFP had made similar promises in 1970−7 and had failed to deliver.[26] None of the opposition parties advanced a credible economic alternative. Indeed, during the campaign SLFP leaders modified its originally rigid attitude to the 'open economy' as they became aware of its popularity.[27]

In the political sphere as well as the economic, the UNP seemed to have had the better of the debate. Jayewardene pointed out that, unlike Mrs Bandaranaike who postponed elections from 1975 to 1977, he had brought forward the date of the election and given the people the right to elect their leader. The UNP spokesmen argued that Mrs Bandaranaike had been tried and found guilty by a judicial tribunal and contrasted this with the SLFP's record of harassment and confiscation of property between 1970 and 1977. Finally, and most effectively, Jayewardene charged the SLFP with 'family bandyism' (nepotism), pointing out that its leadership was drawn from one kinship group.

There was, however, one area in which the SLFP threatened to gain support. That was among the traditional Sinhalese Buddhist leadership. The 'open economy' had also involved the greater opening of the country to Westernising influences such as tourism, television and consumerism. The greater emphasis given to English and the adoption of Tamil as one of the national languages rankled in the minds of the Sinhalese Buddhist traditionalists. A newly formed Council of Sri Lanka Buddhist Societies led by prominent Buddhist monks and laymen presented 25 demands to all candidates.[28] These included the declaration of Sri Lanka as a Buddhist Republic, the reservation of all key posts for Buddhists, a ban on inducements to embrace non-Buddhist faiths, the provision of housing, lands, permits for industries, social service assistance and higher education facilities according to racial quotas, making Sinhalese the sole medium of instruction and the provision of all basic facilities for the Buddhist *sangha* (clergy) by the state. Kobbekaduwa agreed to discuss these demands, but Jayewardene refused. 'The Buddha,' he declared, 'did not preach to any one race and *nirvana* can be attained only by individuals, not by a nation.'[29] He strongly argued that while the government would safeguard the interests of the Sinhalese Buddhist majority, it would also protect minority communities. He was denounced as a traitor to the Buddhists for his pains, but his stand in this matter was also adopted by the two other main candidates.

Any loss of support on this issue was, however, more than counteracted by the 'caste' issue.[30] Since becoming UNP leader in 1973, Jayewardene had integrated elements from the non-*goyigama* castes into his party and given them positions of power. By 1982, the UNP had been transformed from a party of the dominant *goyigama* caste (which was its image in the 1950s) to a political organisation with much wider appeal. On the other hand, the multi-caste SLFP of the 1950s had become increasingly *goyigama*-dominated. In this respect the charge of one UNP leader of humble caste origins that he had been insulted by the SLFP's Anura Bandaranaike owing to his caste, together with the influence of non-*goyigama* Premier R. Premadasa, appear to have had an important impact.

As the campaign progressed, it became clear that the LSSP and NSSP candidates were flagging while JVP rallies attracted large crowds and Ponnambalam was picking up support. Nevertheless, in the end the question was whether Jayewardene would defeat Kobbekaduwa and indeed do so on the first count. The state-controlled radio and three of the four major newspaper groups provided considerable propaganda support for Jayewardene. The fourth major newspaper group, owned by Upali Wijewardane, provided considerable coverage of the opposition viewpoint and often criticised the government until the last few days when it too backed the incumbent President. The Communist Sinhalese daily, *Aththa*, emerged as the chief propaganda news sheet supporting Kobbekaduwa.

A major role was played by television. Although both channels were state-controlled, the Presidential Elections Act decreed that every candidate was entitled to 45 minutes on national television and this was scrupulously adhered to. However, Kobbekaduwa proved singularly inept in the use of television, while the other candidates projected their images well. Jayewardene's own performance was masterly. On the whole, however, campaigning was still in the traditional style with the candidates traversing the country and addressing several meetings each day. Once again the UNP organisation proved superior with twin campaigns in different areas led by the President and Prime Minister. The JVP made excellent use of grass roots support in the south-west, while the SLFP often rested on the organising capabilities of its local notables.

Jayewardene owed his victory to a number of things.[31] Basically more people believed that their economic prospects were better left in the hands of his government. The opposition had failed to put forward a credible alternative to the 'open economy'. Jayewardene also managed to attract considerable support from ethnic and caste minorities. It is also likely that the personal standing of the President and trust in him as a leader played a crucial part. He won pluralities in 22 of the 24 electoral districts of the island and in 132 of the 160 old parliamentary constituencies which were used as counting units. Both in absolute terms and in terms of the percentage of votes

polled, the UNP victory was unprecedented.
Kobbekaduwa did as well as might be expected. His poll of
2,548,438 was 9.5 percentage points higher than the SLFP poll in the
disastrous elections of 1977. Nevertheless, considering the fact that
the SLFP, unlike in 1977, had the support of the CP, MEP and elements of the LSSP and also attracted support in Jaffna in the
absence of TULF competition, the party must have regarded the
results with some concern.

Table 2.1:   Presidential Election, October 1982

		Votes polled	Percentage
J.R. Jayewardene	UNP	3,450,811	52.91
H. Kobbekaduwa	SLFP	2,548,438	39.07
R. Wijeweera	JVP	273,428	4.19
K. Ponnambalam	TC	173,934	2.67
Colvin R. de Silva	LSSP	38,531	0.90
V. Nanayakkara	NSSP	17,005	0.26

Wijeweera of the JVP also failed in his avowed objective to
emerge as the major anti-UNP force. Nevertheless, the JVP clearly
emerged as the major left-wing organisation in Sri Lanka. Ponnambalam also found room for some satisfaction. He gained approximately 40 per cent of the poll in the two major Tamil majority
districts — Jaffna and Batticaloa — and thus made a major impact
on Tamil politics. Indeed the major losers were the TULF which
found that its call for non-participation had a limited impact except
in Jaffna (where valid votes amounted to only 44.16 per cent of the
electorate). As a result of the election the TULF claim to be the sole
spokesman of the Sri Lanka Tamils of the north and east came to be
seriously questioned.

The UNP had advocated a direct presidential election as a measure
which would promote national unity. And despite the divisive riots
of mid-1983, in the immediate aftermath of the election of October
1982, this appeared to have happened. The sole Tamil candidate who
campaigned on a platform of separatism failed to obtain a majority
of votes in any electoral district outside Jaffna. All Sinhalese candidates were constrained to take an all-island perspective rather than
a narrower Sinhalese – Buddhist stand. Even Kobbekaduwa who
made overtures to Sinhalese – Buddhist traditionalist groups proved
sensitive to the wishes of Jaffna Tamils, promising them the repeal

of the Prevention of Terrorism Act and higher prices for subsidiary food crops.[32]

President Jayewardene declared a state of emergency soon after the polls closed, and this had the salutary effect of reducing post-election violence which had been a feature of Sri Lanka politics since the 1960s.[33] A few days after, however, he held that evidence of a plot to assassinate himself and other members of the government had been unearthed. It was alleged that several prominent members of the SLFP including Vijaya Kumaranatunga, son-in-law of Mrs Bandaranaike, were involved and they were taken into custody. President Jayewardene thereupon alleged that a Naxalite (revolutionary Marxist) group had taken over the SLFP and that in the circumstances the holding of a parliamentary election on the basis of proportional representation would allow these elements to secure a third of the seats in Parliament and paralyse government action. He argued that since he had been given a clear mandate by the people to continue UNP policies for the next six years he could not countenance this. Jayewardene therefore proposed to extend the life of the current Parliament by six years through constitutional amendment.[34]

The Constitution of 1978 provided that the life of Parliament could not be extended save by a two-thirds majority in Parliament approved by a referendum, and no measure submitted for a referendum would be deemed approved unless it received a minimum of votes equal to one-third of the registered electorate.[35] Jayewardene was aware that some MPs of his party were less popular than he was and that some were accused of neglect of constituencies and corruption. He therefore demanded and obtained undated letters of resignation from all UNP MPs. The Constitution also specified that any mid-term vacancy in Parliament was to be filled by nominations by the party of the former member, which enabled Jayewardene to decide which UNP MPs would continue in office and which would be replaced.[36]

The opposition was aghast at the decision not to hold a parliamentary election. There is little doubt that there were elements within the SLFP who had advocated violent measures and that there would have been considerable political violence had the SLFP presidential candidate won. But very little concrete evidence of the 'Naxalite assassination plot' was offered at that time or has come to light since. The major reason for opting for the referendum seems to have been a UNP belief that they could not obtain a two-thirds majority under the proportional representation system. Obtaining a bare referendum majority to keep the present five-sixths majority in Parliament for another six years was a more attractive option. The UNP used its parliamentary majority to pass the Fourth Amendment to the Constitution, 142 votes to 4. The crucial phrase stated that, 'unless sooner dissolved the first Parliament shall continue till August 4, 1989 and no longer and shall thereupon stand dissolved . . .'[37] This was achieved swiftly and smoothly, but victory at the referendum was quite another matter.

The Fourth Amendment roused virtually all opposition parties against the government. The minuscule NSSP urged a boycott[38] but Mrs Bandaranaike's SLFP(S) was joined by the LSSP, JVP, MEP, CP and the TC in its political campaign. The TULF also emerged to campaign forcefully against the Fourth Amendment. Mrs Bandaranaike was legally free to campaign on the issues and did so with zest.[39]

The opposition faced certain handicaps. The government further prolonged the state of emergency, declared after the presidential poll, and used its powers to close two opposition newsheets, the Tamil *Suthanthiram* and the Sinhalese *Aththa*, on the grounds of publishing inflammatory material. Moreover, several prominent members of the SLFP(S) including its party Secretary and Vijaya Kumaranatunga and a number of second level organisers were held in custody for various periods before the referendum poll. In certain areas, especially Attanagalla (Mrs Bandaranaike's old electorate, a few miles east of Colombo), there was considerable intimidation and use of force by UNP election workers. In many areas the state machinery was used to assist in pro-amendment propaganda.[40] The opposition parties were also demoralised by their defeat in the presidential election and found it difficult to activate grass roots organisers to oppose a government seemingly entrenched till 1989. Finally, there was an important defection from the SLFP ranks. Maithripala Senanayake's SLFP(M) had supported the Kobbekaduwa's candidature, but they found themselves cold-shouldered by Mrs Bandaranaike after the presidential election and decided to support the UNP on the amendment issue.[41]

The opposition, nevertheless, had certain advantages. First, with six parties arrayed against the amendment and only two supporting it (the UNP and the CWC), the opposition obtained three times as much time on official television as the government. Second, though two newspapers were closed, other party papers were left untouched.

The Communist Party swiftly revived its old daily the *Mawbima* which was *Aththa* under another name. The opposition also made a strong case against the use of a referendum to postpone parliamentary elections. They pointed out that this provision had been introduced into the Constitution to deal with exceptional circumstances and that as the President already had the resignations of all UNP MPs with him, what the people were asked to do was to hand over the right to choose their elected representatives to Jayewardene. Lawyer H.L. de Silva argued, 'There are areas of rights and freedoms where the principle of majority decision is not a valid basis of decision at all. The right to elect representatives is one of those cardinal imperatives.'[42] It was pointed out that this precedent could lead to postponement of future elections too. The government tried to direct attention to other issues. Its spokesmen appealed for a clear majority to deal with the problem of terrorism in the north and to promote accelerated economic development. The price of bread and flour were reduced and the budget scheduled for November 1982, in which some austerity measures were expected, was postponed to March 1983.[43]

In the event, the government won again and the victory in percentage terms was even larger. On the other hand, there was a significant change in the distribution of the votes. The four electoral districts in which Tamils formed a majority or a large component of the population — Jaffna, Wanni, Trincomalee and Batticaloa — decisively rejected the amendment. So did the south-west coast with the districts of Kalutara, Galle and Hambantota having majorities against and Matara approving it only by a whisker. The government also lost ground in all urban areas. The victory of the government was thus due essentially to large majorities recorded in the more conservative areas. The CWC once more delivered the plantation Tamil vote and the SLFP(M) made a distinct impact in Anuradhapura District.

Table 2.2:   Referendum, December 1982

	No. of votes polled	Percentages of valid votes
Yes (Lamp)	3,141,223	54.66
No (Pot)	2,605,983	45.34
Rejected votes	21,456	
Total	5,768,662	100.00
		(= 70.82% of electorate)

The presidential election and the referendum raise the question as to the future of liberal democracy in Sri Lanka. When a presidential system was adopted, some analysts argued that Parliament elected under proportional representation would be a safeguard against arbitary extensions of power, since the President was unlikely to control the two-thirds of seats needed to amend the Constitution.[44] The extension of the tenure of the first Parliament till 1989 renders this safeguard inoperative for a further six years. Moreover, by possessing undated letters of resignation from all UNP MPs, the President has an unprecedented hold over Parliament.

Lester G. Seligman once commented that, 'what distinguishes non-western legislators from western legislators is that the former experience greater deprivation than the latter when they lose office.'[45] This applies not only to legislators but to all those in the bureaucracy who owe their appointments to political favour. They are all liable to what Seligman termed 'high risk' of a sharp fall in both status and income. He argued that, '. . . under conditions of high risk the contest for political office becomes so intense that legal norms buckle under the pressure and coercion and fraud are widely practised.'[46] Sri Lanka has had a long tradition of competitive elections and the verdict of the presidential election of 1982 was accepted by the public with little demur. However, the intimidation and impersonation and other undue uses of state power were significant in some areas during the referendum, and although it may not have affected the final outcome, it strengthens an unhealthy trend towards interference with democratic processes. Moreover, the concentration of power at the apex of the system fosters exaggerated beliefs about leadership qualities. The use of co-option to fill vacancies in Parliament creates a bias towards sycophants and adventurers who court those in power for the sake of political advancement.[47]

The referendum has also in effect excluded the radical SLFP elements and possibly the JVP from Parliament. As Seymour Martin Lipset remarked, 'Wherever new groups become politically active, comparatively early access to the legitimate political institutions tends to win the loyalty of new groups to the system, and they in turn can permit the old dominating strata to maintain their status integrity.'[48] The referendum, by depriving new elements of a chance to participate in the legislature, could have the contrary result.

What seems equally significant is the readiness of the ruling UNP to modify the constitutional structure from time to time for its own short-term political advantage. The Constitution of 1978, with a system of proportional representation including a bonus seat in every electoral district for the party polling the highest total and the elimination from the contest of all those parties failing to gain one-eighth of the votes in the district, was thought to be designed to give an electoral advantage to the ruling UNP. The Constitution itself seemed to be one which was virtually impossible to change without the consent of the UNP which was thought certain of winning at least one-third of the seats under proportional representation.[49]

The First Amendment and the law creating the Presidential Commission of Inquiry which had retroactive powers were seen by the SLFP as a device to exclude Mrs Bandaranaike from politics.[50] The Second Amendment, stipulating that in the first Parliament no MP would lose his seat on expulsion from his party until a majority in Parliament voted for expulsion was also seen as providing a partisan advantage.[51] The ruling party had the majority to punish its own rebellious MPs and to protect any opposition MP who wished to cross to their side. The Third and Fourth Amendments discussed in this article were obviously viewed as similarly conferring political advantages on the ruling UNP. The Constitution which had been perceived by many as a fundamental law was now being increasingly seen as an instrumental device, manipulated by politicians for their advantage.

Opposition spokesmen and other commentators have noted that although the referendum was approved at the national level, it was rejected in many localities. Indeed the opposition gained a majority of votes in 49 of the 160 counting areas which were identical to the old 'single member' constituencies. It was argued that at least constituencies had shown their disapproval of the extension of their MPs' terms without an election. The UNP response was typical of their approach. The government proposed yet another Amendment to the Constitution, the fifth in six years. This Amendment, eventually approved by Parliament on 25 February 1983, specified that if a political party failed to nominate an MP for a vacant seat within thirty days, the Commissioner of Elections would hold a by-election under the old Westminster rules.[52] Jayewardene also decided that UNP MPs from constituencies where the party polled badly at the presidential election and the referendum should resign, and that the party should precipitate by-elections to let the people decide whether to return UNP MPs for their areas. Thus in February 1983 the resignations of 17 MPs were submitted.[53] The opposition was thus challenged to contest by-elections and yet even if they won them all, the UNP would still retain a two-thirds majority in Parliament. Any opposition attempt to resign seats in protest against the extension of the life of Parliament would only precipitate further by-elections, and if the UNP won some of these against an opposition in disarray, it could claim a further mandate from the people. The forms of democracy survive and even flourish, but their substance is attenuated.

Notes

1. On that election see S.W.R. de A. Samarasinghe and C.R. de Silva, 'The Implications', *Sri Lanka Journal of Social Sciences*, iv, 1 (June 1981).
2. Except a President elected by Parliament to fill a vacancy in mid-term.
3. *Daily Mirror*, 27 August 1982.
4. On the rift and reconciliation see news items and commentaries in the *Sun, Island* and *Daily News* during this period.
5. *Tribune*, 14 August 1982.
6. See Samarasinghe and de Silva, 'The Implications', p. 95.
7. *Island*, 21 July 1982.
8. *Sun*, 25 September; *Weekend*, 19 September 1982.
9. *Daily News*, 27 September, 4 October 1982.
10. *Weekend*, 19 September 1982.
11. *Daily News*, 24 September 1982.
12. For example, *Sun*, 27 September; *Daily News*, 24 and 25 September, 4 October 1982.
13. *Sunday Times*, 12 September 1982.
14. *Tribune*, 18 September 1982.
15. *Sun*, 24 September 1982.
16. Ibid.
17. See C.R. de Silva, 'The Tamils and the Constitution of 1978', *Sri Lanka Journal of Social Sciences*, iii, 1 (1980).
18. *Island*, 20 and 26 September; *Weekend*, 26 September; *Lanka Guardian*, 15 September; *Dinapati*, 1 August; *Eelanadu*, 5 August 1982.
19. *Central Bank of Sri Lanka Annual Report*, 1981; *Island*, 11 February 1983 (Speech of the President at the opening of the Third Session of the First Parliament on 9 February 1983).
20. *Tribune*, 18 September 1982.
21. *Island*, 11 January 1983.
22. For example, *Sun*, 27 September; *Daily News*, 4 October 1982.
23. *Tribune*, 18 September 1982.
24. For example, *Sun*, 25 and 27 September; *Daily News*, 22 and 27 September 1982.
25. *Island*, 17 October 1982.
26. *Daily News*, 4 October 1982.
27. *Tribune*, 23 October 1982.
28. *Lanka Guardian*, 15 October 1982.
29. Ibid.
30. On caste and politics in Sri Lanka see J. Jiggins, *Caste and Family in the*

Politics of the Sinhalese, 1947–1976 (Cambridge, 1979).
31. For various analyses of the election results, see *Tribune*, 23 and 30 October; *Lanka Guardian*, 1 November; *Aththa*, 28 October; *Divaina*, 24 October; *Weekend*, 31 October 1982.
32. *Island*, 24 October 1982.
33. *Sun*, 27 October 1982.
34. *Island*, 28 October; *Sun*, 28 October 1982.
35. *The Constitution of the Democratic Republic of Sri Lanka*, Articles 85–87.
36. *Aththa*, 28 October 1982.
37. *Parliament of the Democratic Socialist Republic of Sri Lanka, Fourth Amendment to the Constitution* (Colombo, 1982); *Lanka Guardian*, 15 November 1982.
38. *Lanka Guardian*, 1 November 1983.
39. Ibid.; *Weekend*, 31 October 1982.
40. *Parliamentary Debates*, 26 November 1982, cols. 1977–8; 24 December 1982, cols. 2136–68.
41. *Sun*, 11 December 1982.
42. Ibid., 18 December 1982.
43. Ibid., 18 December; *Island*, 14 December; *Daily News*, 14 December 1982.
44. See, for example, C.R. de Silva, 'The Representation System', *The Ceylon Journal of Historical & Social Studies*, new series, vii, 2 (June – December 1977), p. 32.
45. L.G. Seligman, 'Political Risk and Legislative Behaviour in Non-western Countries' in G.R. Boynton and K.C. Lim (eds.), *Legislative Systems in Developing Countries* (Durham, NC, 1975), p. 91.
46. Ibid., p. 94.
47. Ibid.
48. S.M. Lipset, 'Some Social Requisites of Democracy: Economic Development and Political Legitimacy', *American Political Science Review*, liii, 1 (March 1959), p. 88.
49. See Samarasinghe and de Silva, 'The Implications', p. 163.
50. *The Parliament of the Democratic Socialist Republic of Sri Lanka. The First Amendment to the Constitution* (Colombo, 1978).
51. *The Parliament of the Democratic Socialist Republic of Sri Lanka. The Second Amendment to the Constitution (certified on 26.2.1979)* (Colombo, 1979).
52. *Island*, 26 February 1983.
53. Ibid., 11 February 1983.

3 THE 1982 ELECTIONS AND THE NEW GAULLIST–BONAPARTIST STATE IN SRI LANKA[1]

M.P. Moore

Apart from the novel, if formally constitutional, device of a referendum to extend the life of Parliament, the most remarkable feature of the 1982 elections in Sri Lanka was that they heralded a reversal of the long established pattern of electoral seesawing. For the first time since 1956, seven general elections ago, the voters in October failed to overturn the government. J.R. Jayewardene, leader of the United National Party (UNP), which holds 84 per cent of parliamentary seats, was returned to the presidency with a slightly higher proportion of votes cast than his party had received in the 1977 parliamentary elections (Table 3.1). At the time, this was widely attributed to the disarray of the main opposition party, the Sri Lanka Freedom Party (SLFP), and the ineligibility of its leader and most popular figure, Mrs Sirimavo Bandaranaike, either to stand for the presidency or to campaign on her party's behalf.[2] Mrs Bandaranaike was free to campaign against the extension of Parliament in the December referendum, although her party was in even greater disarray: many members had defected to the UNP at all levels,[3] and her supporters had been imprisoned and legally harassed on charges yet to be proven.[4] The referendum confirmed the electoral ascendancy of the President. While he had gained 52.91 per cent of the votes at the presidential campaign, 54.66 per cent of those voting in the referendum supported his proposal to extend Parliament, albeit on a greatly reduced poll.

This paper examines changes in voting behaviour between (a) the 1977 parliamentary elections and the presidential elections of October 1982: and (b) the presidential election and the referendum of December 1982. Accepting that each was a different kind of election, and that therefore comparisons must be drawn with care, it is argued that the results reflect and illustrate the changing nature of the Sri Lankan polity, and the emergence of what is here termed, for lack of better jargon, a Gaullist–Bonapartist state.

The term 'Gaullist' relates in part to constitutional questions: the

Table 3.1: Results of 1977 Parliamentary Elections and 1982 Presidential Elections

		% Share of valid votes cast in		Party candidate in
		1977	1982	1982 presidential election
United National Party (UNP)	(a)	51	53	J.R. Jayewardene
Sri Lanka Freedom Party (SLFP)		30	39	H. Kobbekaduwa
Lanka Sama Samaja Party (LSSP)		4	1	Colvin R. de Silva
Communist Party (CP)		3	****	—
Nava Sama Samaja Party (NSSP)	(b)	*	neg.	V. Nanayakkara
Janatha Vimukthi Peramuna (JVP)		**	4	R. Wijeweera
Tamil United Liberation Front (TULF)	(c)	7	*****	—
Tamil Congress (TC)		*	3	Kumar Ponnambalam
Others and independents		6***	—	—

Notes:
  * Neither the NSSP nor the TC existed in 1977.
 ** The JVP was not a recognised party in 1977. A few members contested as independents.
*** Includes the Ceylon Workers Congress (CWC) representing Indian Tamil plantation workers, which contested two seats in 1977 (winning one), and supported the UNP in 1982.
**** In 1982 the Communist Party supported the SLFP candidate.
***** The TULF did not participate in the 1982 election.
(a): Mainly Sinhalese parties.
(b): Marxist parties, mainly Sinhalese.
(c): Sri Lanka Tamil parties.

formal subordination of the party-oriented legislature to a directly elected President. More importantly, it indicates that the President has the capacity to exercise his formal powers by virtue of having established an identity and a following which is both partly independent of and broader than that of his party, even while he continues to dominate the party through his control over the top party 'apparatchiks', none of whom are elected MPs. This 'Gaullist' element in the new polity has been evident for some years. The recent elections, especially the referendum, indicate the appropriateness of coupling with this the term 'Bonapartist'. The President has at least temporarily succeeded in reducing the level of political militancy of a population formerly ranking as one of the most politicised in the world.[5] He has also either neutralised within his coalition or isolated the leading elements of the political – ideological movements which have, over recent decades, made the running in Sri Lankan politics — Sinhalese – Buddhist 'nationalism',[6] the more specific regional-cum-ethnic revivalism of Kandyan Sinhalese Buddhists, the militant separatism of the Sri Lankan Tamils, and the popular radicalism (Marxism) of the Low Country Sinhalese. He has obtained in a way directly reminiscent of Marx's analysis of the Bonapartist polity of Louis Napoleon, the consent of the small-scale farming population ('peasantry') for the continuance of the President's personal rule and for a cessation, in his favour, of inter-party electoral competition. And, at least until the violence of mid-1983, he had aligned himself firmly with ethnic minorities — the Indian Tamils, Sinhalese Christians, Muslims and the anti-separatist Sri Lanka Tamils of the east coast, especially near Batticaloa — whose demands are for protection and material favours from the state rather than, as in the case of militant Sinhalese Buddhists and Sri Lankan Tamils, for (provocative) changes in the form and symbols of the polity — a 'Buddhist state' and a separate Tamil state respectively.

The Presidential Election of October 1982

Although the outcome of this election violated established patterns, there was no such novelty about the pattern of party competition. Despite the new Constitution and electoral system, the pattern of party electoral support was in general very much as it has been since the emergence of the SLFP in the 1950s. In sum, most voters from the majority Sinhalese community supported either the UNP or the SLFP. Among the Sinhalese, support for the SLFP and, in the densely populated south-western lowlands, support for the various Marxist parties, came disproportionately from rural Sinhalese Buddhists, while urban and Christian Sinhalese were more likely to support the UNP. Sri Lanka Tamil votes went mainly to Tamil parties demanding administrative and political devolution or autonomy for the Tamil areas, but with significant marginal competition from the 'Sinhalese' parties, especially outside the Jaffna peninsula, the heartland of Sri Lanka Tamil society. Finally, other ethnic minorities — Muslims, Indian Tamils (mainly estate labourers),

Sinhalese Christians (mainly Catholics), Malays and Burghers (descendants of the Dutch)[7] — were wooed by both main 'Sinhalese' parties, but more successfully by the UNP, and with more or less explicit concern for communal interests. Within this pattern of overall stability, over recent decades there have been a number of consistent trends. Two in particular were further accentuated or confirmed by the results of the 1982 elections. The first is the electoral decline of the established Marxist parties[8] and their partial replacement by the Janatha Vimukthi Peramuna (JVP), now organised on a 'parliamentary' basis around the leadership of Rohana Wijeweera, who led the formerly revolutionary JVP into the 1971 insurgency.[9] The second is the continuing decline of independent non-party voting. Admittedly voters did not have the option of voting for independents in 1982. However, except the special case of the Sri Lanka Tamils (see below), voter turnout was elsewhere almost as high as in 1977 (columns (d)–(f) of Table 3.2), indicating that few of the voters were strongly attached to independent politicians rather than national parties.

The concern of this paper is, however, not with the continuity of electoral behaviour between 1982 and previous years, but with the fact that there were some significant marginal shifts in 1982 compared to 1977. In so far as one can identify the causes of shifts from aggregate data on voting patterns relating to electoral districts and parliamentary electorates, the data very strongly suggest that ethnic group identification was the main cause of these shifts. In sum, the UNP suffered a relative *loss* of support from Sinhalese Buddhists and became more dependent on the support of the ethnic minorities, although rather ambiguously so in the case of Sri Lanka Tamils. The evidence for this claim and its significance for Sri Lankan politics are discussed below.

Interpreting the Statistics

The statistical analysis below is based on comparisons of voting in the 1977 parliamentary and the 1982 presidential elections. Such a method raises four actual or potential problems.

The first arises from the change in the Constitution and electoral system, and the fact that one is not quite comparing like with like. In 1977 voters were choosing an MP partly at least to represent local interests. They had the option of voting for independent candidates representing particular local interests. In 1982 the voters comprised a single national electorate voting for the President. The impact of this

Table 3.2: Changes in Electoral Behaviour and their Determinants by Electoral District, 1977 Parliamentary and 1982 Presidential Elections

Electoral district	% of the population by ethnic group, 1981 — Sinhalese Buddhists[1] (a)	Sri Lanka Tamils (b)	Other[2] (c)	% of the electorate voting 1977 (d)	1982 (e)	(f)	UNP party bloc[3] 1977 (g)	1982 (h)	Other Sinhalese party bloc[4] 1977 (i)	1982 (j)	(k)
Group A[5]											
Colombo	71	10	19	80	78	0.98	57	58	34	42	1.01
Gampaha	71	3	26	88	83	1.06	54	53	45	47	0.97
Kalutara	84	1	15	88	85	0.96	54	50	35	50	0.94
Kandy	74	5	21	88	86	0.97	54	60	34	40	1.11
Matale	79	6	15	90	86	0.96	63	58	36	42	0.92
Galle	94	1	5	87	82	0.95	54	50	40	50	0.93
Matara	95	1	4	86	84	0.97	55	49	42	51	0.89
Hambantota	97	0	3	88	82	0.95	56	46	40	54	0.83
Digamadulla[8]	37	20	43	88	79	0.90	45	56	26	39	1.27
Kurunegala	90	1	9	90	86	0.97	57	56	40	44	0.98
Puttalam	48	1	51	87	81	0.93	56	59	40	41	1.06
Anuradhapura	90	1	9	88	85	0.96	53	50	45	50	0.94
Polonnaruwa	90	2	8	85	83	0.97	58	56	39	44	0.97
Badulla	68	6	26	88	86	0.98	59	59	38	41	1.00
Moneragala	93	2	5	85	82	0.97	55	49	42	50	0.90
Ratnapura	85	2	13	89	86	0.97	53	51	41	49	0.96
Kegalle	85	2	13	88	84	0.96	55	57	43	43	1.03
Group B[6]											
Nuwara Eliya	35	13	65	87	86	0.98	57	63	33	37	1.10

Table 3.2 — continued

Electoral district	% of the population by ethnic group, 1981			% of the electorate voting		(e)/(d)	% of valid votes cast for				(h)/(g)
	Sinhalese Buddhists[1]	Sri Lanka Tamils	Other[2]	1977	1982		UNP party bloc[3]		Other Sinhalese party bloc[4]		
							1977	1982	1977	1982	
	(a)	(b)	(c)	(d)	(e)	(f)	(g)	(h)	(i)	(j)	(k)
Group C[7]											
Jaffna	0	95	5	82	44	0.54	3	21	3	39	7.93
Wanni[9]	7	60	33	86	59	0.69	31	46	neg.	37	1.51
Batticaloa	3	71	26	89	70	0.78	26	40	28	21	1.57
Trincomalee	32	34	44	86	70	0.82	47	49	25	41	1.03
Sri Lanka	69	13	18	87	80	0.92	51	53	36	44	1.04

Sources: As in note 1 and columns (a)–(c) from *Census of Population and Housing, Sri Lanka — 1981 Preliminary Release No 1*, Department of Census and Statistics, Colombo (1981), Table 1.

Notes:

1. The 1981 census figures are not cross-tabulated by ethnic groups and religions. However, it is quite justifiable to follow the procedure used here and assume that virtually all Buddhists are Sinhalese Buddhists. At the 1946 census 99 per cent of all Buddhists were Sinhalese (calculated from data in *Census of Population, 1971 Sri Lanka, General Report*, Department of Census and Statistics, Colombo (1978), pp. 79, 89).

2. The 'other ethnic groups' category includes, in order of quantitative importance: Sri Lanka Moors, Indian Tamils, Sinhalese Christians, Malays, Burghers and Indian Moors.

3. The 'UNP party bloc' comprises the UNP and the small Ceylon Workers Congress (CWC). (See notes to Table 3.1.)

4. The 'other Sinhalese party bloc' comprises, in 1977, the SLFP, LSSP and CP, and in 1982 the SLFP, LSSP, JVP and NSSP (for details see notes to Table 3.1).

5. Group A electoral districts are those in which neither Sri Lanka Tamils nor estate Tamils are represented in large numbers. They comprise all districts in which Sinhalese Buddhists are in the majority plus Digamadulla, where Muslims are the largest single group and Puttalam, where Sinhalese Christians comprise about a third of the population, giving the Sinhalese (Buddhist and Christian) a large overall majority.

6. Nuwara Eliya is the only district to have a very large proportion of estate Tamils — 47 per cent of the population.

7. Group C electoral districts are those in which Sri Lanka Tamils account for a third or more of the population.

8. The Digamadulla electoral district corresponds to Amparai administrative district.

9. The Wanni electoral district comprises the administrative districts of Mannar, Vavuniya and Mullaitivu.

change in the electoral system was almost certainly greatest among Moors and Indian Tamils. For they have a certain tradition of local community solidarity in politics, electing community leaders who then use their parliamentary voting power to obtain from the government of the day assistance for their own communities.[10] However, these minorities comprise only a small proportion of voters and, more importantly, had even by 1977 been to a large extent inducted into the dominant pattern of party competition at electorate level. Apart from one Sinhalese independent MP who immediately joined the SLFP[11] and S. Thondaman, the leader of the Ceylon Workers Congress (CWC) — the trade union-cum-political party representing most Indian Tamil estate workers — who immediately became a Cabinet member, the MPs elected in 1977 represented only the UNP, the SLFP and the Tamil United Liberation Front (TULF), the separatist Sri Lanka Tamil party. With the exception of those voting from Sri Lanka Tamil parties, in both 1977 and 1982 the great majority of voters were consciously voting for a government. The evenness of electoral swings over the island supports this view (see column (k), Table 3.2, and the text below).

The second problem in interpreting electoral data concerns the drawing of inferences about which categories of voters changed parties and why they did so. In the absence of information on the voting behaviour of a sample of individual voters[12] one must beware of committing the 'ecological fallacy' of, for example, assuming that a shift to the UNP in districts in which minority groups are numerous is in fact the result of changes in voting behaviour by members of minority groups rather than Sinhalese Buddhists. A related issue is the danger of assuming that changes in voting behaviour by, for example, Sinhalese Buddhists, are due to their ethnic identity and not to some other unrelated factor. These problems are dealt with below.

The third and more concrete problem of statistical interpretation lies in the large-scale abstention from the polls by Sri Lanka Tamils in 1982. This was the result of the TULF's decision not to participate. Analysis would have been easier if the TULF had in fact called for a boycott, for abstentions would then be a measure of their strength. Not only did they stop short of calling a boycott, but the standard of Tamil separatism was actually borne in the presidential contest by Kumar Ponnambalam, a prominent non-TULF politician of the Tamil Congress (TC). There is then no clear criterion for measuring either electoral support for the policy of a separate Tamil state

Table 3.3: Changes in Electoral Behaviour in Group C ('Sri Lanka Tamil') Districts between the 1977 Parliamentary and 1982 Presidential Elections

Electoral district	% of Sri Lanka Tamils in 1981 population[1]	% of total number of registered electors voting for										Independents	% of electors abstaining		
		UNP			Other Sinhalese parties[2]			Tamil parties[3]						
		1977	1982	$\frac{(c)}{(b)}$	1977	1982	$\frac{(f)}{(e)}$	1977	1982	$\frac{(i)}{(h)}$	1977	1977	1982	$\frac{(l)}{(m)}$
(a)	(a)	(b)	(c)	(d)	(e)	(f)	(g)	(h)	(i)	(j)	(k)	(l)	(m)	(n)
Jaffna	95	2	10	4.6	2	17	8.2	59	18	0.3	18	18	56	3.0
Wanni	60	26	28	1.1	neg.	22	39.4	46	10	0.2	12	14	41	2.8
Batticaloa	71	22	28	1.3	24	14	0.6	40	27	0.7	–	12	30	2.5
Trincomalee	34	40	34	0.8	21	28	1.4	23	8	0.3	neg.	14	30	2.1

Notes:
1. Corresponds to column (a) of Table 3.2.
2. Almost entirely SLFP.
3. Relates to the TULF in 1977 and the TC in 1982.

or the relative electoral strength of the two main Tamil parties. Such conclusions as can be drawn about Sri Lanka Tamil voting in 1982 compared to 1977 are based on treating separately the four (Group C) electoral districts in which Sri Lanka Tamils form a third or more of the population. These districts are excluded from the statistical analysis because of the comparability problems caused by large-scale abstentions in 1982 (see Tables 3.2 and 3.3 and Map 3.1).

Nuwara Eliya District (Group B) has also been excluded from statistical analysis, but for a different reason. This is the only district in which Indian Tamils form a large proportion of the population — 47 per cent in 1981 (column (e), Table 3.4). The problem here is that in the case of Indian Tamils, one cannot infer voting strength from population numbers, since only a minority have Sri Lankan citizenship. Details are not available at district level on the number of Indian Tamils who have citizenship and/or who are enrolled on electoral registers. Only in the Nuwara Eliya case would the counting of all adult Indian Tamils as potential voters seriously jeopardise statistical analysis. Nuwara Eliya has, therefore, been treated separately, but in the knowledge that Indian Tamils comprise an important fraction of its electorate.

Table 3.4: Changes in Electoral Behaviour between the Presidential Election of October 1982 and the Referendum of December 1982

Electoral district	% of 'yes' votes at referendum	No. of persons voting at referendum as % of no. voting at presidential election	Proportion of 'yes' votes at referendum as % of UNP share of votes at presidential election	% of votes cast in all general elections, 1947–77, going to Marxist parties[1]	% of estate Tamils in the population, 1981
	(a)	(b)	(c)	(d)	(e)
Group A					
Colombo	53	83	92	29	1
Gampaha	58	82	109	8	neg.
Kalutara	49	82	98	30	4
Kandy	62	88	104	4	9
Matale	73	93	126	1	7
Galle	47	82	94	22	1
Matara	51	87	103	28	2
Hambantota	45	82	98	12	neg.
Digamadulla	59	96	105	4	neg.
Kurunegala	62	87	111	5	neg.

Table 3.4—*continued*

Electoral district	% of 'yes' votes at referendum	No. of persons voting at referendum as % of no. voting at presidential election	Proportion of 'yes' votes at referendum as % of UNP share of votes at presidential election	% of votes cast in all general elections, 1947–77, going to Marxist parties[1]	% of estate Tamils in the population, 1981
	(a)	(b)	(c)	(d)	(e)
Puttalam	60	83	102	2	1
Anuradhapura	68	87	137	5	neg.
Polonnaruwa	58	83	104	1	neg.
Badulla	70	90	119	9	21
Moneragala	64	87	130	4	3
Ratnapura	58	88	114	21	11
Kegalle	57	87	100	19	6
Group B					
Nuwara Eliya	73	93	115	2	47
Group C					
Jaffna	9	133	42	9	2
Wanni	34	106	74	1	15
Batticaloa	39	100	98	2	1
Trincomalee	43	98	88	1	3
Sri Lanka	55	88	103	14	6

Note:
1. Includes all main recognised Marxist parties from 1947: LSSP, CP, the Mahajana Eksath Peramuna (from 1959 onwards), and the now defunct Bolshevik–Leninist and Viplavakari Lanka Sama Samaja parties.
Sources: as in note 1, Table 3.2.

Statistical Analysis: Group A Districts

Group A comprises all electoral districts except those in Groups B and C which have been treated separately for reasons given above. Sinhalese Buddhists form the majority or the overwhelming majority of the population in all but two of the 17 Group A districts. In Puttalam District a substantial Sinhalese Catholic population makes Sinhalese, both Buddhists and Catholics, the majority group. Digamadulla District has substantial populations of Moors, Sinhalese and Sri Lanka Tamils.

In columns (g)–(j) in Table 3.2, figures are given on the division of votes in 1977 and 1982 between two party blocs. The first, the 'UNP bloc', comprises the UNP and the CWC, the party of the Indian

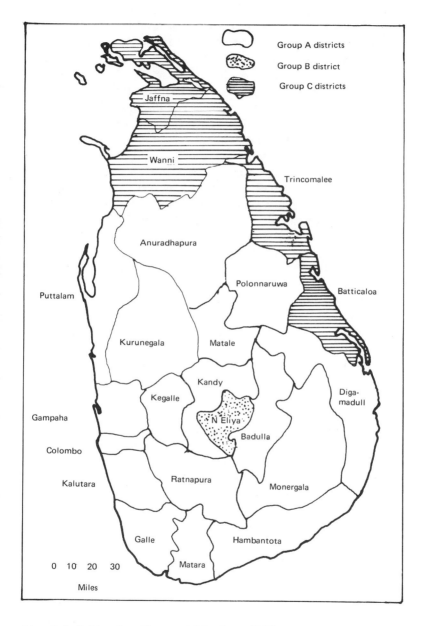

Map 3.1: Sri Lanka: Electoral Districts, 1982

Tamil estate workers, which is of major significance only in Nuwara Eliya District. The CWC was tacitly allied to the UNP in 1977 and very firmly and explicitly so in 1982. The second bloc, the 'Other Sinhalese party bloc', comprises the SLFP and the various Marxist parties which have tended to ally with the SLFP and which share the same rural Sinhalese Buddhist electoral base.[13] The stability in the pattern of electoral competition between these two blocs is illustrated by the following results. In 1977, the Group A districts elected 129 UNP MPs and seven SLFP MPs. Had the 1982 presidential vote been 'translated' into a parliamentary vote on the old constituency basis, the party position would be much the same, the UNP having lost eight seats to the SLFP, but winning another two from them.[14] The main point here, however, is that between the two elections, there was a small but nationally very uniform relative shift of votes from the UNP bloc to the 'Other Sinhalese party bloc' (essentially to the SLFP) in areas dominated by Sinhalese Buddhists. This, on a district basis, is illustrated by regression 1 in the appendix: compared to 1977, the UNP bloc share of valid votes cast in 1982 tended to fall, in a statistically very significant fashion, in proportion to the percentage of Sinhalese Buddhists in the district populations. This shift thus accentuates the previous pattern, illustrated by regression 2, in which the strength of UNP bloc electoral support was inversely related to the proportion of Sinhalese Buddhists in the population. Regression 3 illustrates the obverse of the relative shift between 1977 and 1982: compared to 1977, the UNP bloc share of valid votes cast in 1982 increased, in a statistically very significant fashion, in proportion to the percentage of all minorities. It is important to note that this relative shift of votes to the UNP bloc is in a statistical sense better explained by regression 3 than by regression 4. In the latter the explanatory variable is the proportion of the district populations comprising 'other minorities', that is, neither Sinhalese Buddhists or Sri Lanka Tamils. The conclusion to be drawn is that in Group A districts at least — those outside the main Sri Lanka Tamil areas — Sri Lanka Tamil voters tended to support the UNP more strongly in 1982 than in 1977.

At this point, one might raise the question of the 'ecological fallacy' mentioned above. How can one be sure that the shift away from the UNP in districts dominated by Sinhalese Buddhists was the result of Sinhalese Buddhist voters themselves, and not members of other groups, shifting their support from the UNP? Conversely, was it indeed the votes of groups other than Sinhalese Buddhists which explained the relative shift to the UNP in the district where these groups were numerous? In the absence of the conclusive proof that only statistics on individual voting behaviour could provide, one can, in two stages, demonstrate the overwhelming plausibility of the claim that these observed inter-party shifts were indeed the result of changes in ethnic group behaviour of the kind posited above, and basically because of ethnic group considerations.

In the first place, it is clear from an examination of Table 3.2 that in the 'extreme' cases of Group A districts with either very high or very low proportions of Sinhalese Buddhists — Hambantota and Digamadulla respectively — the observed relative shifts of votes between party blocs could not have been achieved without Sinhalese Buddhists switching from the UNP bloc in Hambantota and members of other ethnic groups shifting to the UNP bloc in Digamadulla. This is *prima facie* evidence in support of our claim, all the more so as the relative party position at electorate level was very much the same in 1982 as in 1977. Had there been a great deal of complex switching of votes between parties then, since different ethnic groups are unequally concentrated in different electorates, many more electorates would have 'changed hands', in a figurative sense, in 1982.

In the second place and rather more importantly, the shift of Sinhalese Buddhist votes to the SLFP and minorities' votes to the UNP conforms very much to expectations based on government policies and on political issues before and during the campaign. In various ways, the minorities had good reason to be relatively more pleased than Sinhalese Buddhists with UNP policy. The minorities tend to be more urbanised, more concentrated in the Colombo area, and more engaged in non-agricultural activities, especially commerce, than Sinhalese Buddhists.[15] The free market economic policies of the UNP since 1977 have tended to benefit them, albeit with many exceptions, especially among poor Muslims in North Colombo. At the same time, opportunities for foreign travel benefit groups like Sri Lanka Tamils and Burghers with foreign connections, and the UNP government's policy on admissions to higher education institutions has been less slanted in favour of rural Sinhalese-educated students than was that of the previous SLFP-led government. Even more concretely, the question of the UNP government's alleged 'softness' towards non-Buddhists was a significant political issue in the year prior to the election. President Jayewardene had taken a relatively firm and very public line in quashing

Sinhalese Buddhist militancy in his own party, expelling from the party — and thus, under the 1978 Constitution, from Parliament — the MP for Panadura for public expressions of Sinhalese Buddhist chauvinism, and severely reprimanding the District Minister for Ratnapura for less-than-total opposition to Sinhalese communal violence in his district in 1981.

On the other side, there has recently emerged a network of militant Sinhalese Buddhists, including some priests, who have openly attacked the President for dereliction of duty towards Buddhism and for appointing too many Christians to senior posts. In early 1982, a public meeting at which these kinds of points were being made was broken up by what were officially described as loyal UNP members enraged at attacks on the President. As C.R. de Silva has shown in the preceding essay, all candidates during the presidential election campaign were presented with demands from the Council of Sri Lankan Buddhist Societies to make Sri Lanka a fully Buddhist state. It is significant, however, that the most sympathetic response came from the SLFP candidate.[16] It is widely believed that these Buddhist militants have close connections to the SLFP.

The statistical analysis summarised above indicates a relative swing of Sinhalese Buddhists to the SLFP between 1977 and 1982, and a corresponding movement of members of minorities to the UNP.

The Group B District — Nuwara Eliya

Nuwara Eliya District has been treated separately because of the weight there of Indian Tamil voters, whose precise numbers are unfortunately unknown. However, the election results there — a very strong swing to the UNP bloc (Table 3.2) — conform very closely to conclusions derived from the analysis of Group A districts. For a very close political alliance has been forged since 1977 between the UNP and the CWC, the main representative of the Indian Tamil estate labour force. The leader of the CWC, S. Thondaman, is the sole CWC MP, and represents a Nuwara Eliya electorate. As Minister of Rural Industrial Development since 1977, he has been able to direct additional resources to his community, partly through his control of the livestock industry, for commercial dairying is an important secondary source of income for the estate populations of the tea-growing areas. President Jayewardene has also taken an unprecedently favourable public stance towards the Indian Tamil community, calling for example for their full integration into Sri

Lankan society in a speech made only a few weeks before the election.[17] The Indian Tamil voters appear to have responded very positively by throwing their full weight behind him.

Group C ('Sri Lanka Tamil') Districts

In these four electoral districts with a third or more Sri Lanka Tamils in their populations, interpretation of the 1982 results is complicated by the behaviour of the Tamil parties. The main Tamil party, the TULF, decided not to participate, and thus led many of its supporters to abstain. Yet the TULF stopped short of calling for a total boycott of the polls, and left its supporters free to vote for another Tamil candidate, Kumar Ponnambalam, who also called for a separate Tamil state. Little can be said directly about changes in the degree of support either for Tamil separation or for the TULF. However, some significant conclusions can be drawn from the figures in Table 3.3, which in this case relate to the total electorate rather than, as in Tables 3.1 and 3.2, to those actually voting.

These conclusions derive from contrasting changes in voting patterns between the districts of Jaffna and Wanni on the one hand and Batticaloa on the other. (The results in Trincomalee District do not fall into any clear pattern and are very hard to interpret.) It can be seen from Table 3.3 that in 1977 Batticaloa voters very much more integrated into the national, as opposed to the Sri Lanka Tamil, pattern of party competition than were those in Jaffna and Wanni. In Batticaloa 46 per cent of the electorate voted for the Sinhalese parties, and only 40 per cent for the TULF, the recognised Tamil party contesting at that time. The corresponding figures for Jaffna and Wanni were 4 per cent and 59 per cent, and 15 per cent and 46 per cent respectively. This reflects a long-standing difference — and even antagonism — between two Sri Lanka Tamil populations oriented to two different urban complexes: Jaffna on the one hand and Batticaloa on the other. Jaffna, the larger of the two and the main centre of Sri Lanka Tamil culture, has always been the home of Tamil separatist sentiment, while the Batticaloa Tamils have been more favourable to the idea of continuing to live in a unitary, Sinhalese-dominated state. Batticaloa Tamils have tended to give substantial support to the UNP.[18]

The significance of the 1982 results lies in the fact that they illustrate an increasing polarisation between Jaffna and the Wanni on the one hand, and Batticaloa on the other. This polarisation was expressed in the changing ratios between the votes cast for the two

main Sinhalese party blocs. Since almost all the votes cast for these
blocs in these districts were, especially in 1982, either for the UNP or
the SLFP, we will henceforth talk in terms of these parties themselves rather than of the blocs which they dominate elsewhere in the
island.

In 1977, the number of votes obtained by the SLFP and the UNP
in Batticaloa District were approximately equal (Table 3.3). In 1982
the district as a whole swung very strongly to the UNP relative to the
SLFP: the percentage of UNP votes to SLFP votes was 92 per cent in
1977 and 200 per cent in 1982. This was mainly because the SLFP
vote fell by 50 per cent in absolute terms (Table 3.3). A swing of this
size, in a district in which Sri Lanka Tamils comprise 71 per cent of
the population, must certainly owe something to changes in voting
behaviour by Sri Lanka Tamils. The results strongly suggest that in
Batticaloa, Sri Lanka Tamils and also Sri Lanka Moors (who comprise another quarter of the district population) behaved like minorities elsewhere in the island and between 1977 and 1982 switched from
the SLFP to the UNP.

Jaffna and Wanni Districts behaved in the opposite fashion.
While the proportion of the total electorate voting for the UNP
increased to a small extent, the SLFP vote increased dramatically
from a very small base. In 1977, the number of votes obtained by the
UNP and the SLFP in the two districts collectively were 31,000 and
5,000 respectively. In 1982 they numbered 81,000 and 101,000,
increases of 160 per cent and 1,719 per cent respectively. How is this
big increase in SLFP support from Sri Lanka Tamil voters in Jaffna
and Wanni to be explained? It appears that the answer is two fold.

First, the UNP government, despite the President's generally successful attempts to project himself as the guardian of the ethnic
minorities, has come into open and violent political confrontation
with both the TULF and Tamil separatist sentiment generally. This
is manifested both in the increasing repression associated with the *de
facto* 'occupation' of Jaffna and Wanni Districts by the armed
forces and, more particularly, in the violence in Jaffna in 1980 and
1981 stemming in large part from attempts by the government to
manipulate the results of the 1980 elections to the Jaffna District
Development Council in favour of UNP candidates. The vote for the
SLFP may have been in part an expression of protest against the
UNP government, and was no doubt in part motivated by
Kobbekaduwa's promise to repeal the anti-terrorist laws. This is,
however, not a complete explanation, for abstention or voting for

the TC candidate were other and perhaps more convincing modes of expressing the same sentiments. A second and more concrete reason for Tamil support for the SLFP can be found in material interests. The reason, as President Jayewardene has reportedly said, lies in 'potatoes, chillies and onions'. The rural areas of Jaffna and, to a lesser extent, parts of the Wanni, specialise in the production of these and other high-value vegetables. During the rule of the 1970–77 SLFP-led government, in which Hector Kobbekaduwa was Minister of Agriculture, imports of various vegetables and other so-called 'subsidiary food crops' were severely restricted or banned. Producer prices reached unprecedented heights, only to collapse after the UNP government permitted unrestricted imports.[19] It is reported that Kobbekaduwa's election campaign promises to restore these import restrictions evoked a favourable response from Tamil farmers, for the five Jaffna electorates in which Kobbekaduwa topped the poll appear to correspond to those areas where vegetable cultivation is more important.[20] By contrast, he obtained fewer votes than both the TC and the UNP candidates in Jaffna town and the adjacent suburban Nallur electorate.

Implications of the Presidential Election

There is little doubt that ethnic group identification was the main basis of changes in electoral behaviour in Sri Lanka between 1977 and 1982. It is tempting to describe this as a partial reversion to the (rather turbulent) politics of the late 1950s and early 1960s, when ethnic (and caste) considerations seem to have been more salient in political conflict than they were in the more materialist politics of the late 1960s and 1970s. But, even leaving aside the question of the depth and permanency of these recent changes, it is clear that history is not repeating itself exactly. The SLFP had, by mid-1982, again become more closely identified with Sinhalese Buddhist sentiment. But its candidate, Kobbekaduwa, signally failed to make gains among one group of Sinhalese from whom he expected much — the rural Kandyans whom he once represented in Parliament, who gained most from his land reforms in the early 1970s[21] and to whom he made special appeals in 1982. Not only did he fail to gain more votes than Jayewardene in the electorate which he (Kobbekaduwa) represented between 1970 and 1977, but the Kandyan districts generally failed to rally to him. Indeed, Kobbekaduwa's share of the vote in 1982 was very significantly less than 'expected' on the basis of the regression results (report in the appendix) in two of the main

Kandyan districts, Kandy and Kegalle. Antipathy between Kandyan and Low Country Sinhalese, which might have helped Kobbekaduwa, appears to have waned considerably.

Also in contrast to the earlier period, the Sri Lanka Tamils appear by late 1982 to have become polarised in their attitudes towards the Sinhalese-dominated polity. Those centred upon Jaffna had become somewhat more hostile to the UNP, the Sinhalese party with which they have traditionally felt the greater affinity (or the least antipathy). The Sri Lanka Tamils elsewhere in the island had identified themselves even more clearly with the UNP and the other minority groups. However, those concerned about the future of Sri Lanka as a unitary state may perhaps take heart from the fact that a substantial fraction of the Jaffna-centred Tamils were still prepared to engage in national electoral politics on a transactional basis. Their support for the SLFP candidate over the question of vegetable prices suggests that they were prepared to respond positively to appeals to their material self-interest.

The Referendum of December 1982

Statistics on the voting pattern at the referendum, with some comparisons with the previous presidential poll, are given in Table 3.4. Before dealing with the main implications, we might note that among the Sri Lanka Tamil voters (Group C districts) one trend identified above was further accentuated. Compared to the presidential election, voter turnout increased in all Group C districts except Trincomalee, where it fell fractionally (column (b), Table 3.4). For, at the referendum, the main Sri Lanka Tamil party, the TULF, joined with all opposition parties except a splinter of the SLFP to call for a 'No' vote. The Sri Lanka Tamils responded positively, above all in Jaffna District, where 91 per cent voted 'No' (column (a), Table 3.4). The point of immediate significance is, however, that the actual shift of Sri Lanka Tamil voters away from the President and his party, as measured in column (c) of Table 3.4, was greatest in Jaffna and lowest (in fact negligible) in Batticaloa. The Tamils of Batticaloa indicated even more firmly that they see their future within a unitary Sri Lankan state rather than the Tamil *Eelam*.[22]

The main points of significance in the referendum voting pattern, however, lie in Group A and B districts. A point of entry for analysing the results in these districts is a comparison at district level of the stability of the 'UNP' share of the vote between (a) the 1982 presidential election and the 1977 parliamentary election and (b) the 1982 referendum and the 1982 presidential election. Here the 'UNP' vote is defined as the percentage of the vote given: to the 'UNP bloc' (UNP and CWC) in the 1977 parliamentary election; to Jayewardene in the 1982 presidential election; and in favour at the 1982 referendum. The presidential poll and, even more, the referendum were of course not purely party contests. 'Stability' relates to the extent to which the changes in the UNP vote at district level deviated from the pattern of changes in the UNP vote at the national level between each succeeding pair of elections. In fact the coefficients of variation between, respectively, the 1977 parliamentary elections and the 1982 presidential election, and the presidential election and the referendum, were almost identical.[23] In other words, leaving out self-cancelling mutual switches of votes between the 'UNP' on the one side and the 'non-UNP' on the other, there was just as much net electoral volatility in the two months between the two 1982 elections as there was in the 63 months between the 1977 parliamentary elections and the 1982 presidential poll. This in itself is not surprising. For after all the referendum was a distinctively different kind of election from the others. It was not directly about choosing a government, and the constitutionality or moral validity of the referendum was naturally made into a major issue by the opposition.

The actual changes by district in support for the UNP between October and December 1982 are given in column (c) of Table 3.4. A very clear pattern emerges. When standardised for the overall national swing to the UNP, there was either no swing to the UNP or a swing away in seven districts: Puttalam, Colombo, Kalutara, Kegalle, Galle, Matara and Hambantota. As the map shows, these districts form a homogeneous block along the densely populated south-western coastline. They are not distinguished from other Group A and B districts by such variables as literacy levels, rates of school attendance or the proportion of Sinhalese Buddhists in the population. There are, however, at least three related sets of characteristics which they have mainly or entirely in common. First, all except Kegalle are populated mainly by Low Country Sinhalese, while all the other districts swinging to the UNP, except Gampaha, are populated mainly by Kandyan Sinhalese. Secondly, in all these districts except Hambantota, the rural populations are relatively heavily engaged in non-agricultural activities, and engaged in farming on a part-time basis. By contrast, the districts swinging to the UNP are characterised by either estate production or, more importantly, small-scale 'peasant' farming.[24] Thirdly, and most clearly and significantly, all of the districts swinging away from the UNP are those with a long tradition of (minority) electoral support for Marxist political parties (column (d), Table 3.4). Indeed, as regression 5 in the appendix illustrates, the absence of a tradition of Marxist voting is a statistically significant explanation of the extent of the electoral swing to the UNP between the two 1982 polls. The most dramatic illustration is the contrasting behaviour of the two adjacent districts of Colombo and Gampaha, until 1978 united as the old Colombo administrative district. Colombo, with a strong minority Marxist tradition, while at the same time one of the main traditional strongholds of the UNP,[25] swung markedly away from the UNP. Gampaha, a traditional stronghold of the SLFP[26] and with no comparable Marxist tradition, swung markedly to the UNP.

In fact the swing to the UNP between the two 1982 elections was most marked in the traditional SLFP areas, Gampaha and the Kandyan Districts, especially the Dry Zone districts of Anuradhapura, Matale, Moneragala and Kurunegala.[27] Until recently 'most of the Dry Zone has remained an SLFP stronghold'.[28] Despite the fact that the 1982 presidential elections appeared to confirm the demise of the Marxist vote, it was in the traditional Marxist areas that the electorate dissented at the referendum proposal and tended to stay at home more than elsewhere.

There is an explanation for this pattern which must be regarded as overwhelmingly plausible unless a better one is found. The areas with a history of Marxist voting — more or less the Low Country Sinhalese districts except Gampaha — have also been politically much better organised and vocal, and the nurseries of almost all new political and ideological movements among the Sinhalese for the past century. More so than elsewhere, the electorates were unwilling to cede their political rights to the presidential leadership. They responded to the opposition parties' case that the referendum was an undesirable constitutional innovation, even if they tended to support the UNP in October. The referendum voting, to a greater degree than the presidential election, was in part about issues other than party: it was almost the desirability of conceding established political rights to the President. The small-farming or peasant populations of the Kandyan areas responded to J.R. Jayewardene's referendum in ways which vividly recall, albeit with reservations about the dramatic language, Marx's analysis of the support given to Louis Bonaparte by the French peasantry:

> They cannot represent themselves, they must be represented. Their representative must at the same time appear as their master, as an authority over them, as an unlimited governmental power that protects them against the other classes and sends them rain and sunshine from above. The political influence of the small-holding peasants, therefore, finds its final expression in the executive power subordinating society to itself.[29]

As one might predict on the basis of Marx's analysis, in Sri Lanka it was the smallholder or peasant rural populations, as opposed to the peri-urban 'rural' populations of the Low Country, who were pleased to bring themselves under the wing of the presidential (or executive) power. It is not inappropriate here to mention the present author's own work on the theme of the failure of the Sri Lankan peasantry to use their massive electoral power to pursue their class interests.[30]

The final point about the referendum result relates to the Indian Tamil vote. There is a clear relationship between the proportion of Indian Tamils in the district populations and a swing to the UNP between October and December, even if this is not statistically significant (regression 5 in the appendix). There is an equally clear, if once again not very close, tendency for voter turnout between October and December 1982 to fall least in the Group A and B districts with high proportions of Indian Tamils in the population (columns (b) and (e) of Table 3.4). Except in Nuwara Eliya, the Indian Tamil proportions of the electorates are so small that their behaviour is unlikely to show through very clearly in aggregate statistical analysis. Such statistical observations as one is able to make do, however, accord very closely with observers' claims that at the referendum the CWC political machine marched out Indian Tamil voters to support the President even more effectively than in the presidential election.[31] The rewards were not long in coming. In a major reversal of land policy, the Minister of Lands met the CWC leadership in January 1983 and agreed that non-citizen Indian Tamils occupying crown lands in the northern Sri Lanka Tamil districts would not be evicted as was previous practice, but would be granted annual occupancy certificates.[32]

J.R. Jayewardene's victories at the presidential election and the referendum appeared in late 1982 to be even greater than the electoral statistics indicated. He seemed to have fashioned a polity, a political atmosphere and an electoral coalition which promised considerable stability in the immediate future. The Muslim, estate Tamil and Christian communities seemed solidly behind him. The Sri Lanka Tamils were sufficiently split that the demand for a separate Tamil state could be even more clearly seen to be confined to the Jaffna peninsula. Both Tamil separatism and Sinhalese Buddhist militance, although always potential threats to the political order, seemed in the short term at least to have been contained. And the electorate as a whole appeared to have been persuaded to endorse a lull in inter-party electoral competition. Provided that the endemic violence practiced in the Sri Lanka Tamil areas by separatist guerrillas and the armed forces did not escalate out of control, provided that Sinhalese chauvinists did not turn again to anti-Tamil violence and provided that the President himself remained alive or arranged a powerful successor, then the prospects seemed right for the kind of political stability that is required for his economic programme to have some chance of success.

Appendix: Statistical Analysis of 1982 Election Results by Electoral Districts: Group A Districts Only.

1. Group A Districts; 1982 Presidential Poll

The variables are:

a — % of Sinhalese Buddhists in the district population, 1981 (= column (a) of Table 3.2).

c — % of 'other minorities' in the district population, 1981 (= column (c) of Table 3.2).

p — % of all ethnic group except Sinhalese Buddhists in the district population, 1981 (= 100 — variable a = sum of columns (b) and (c) of Table 3.2).

k — $\dfrac{\text{UNP bloc share of valid votes cast in 1982}}{\text{UNP bloc share of valid votes cast in 1977}}$ (= column (k) of Table 3.2).

$$1 - \frac{\text{UNP bloc share of valid votes cast in 1982}}{\text{'Other Sinhalese party bloc' share of valid votes cast in 1982}}$$

$$\left\{ = \frac{\text{column (h) of Table 3.2}}{\text{column (j) of Table 3.2}} \right\}$$

Regression 1 — $k = 1.3805 - 0.0050$ a $R^2 = 0.71$, $p < 0.005$, $n = 17$

Regression 2 — $1 = 1.9378 - 0.0092$ a $R^2 = 0.52$, $p < 0.005$, $n = 17$

Regression 3 — $k = 0.8802 + 0.0050$ p $R^2 = 0.71$, $p < 0.005$, $n = 17$

Regression 4 — $k = 0.8894 + 0.0056$ c $R^2 = 0.57$ $p < 0.005$, $n = 17$

2. Group A and B Districts (except Anuradhapura): 1982 Referendum

The variables are:

$$y - \frac{\text{\% of 'yes' votes at the 1982 referendum}}{\text{\% of valid votes cast for UNP nominee at 1982}} \times 100$$

Presidential election (= column (c) of Table 3.4).

x_1 – % of Indian Tamils in district population, 1981 (= column (e) of Table 3.4).

x_2 – % of all valid votes cast in all general elections, 1947–77, going to Marxist parties (= column (d) of Table 3.4).

Regression 5 —
$y = 112 + 0.231x_1 - 0.509^*x2$ $R^2 = 0.37$, $* = p < 0.025$, $n = 17$
$\quad\quad (0.17) \quad\quad (2.34)$

Notes

1. The sources of the electoral data used in this paper are as follows: G.P.S.H. de Silva, *A Statistical Survey of Elections to the Legislatures of Sri Lanka 1911–1977* (Colombo, 1979); *Ceylon Daily News Eighth Parliament of Sri Lanka 1977* (Colombo, 1977); *Island*, 22 October and 25 December 1982; *Daily News*, 25 October 1982; and *Sri Lanka News*, 30 December 1982. The term 'Gaullist' in the title of this paper is borrowed from A.J. Wilson, *The Gaullist System in Asia — The Constitution of Sri Lanka (1978)* (London, 1979). The author is grateful to James Manor for comments on an earlier draft of this paper.
2. Only one of three or four factions of the SLFP actively supported the campaign

of the party's presidential nominee, Hector Kobbekaduwa.

3. Other leading SLFP figures had not formally defected to the UNP, but were throwing their support behind the President.

4. The most notable case was Vijaya Kumaranatunga, Mrs Bandaranaike's son-in-law, and a key figure in the faction of the party which had actually supported the SLFP candidate in the presidential campaign.

5. J.P. Jupp, *Sri Lanka: Third World Democracy* (London, 1978), p. 189 and *passim*.

6. For some discussion of the conceptual problems involved in talking of 'nationalism' of the various Sri Lankan ethnic groups, see M. Roberts, 'Meanderings in the Pathways of Collective Identity and Nationalism' in M. Roberts (ed.), *Collective Identities, Nationalisms and Protest in Modern Sri Lanka* (Colombo, 1979).

7. Jupp, *Sri Lanka: Third World Democracy*, especially chs. 2, 3, 5 and 7.

8. The oldest and, until recently, the largest of the Marxist parties, the Lanka Sama Samaja Party (LSSP) suffered a humiliating rebuff in 1982 when its presidential candidate, Colvin R. de Silva, obtained less than 1 per cent of the vote despite being a well-known and respected public figure. The Communist Party did not contest the election, and supported the SLFP candidate.

9. The core of JVP support lies in the south-western lowlands, the established base of Marxist electoral support (Jupp, *Sri Lanka: Third World Democracy*, ch. 3).

10. Ibid., ch. 5.

11. R.P. Wijesiri, the second MP for the two-member Harrisspattuwa electorate. He was to rejoin the UNP after the 1982 presidential election.

12. Sri Lanka has no public opinion polls.

13. For details of the Marxist parties see the notes to Table 3.1. For an account of the history of their relationships with the SLFP see Jupp, *Sri Lanka: Third World Democracy*, ch. 3.

14. 'Old' parliamentary constituencies because the next parliamentary elections will be on a proportional representation basis at the district level. Included in the figures is the one independent MP who joined the UNP immediately after the election — see note 11.

15. M.P. Moore, 'The State and the Peasantry in Sri Lanka', D. Phil thesis, University of Sussex, 1981, p. 40.

16. For details see *Lanka Guardian*, 15 October 1982.

17. See *Observer*, 12 September 1982.

18. In 1977 Jaffna district returned 11 MPs, all Tamils and all from the TULF. Wanni also returned TULF members in each of its three electorates. Trincomalee district returned one Sinhalese and one Muslim MP (both UNP), and one Tamil TULF MP. Batticaloa district, despite the fact that Sri Lanka Tamils comprise 71 per cent of the population, gave very substantial support to the UNP. Of the four MPs returned, two were Tamil TULF men, one a Tamil UNP man, and one a Muslim UNP man. One of the TULF MPs, the first member for Batticaloa, defected almost immediately to the UNP. Details in . . . *Eighth Parliament of Sri Lanka*, pp. 132–51.

19. See Moore, 'The State and the Peasantry in Sri Lanka', pp. 210–13.

20. These are the electorates of Kankesanturai, Manipay, Kopay, Uduppiddy and Point Pedro. See *Daily News*, 25 October 1982.

21. See Moore, 'The State and the Peasantry in Sri Lanka', ch. 4.

22. *Eelam* is the Tamil term for the Tamil homeland.

23. The coefficients of variation were 10.37 per cent and 10.08 per cent respectively. For reasons given in the text above, the Anuradhapura District data were excluded from this calculation.

24. See Moore, 'The State and the Peasantry in Sri Lanka', ch. 6 and *passim*.

25. Jupp, *Sri Lanka: Third World Democracy*, ch. 7.

26. Ibid.

27. Polonnaruwa, also a Dry Zone district, did not swing to the UNP very strongly.

28. Jupp, *Sri Lanka: Third World Democracy*, p. 197.

29. K. Marx, *The Eighteenth Brumaire of Louis Bonaparte* (Moscow, 1972), p. 106.

30. Moore, 'The State and the Peasantry in Sri Lanka'.

31. *Lanka Guardian*, 1 January 1983 and *Daily News*, 25 December 1982.

32. *Sri Lanka News*, 20 January 1983. For the background of the former refusal of Sri Lankan parties and governments to grant any land rights to Indian Tamils see V. Samaraweera, 'Land as "Patrimony": Nationalist Response to Immigrant Labour Demand for land in Early Twentieth Century Sri Lanka', *Indian Economic and Social History Review*, xiv (1977).

4 THE ELECTIONS OF 1982

Lalith Athulathmudali

In 1982, Sri Lanka experienced two unique elections — unique in the country's constitutional history and unique to the people. Sri Lanka is a nation with long experience of democratic thinking and democratic systems. Ever since the people achieved universal franchise in 1931 they have been accustomed to periodic and systematic multi-party elections. Governments of differing political and socio-economic views have come and gone peacefully.[1] Perhaps an ingrained tolerance brought about by our religious and cultural traditions has created within our people a desire and respect for peaceful and just means of government, rather than for the revolutionary experiences not uncommon among many of the developing states. In numerous spheres, radical changes have been effected throughout the years — but through the democratic process. Our single attempt to change by revolutionary methods was short-lived and disastrous, leaving behind regrettable memories in the minds of both insurgents and the authorities.[2]

To understand the nature and results of the elections of 1982, one must understand the political and socio-economic background of the country, especially that which has prevailed since 1977. Statistics and statistical analyses become a forte of politicians and economists when events of national importance occur. Yet these are only a reflection of the thinking and feeling of the people, individually and in groups who form the electorate — of their socio-economic and political perceptions, their experiences of the past and their hopes for the future.

In Sri Lanka, the national election of 1977 marked the beginning of a period of significant changes. Politically, the overwhelming victory of the United National Party (UNP) resulted in a stable government. Economically, it brought about a radical change from the closed policies of the previous regime. The dominant features of that economy had been an overprotected internal trading system with rigid import and fiscal controls and increasing nationalisation of resources and services. These had created a package resulting in a near-zero growth rate and ever increasing unemployment.[3] Since

1977 there has been a systematic opening up of our economy, linking it with the world's economy.[4] Imports have been liberalised, subsidies curtailed to bearable limits and strong incentives provided to local entrepreneurs. The protectionism which had fostered inefficient domestic industries was lifted and uneconomic ventures into nationalisation halted.[5] The possibilities for various schemes for earning foreign exchange were pursued. Priority has been given to a planned export drive and incentives provided for tourism and foreign employment of our citizens. In the creation of the Greater Colombo Economic Commission (Free Trade Zone) and the Mahaveli River Development Scheme the government sought solutions for urgent problems.[6] At the time when even developed countries are faced with severe unemployment problems Sri Lanka's achievement between 1977 and 1982, of halving the number of persons unemployed, is indeed remarkable.[7]

One result of these activities was the creation of new social and economic groups of significant size and importance. All of these groups — the new thinking that fostered them and that they in turn engendered — inevitably influenced the political scene and the elections of 1982.

In their experimentation with new economic policies the government had, in the first two years of office, run into some problems — understandable when attempting to effect a new growth strategy within an uncongenial international economic environment. Inflation rose to unprecedented heights by early 1980, especially when a currency depreciation had to be introduced. Subsidies had to be re-targeted, resources switched from investment in long-term, slow-gestation schemes to short-term, less capital-intensive ones with rapid gestation.

However, by 1982 greater stability had been achieved. The government's appraisal of the situation and the decisive measures adopted saw inflation shrinking to a one digit figure. The creation of a very large number of employment situations was a significant factor. The remarkable achievement of changing from a major rice-importing country to one nearly self-sufficient in this staple was a contributory factor towards increased productivity.[8] Moreover, the consumer, who had for long been starved of even essential commodities, appreciated the new horizons brought into view by the open market policy adopted since 1977.

It is, then, apparent that a host of economic, social, political and psychological factors were in operation at the time when the decision was made to hold an election new to the people in many ways — new in that it brought about a direct election of the executive head and new in the method it incorporated of the single transferable vote.

To effect this decision, it was necessary to amend the existing Constitution only as to advance the date of the election. According to the 1978 Constitution a presidential election was to be held every six years. In August 1982, a constitutional amendment was made in Parliament that enabled the President, if he so wished it, to call for an earlier mandate and shorten his period by one year. Within Parliament and outside, many interesting views were expressed regarding this proposal. The main thrust of the parliamentary criticism of this proposal was on the grounds that it caused an infringement on the constitutionally established 'Sovereignty of the people' in that it (a) shortened the period of presidency which had been set at six years in the 1978 Constitution and (b) infringed on the people's use of the franchise.

It was contended that by seeking to reduce the period of office of the President, the sovereignty of the people to determine that tenure as set out in the 1978 Constitution was jeopardised. A panel of three Judges of the Supreme Court sat in adjudication. The Attorney General submitted that the proposed amendment was constitutional — and that it in no way alienated the sovereignty of the people; in fact, he contended that it provided more opportunities for the people to exercise their franchise.[9] The amendment, further, does not force the President to change his tenure at the end of four years. It only empowers him to appeal for a mandate before the end of his fixed term. The Attorney General also held that the proposed amendment in no way infringed upon the franchise. The Supreme Court decided that there was no infringement of fundamental rights.

There were many reasons for the advancement of the presidential election by 15 months. The party in power had, no doubt, a well organised set up while the opposition parties were in disarray. Yet fair play was exercised, especially in media-use, each candidate assigned equal time to speak for himself and his party on television and freedom to express himself in the national newspapers.

On 22 October 1982, Sri Lanka's first presidential election was held. Over eight million people went to the polls. A number of interesting features emerged. There were presidential candidates from even among those parties who opposed the concept itself. A very high percentage of votes was polled, totalling 81.1 per cent. In 21 of the 22 electoral districts the UNP obtained clear majorities. A comparative analysis of the 1977 and 1982 elections indicates the increasing popularity of the UNP — which polled 52.9 per cent of the total votes in 1982 as against 50.6 per cent in 1977.[10] The election itself was a peaceful one — and there is little doubt that despite its complexity and strangeness, it caught and held the imagination of the people. Sri Lanka's people have always been singularly mature in the ways of politics. A comparative analysis of voter-participation in national elections indicates the interesting fact that Sri Lanka showed a voter turnout in 1977 of 86.7 per cent. India's turnout in 1980 was 57.0 per cent. The United Kingdom's percentage in 1979 was 76 and the USA's 54. Our own general elections also record a steady increase in voter participation: 69 per cent in 1956, 75.9 per cent in 1960, 85.2 per cent in 1970 and 86.7 per cent in 1977. During these last three decades, as many as nine different political parties have been represented in our Parliament. Yet an analysis of votes polled at the three general elections held during this period shows an increasing concentration of votes for two or three major parties. Between 1960 and 1970, the UNP and the Sri Lanka Freedom Party (SLFP) collected 68 per cent to 75 per cent of the votes between them. In 1977 these two parties totalled over 80 per cent of the votes cast.

The result of the presidential election was an overwhelming victory for J.R. Jayewardene, the leader of the UNP. It was clear, then, that the country wanted him as its executive head and that the people approved the policies of his party. The next question was that of the legislature. To decide on this the method of ascertaining the people's opinion by a referendum was proposed — a referendum whereby the people could decide whether or not they wanted the existing Parliament to continue for a further period. This proposal aroused some controversy. Critics of the government argued that it was unconstitutional and dictatorial.

The question of extending the life of Parliament has had an interesting history in Sri Lanka. The 1972 Constitution had made it possible for Parliament to extend its own period if two-thirds of its members voted in favour — and, in fact, they did so. The 1978 Constitution, however, provides a special clause whereby such an extension is possible only if it is the wish of the people. The referendum is expressly provided for as the means of allowing the people directly to decide on matters, such as this, which are of crucial national importance.[11]

The legality of the method, then, cannot be doubted as it is clearly provided for in the present Constitution. Moreover, at the time of its introduction there was absolutely no opposition to it from outside or inside Parliament, since it was an obvious improvement on the earlier method whereby the people were not consulted. The more pertinent question posed was 'Is it correct to use the referendum at this juncture?' The question which answers this question is 'Who is to decide this?' The political critics who posed the question believed that they should decide but the government thought that it was the people who should decide and the referendum was an opportunity for them to do just this.

The government's opponents, however, held that a referendum *per se* was undemocratic and that this particular referendum at this juncture was dictatorial. They interpreted it as an attempt to keep the reins of power by unfair means. On the other hand, the government held that their proposition to hold the referendum was not, in any way, a refusal to hold an election. If the majority of the people said 'No' at the referendum, they were assured of a general election. The referendum, as envisaged by them, had the same status as a parliamentary election. Moreover, the political situation at the time emcompassed a pervasive fear of an anti-democratic 'Naxalite' type of movement arising from within certain opposition parties. The growth strategy of the post-1977 period had paid dividends and fruitless delays and expenditure would be extremely harmful. Thus, practical politics made the referendum a timely instrument.

The principles and methods of a democratic election were fully observed at this referendum — the same freedom and secrecy laws, the same rights to campaign. Even opposition members who had been deprived of civic rights had the right to contest. Perhaps it was a lack of knowledge of a referendum, *per se*, which created many of the doubts expressed. Yet the historical development of this method establishes it as an entrenched instrument of the democratic system. It was first used in Massachusetts in 1778 and spread in the nineteenth century to Switzerland, France and Italy. Many countries which did not want a referendum have now made use of it. Britain has resorted to it twice in the last ten years. In France and Italy constitutional amendments are possible only by referendum.

The referendum, then, is a direct consultation of the people, which is the essence of democracy. The established concept of people's 'representatives' is a logical growth from the first gathering of citizens in the Athenian democracy. When an issue of crucial national importance arises to go back to the people is a direct democratic method.

The December 1982 referendum gave the people of Sri Lanka the option of avoiding a crisis in the country as well as in the Constitution — a means of avoiding a situation where the President was of one party and Parliament of another. The political wisdom of our people was indicated when the referendum resulted in a definite 'Yes' to the question as to whether the Parliament in power should continue or not. Of the votes polled, 54.6 per cent were in favour of an extension of the present Parliament — this being an even higher percentage than that polled by J.R. Jayewardene at the presidential election.[12] It is relevant to note that at such a referendum the opposition could have combined against the government, a situation which is unlikely to have occurred if a general election had been held.

After the victory of the ruling party at the two elections of 1982, in those electorates where the party had shown losses, the people were given a further opportunity to elect new representatives, if they so desired. In May 1983, by-elections were held in those 18 electorates. In 14 of them the UNP gained clear majorities — thus reconfirming the people's confidence in the government.

The 1982 referendum proved that our people are politically mature enough to be unmoved by slogans and grandiose promises. It also indicates that they appreciated the pressing need for a legislature which could and would work with the President. The election of a politically-opposed Parliament would have no doubt resulted in a permanent stalemate. The people had assessed in practical terms the growth already achieved and they preferred to give a chance to established methods with proven success rather than to change for the sake of change — a mistake they had made all too often during the last three decades.

Notes

1. See the information in note 4 of the Introduction to this volume.
2. In April 1971, a small group of discontented youth led a totally unexpected attack against the armed forces. The movement, which was obviously backed by the radical left parties, spread throughout the island. The government at that time under Mrs Sirimavo Bandaranaike declared a State of Emergency. The uprising was short lived but bloody. It resulted in the emergence of a new left-wing party, the Janatha Vimukthi Peramuna.

3. According to statistics recorded by the Central Bank of Sri Lanka, between 1970 and 1977, a growth rate of 3.5 per cent occurred. Between 1977 and 1982, the average annual growth rate was 6 per cent.

4. Further material on the revival of the economy after 1977 is presented in the Introduction to this book.

5. State Trading Corporations were set up with absolute monopolies in a number of essential items, for example textile imports, imports of food items such as dried fish, tinned fish, dhal, onions, etc. The ostensible purpose of this was to foster domestic industries. However, the resulting blanket protectionism produced low-quality products, an illogical pricing system and persistent shortages. Nationalisation of the plantation business led to the demoralisation of this vital sector and the consequent downward trend in both productivity and profit.

6. 'A special, autonomous statutory body, the Greater Colombo Economic Commission (GCEC) is the authority for the Sri Lankan Investment Promotion Zones. The GCEC's objectives are to promote export oriented foreign investment, create employment opportunities and increase export earnings. The GCEC has complete jurisdiction over a 415 square kilometre area just north of Colombo, which accommodates the three Investment Promotion Zones . . . The GCEC can grant exemptions from or modify the application of certain Laws of the country, in order to offer investors a suitable and attractive incentive package' (*Sri Lanka's Investment Promotion Zones*, December 1979).

7. Commenting on the employment situation just prior to the adoption of the new economic policies, a Ministry of Plan Implementation document of November 1980 states that 'by the end of 1976 over one million persons were unemployed out of a total work force of 5.25 million'.

8. The Department of Census and Statistics provided the following figures on paddy production:

Year	Extent sown ('000 hectares)	Net extent harvested ('000 hectares)	Production ('000 m tons)	Yield per hectare ('00 kg)
1969	692	530	1,374	25.9
1970	759	611	1,616	26.4
1971	727	590	1,396	23.6
1972	727	543	1,312	24.1
1973	725	571	1,312	22.9
1974	826	681	1,602	23.5
1975	696	509	1,154	22.7
1976	724	541	1,252	23.1
1977	828	666	1,677	25.2
1978	876	724	1,891	26.1
1979	839	697	1,917	27.5
1980	845	728	2,133	29.2
1981	877	740	2,230	30.1
1982	845	661	2,156	32.6

9. 'The learned Attorney-General countered the argument of the Petitioners by his submission that the proposed Amendment, far from alienating the sovereignty of the People, enhances the franchise which is one of the components of the sovereignty, by providing for more opportunities for the People to exercise their franchise' (*Parliamentary Debates (Hansard)*, 26 August 1982).

10. For a district-by-district breakdown in the changes in the UNP's vote between 1977 and 1982, see *Economic Review* (December 1982).

11. Article 86 of the Constitution states: 'The President may, subject to the provisions of Article 85, submit to the People by Referendum any matter which in the opinion of the President is of national importance.'

12. For data on this point, see statistics in Chapter 2 of this volume and, for a province-by-province breakdown, see *Economic Review* (December 1982).

5 THE CONDUCT OF THE REFERENDUM

'Priya Samarakone'

The referendum of December 1982 was presented by leading government figures as a 'high point of democracy'[1] and a fresh mandate for the United National Party (UNP) to govern. The purpose of this paper is to challenge these assertions and to argue, first, that the referendum campaign and the poll itself were conducted in a manner that violated acceptable and well-established rules of electoral practice, and second, that this brings into question the very validity of the government's victory (54.66 per cent for, 45.34 per cent against) in favour of extending the life of the present Parliament.

It should be stressed at the outset, however, that even if the 'yes' vote in the referendum were genuine, the government's decision to hold the referendum was extremely dubious on democratic grounds. This was not just because the government was abandoning parliamentary elections on the principle of proportional representation which it had introduced. It is also because under the law, success in a referendum required only a simple majority in the country as a whole, provided a minimum of one-third of the registered vote was obtained. In other words, by this means the government could in theory have kept its 84 per cent of the seats in Parliament by obtaining the votes of less than 17 per cent of the total electorate. In the event, it kept its massive parliamentary majority with the votes of 38.7 per cent of the total electorate. It was to avoid such extreme incongruities that the government had introduced proportional representation in 1978. It was to *reproduce* such an incongruity that it set aside proportional representation in favour of a referendum in 1982.

Part One of this paper examines the reasons that the referendum was held, while Part Two discusses events during the referendum campaign. This is followed in Part Three by an assessment of doings on polling day itself. In the final section, an analysis of the results supports the cumulative evidence that the referendum of 1982 was a massive exercise in political engineering. The results also indicate, however, that despite these efforts to manipulate the outcome of the referendum, the voters of Sri Lanka managed to express considerable opposition to the government's proposal to postpone elections by six years.

Part One: The Reasons for the Referendum

On 22 October 1982, the day after the results of the presidential election were announced, President J.R. Jayewardene told foreign correspondents that he planned a post mortem on them before deciding the date of the next parliamentary election. 'In any case,' he added, 'I must have it before July 1983. It's a question of a few months.'[2] It appears that it was this post mortem which caused the President to effect a complete *volte face* a few days later and make the startling announcement that he had decided instead to hold a referendum, before the end of the year, to ask the electorate to agree to an extension of the incumbent Parliament for six years. The reason given for this change of mind was that soon after the presidential election, he 'had information' that one faction in the Sri Lanka Freedom Party (SLFP) 'had decided to assassinate (him) and a few other Ministers, Mr Anura Bandaranaike, Armed Service Chiefs and others, do away with the Constitution and imprison Mrs Bandaranaike . . .' and he wished to prevent people 'entering parliament in large numbers'.[3] This assassination 'conspiracy' came to be referred to as the 'Naxalite plot', one more in a series of such plots which the UNP has managed to unearth, forestall or anticipate at various difficult moments during the period that it has been in power.[4]

What the post mortem on the results did in fact reveal was that while the government had won 52.91 per cent of the valid votes cast and polled 0.99 per cent more of the valid vote than in 1977, the SLFP had increased its share by over 9 per cent from 29.72 to 39.07 per cent.[5] It further showed that the government received only 42.37 per cent of the total registered vote as opposed to 48.62 per cent in 1977. Moreover, many of these votes were a response to Jayewardene's personal standing against a weak opposition candidate. At a parliamentary election, where proportional representation operated on a district list basis, unpopularity of local politicians might well have worked against Jayewardene's United National Party.[6] Even if that did not occur, a crude projection of presidential election patterns gave the SLFP at least 70 seats in a Parliament of 196.

This strong showing by the main opposition party probably came as a shock to the President who had spoken in the following confident terms during the presidential election campaign:

We are contesting this election to win and at a time most favourable to us. We intend . . . to demolish and completely destroy the opposition politically. After that I say to you, roll up the electoral map of Sri Lanka. You will not need it for *another ten years.*[7] (italics added)

But the SLFP was not demolished. Despite terrible disadvantages, it obtained over $2\frac{1}{2}$ million votes, while Jayewardene with his strategic superiority, a united party, and all the advantages of control over the full range of government machinery, polled just under $3\frac{1}{2}$ million.

Migara, a political columnist popularly believed to have close access to the President, gives some indications of what may have been the actual thinking of the UNP leadership at this time:

. . . the SLFP won 39 per cent of the votes despite all its drawbacks. A relatively unknown Presidential candidate, Mrs Sirima Bandaranaike not in the campaign and Anura Bandaranaike and his loyalists not too interested in the campaign. The defection of party stalwarts, the disillusionment of its rank and file and the years of organisation(al) neglect due to the split in the party since Mrs Bandaranaike's disenfranchisement two years ago . . . electorate-wise, considering the wide gap between the personalities and experience of the candidates which certainly made a tremendous impact on the votes, the results are not too adverse where the SLFP as a party is concerned.[8]

In the course of the referendum campaign, many reasons were advanced for holding it, but the President himself probably revealed the main one when he said in a moment of candour:

I found the SLFP polling 3 million *without* Mrs Bandaranaike campaigning in the presidential election.[9] So I thought I should tell the people do you want us or do you want 50 to 60 Communist-sponsored Naxalites (revolutionaries) in parliament? . . . Is a country democratic if one of its major political parties is composed of terrorists *who might win the next election* and be the government?[10]

The referendum was invoked as a means of saving the nation from 'a Naxalite type of people, bent on violence'.[11] The need to protect a peaceful and stable democracy was adduced as a reason for a diminution rather than an enhancement of the democratic process. The essence of the so-called 'Naxalite plot' was that the power balance in Mrs Bandaranaike's party had swung in favour of a caucus of some of its left-leaning personalities, including the presidential candidate, Kobbekaduwa, and Mrs Bandaranaike's son-in-law, Vijaya Kumaranatunga. However, the report of the CID investigation into the 'Naxalite plot' later showed that there was little more to it than intra-party squabbles and manoeuvres and no basis whatsoever for charges in a court of law — much less a conspiracy to assassinate UNP and SLFP leaders.[12]

Part Two: The Campaign

Once the decision to hold the referendum had been made, the government immediately took a series of steps which profoundly affected the nature and conduct of the referendum campaign. These included the continuation of the emergency; the illegal 'lamp' campaign; the attacks on and the arrests of SLFP organisers; the banning of oppostion newspapers and the sealing of presses; the government manipulation of the state-owned media; the harassment and intimidation of various elements who campaigned for a 'no' vote at the referendum.

The Emergency

On 20 October, a state of emergency had been proclaimed, ostensibly for the purpose of checking post-election violence after the presidential poll. In the past, such violence had broken out after almost every election, on an increasing scale — but, hitherto, in every case, power had in fact changed hands. Thus it was invariably the victors, endeavouring to settle scores with their recent oppressors or rivals, who took the law into their own hands and went on the rampage in the first heady days of victory. This time, however, power had *not* changed hands and the violence, if any, should have been minimal and quickly brought under control. Nevertheless, it is reliably reported that even government MPs were perpetrating acts of outrage and the police were powerless to intervene.[13] It is difficult, therefore, to accept that the emergency on this occasion ever actually served the purpose for which it was originally proclaimed.

On the contrary, it could be argued that it was the government party alone which benefited from the state of emergency — for there is no doubt that while it did not protect the defeated parties from reprisals, it did, in many cases, assist government party politicians and supporters in punishing opposition workers. Above all, it enabled the government to undermine and almost paralyse any effective campaign against the extension of the life of the existing Parliament.[14] Under emergency regulations important opposition newspapers were banned, printing presses were sealed, opposition meetings were restricted and many opposition organisers and supporters and other critics of the government detained or arrested and interrogated.[15] On 15 December, the Minister of State announced that the situation had returned to normal and the emergency would be allowed to lapse on 19 December. However, it was renewed as soon as it lapsed and, for the first time, the people of Sri Lanka went to the polls while a nationwide state of emergency prevailed.

The Ubiquitous 'Lamp'

Contrary to all the rules of election practice in Sri Lanka, a massive and highly expensive propaganda and advertising campaign was carried out by the UNP throughout the entire pre-referendum period. The most dramatic aspect of this was what we might call the 'lamp campaign'. The symbols to be employed in a referendum in Sri Lanka are a 'lamp' and a 'pot'. A vote for the 'lamp' meant 'yes'; a vote for the 'pot' meant 'no'. The 'lamp' indicated agreement to the extension of the existing Parliament for six years without a general election.

Overnight, just before the referendum was promulgated, thousands of large green (the colour of the ruling party) durable banners, depicting a 'lamp' with a cross marked against it, appeared on lamp posts, buildings and buses throughout Colombo and most other parts of the country — probably everywhere except in Jaffna.[16] They were clearly 'factory'-produced in hundreds of thousands, and thereafter speedily and efficiently distributed to allocated areas through a massive, organised network of people and vehicles. Each poster even had a location printed on it, indicating precisely where it was to be hung. For many people, this was the *only* symbol they would see.

The Referendum Act states that such a display of symbols in any place to which the public have access, except premises where a meeting is to be held and then only on the day of the meeting, is an offence, and 'any police officer may take such steps and use such force, as may be reasonably necessary' to seize and remove any such offending symbol, poster, etc.[17] Moreover, under the emergency, no poster could be publicly 'affixed' or leaflets distributed 'among the public' without permission of the Inspector General of Police (IGP) or another authorized officer.[18]

Complaints were made to the Elections Commissioner about this flagrant violation of the law and the IGP wrote to local authorities about offences under the Act.[19] Subsequently, on 2 December, he issued instructions to all police divisions that 'party organisers be asked to remove all flags, banners, posters, etc., displaying referendum symbols'.[20] In some areas, the police were able to carry out orders, but many apparently feared reprisals from politicians and, for the most part, the illegal banners were allowed to remain.[21] Another order from the IGP two weeks later was equally ineffective. Newspapers report, however, that certain opposition supporters were arrested for allegedly displaying a 'pot' poster and one even in the act of removing a 'lamp' poster.[22] Citizens outraged by this blatant flouting of the law, were too intimidated by the general atmosphere of lawlessness to dare to remove posters themselves. In fact, when a lady in the Nuwara Eliya District protested at the forcible implantation of a 'lamp' banner in her garden by a mob, she was threatened with being bombed. Complaints to the local UNP branch treasurer and the police resulted in *her* being remanded.

Posters advertising meetings to promote the 'lamp' campaign were put up on many public buildings, even on the General Post Office facing the entrance to President's House. They were particularly in evidence in the vicinity of the Courts at the entrance to the Supreme Court, the Magistrate's Court and the Bar Association building. 'Lamp' banners swung from posts along the Parliament drive. 'Lamp' floats and banners decorated the street where the Prime Minister has his private residence. At the entrance to the main Colombo railway station a huge placard exhorted travellers and commuters to 'Vote for the Lamp to create a society free and just, jobs, food, shelter and clothing a-plenty'. Even the railway time-table boards were covered by posters advertising 'lamp' meetings. At night, enormous illuminated 'lamps' and portraits of the Prime Minister brightened the usually dimly-lit streets in many districts. All of this was illegal.

A few days before the poll, a fresh rash of posters covered the city (including the wall of the Prime Minister's official residence, adjacent to a large police station). They advertised a 'Referendum Victory Rally' ('A New JR Era') for the 19th, and carried a large portrait of the President, flanked by the Prime Minister and a 'lamp'. They also bore the legend: 'Not to be displayed in public places'. They were in fact displayed in *thousands* everywhere.

Posters depicting the 'pot', on the other hand, were seldom if ever in evidence in most parts of the country.[23] 'Pot' supporters lacked both the resources to produce such massive quantities of expensive posters and the immunity from the law which 'lamp' supporters seemed to enjoy. Moreover, it seemed futile to attempt to put up illegal posters which the police or government supporters would have immediately removed.

The 'lamp' poster campaign is symbolic of two trends which emerged during this period. One was the attempt to black out as much as possible of the opposition's campaign; the other was the increasing partisanship of the police, which rendered opposition workers and 'pot' voters extremely vulnerable in the face of intimidation by government supporters.[24] The 'lamp' campaign exerted tremendous pressure on the electorate. The massive display of the 'lamp' and blatant violation of electoral rules despite orders from the IGP, created a sense that the government party was omnipotent and that no one, not even the police or the Elections Commissioner, much less the opposition, could do anything to halt the inexorable momentum of government power. It provided a subtle but all-pervasive backdrop of intimidation, and exercised psychological pressure in favour of a 'yes' vote.

The Attack on the SLFP

Even more serious than this propaganda campaign was the frontal assault on the main opposition party, the SLFP led by Mrs Bandaranaike. The surprisingly strong showing of the SLFP candidate in the presidential election left the ruling UNP with the problem of what to do about the SLFP's apparently durable support base. How was it, for instance, to reduce the vote in traditional SLFP strongholds like Attanagalla, which Mrs Bandaranaike had retained by a majority of over 10,000 in 1977 despite an island-wide rejection of her party? The problem was tackled at two levels; at the grassroots by directly interfering with the voters and the voting process, and at the national level by harassment of SLFP cadres and a concerted attempt to paralyse its organisational network.

Much of the credit for the SLFP showing in the presidential poll went to the organisational work of its General Secretary, Ratnasiri Wickremanayake, the energetic campaigning of one of its Assistant Secretaries, Vijaya Kumaranatunga, and the strong backing provided by party Vice President T.B. Ilangaratne. Credit was also given to *Aththa*, a popular and widely-read Communist Party (CP) newspaper which gave wholehearted support to the SLFP candidate. The referendum also saw the return of Mrs Bandaranaike to the hustings — her civic disabilities not extending to her participation in a referendum campaign. These factors added up to a serious challenge to the government, especially on an issue about which many traditional UNP voters had their doubts. It appears, therefore, that tactical expediency rather than any supposed threat to the nation dictated the arrests and detention of key SLFP organisers and the closure of *Aththa* under emergency regulations.

The efficient functioning of the SLFP General Secretary was essential to the party's contribution to the referendum campaign. On 10 November, he was asked to report to the Criminal Investigation Department of the police (CID) with a list of the SLFP's 22 district organisers and polling agents. Upon doing so, he was taken into detention at an Army Camp and only released, conditionally, on 24 November. He was finally charged, along with ten others, with conspiracy two years earlier to commit acts of violence against the state. It is extraordinary that the authorities did not see fit to take action on this until a time when it proved to be extremely useful in disrupting the SLFP referendum campaign.[25]

Assistant Secretary Kumaranatunga seems to have been identified as a major 'villain' and singled out for special treatment. A popular film star and forceful speaker, he has also proved a tough and energetic campaigner. He and his wife, Chandrika[26] were named the 'main culprits' in the so-called 'Naxalite plot', 'to assassinate the Head of State', create 'widespread violence' and 'tear up the Constitution'. The nature of the evidence given in support of this by the Prime Minister is indicated by a comment in the state-owned *Sunday Times*:

. . . Mr Premadasa referred in particular to a statement made by Mrs Chandrika Kumaranatunga at a meeting where she had referred to President J.R. Jayewardene as 'a dog'. This one statement alone discloses to what low depths the SLFP Presidential campaign had sunk and with what venom and vengeance they had planned post-election violence.[27]

Apparently unaware of the illogicality and implications of his statement, a pro-government columnist in the *Weekend* of 7 November wrote:

According to some high-ranking ministers, the indications now point towards an intention by those supporters to follow a pattern similar to those of Adolf Hitler's Reichstag fire.

Some days earlier, the President himself had stated that 'their actions, which amount to a coup, are now being investigated by the Police'.[28] Yet an examination of the nature of the investigations carried out suggests that either the investigators did not do their jobs properly, or they did not take the plot story seriously.

The interrogation of Kumaranatunga and his wife had little or nothing to do with the so-called plot itself, as judicial submissions and the investigation report itself show. The main aim of the questioning was to obtain information about the organisational structure and other internal matters of the SLFP, which material, in fact, forms the bulk of the investigation report. Finally on 19 November, Kumaranatunga was detained and kept in virtual solitary confinement in Welikada Jail from 25 November. It appears that he was not questioned at all while in detention and was only released in mid-January, long after the campaign was over. No charges were preferred against him.

The fact that so much was made of the 'Naxalite plot' while it apparently formed so small a part of the CID investigation, is strange, to say the least. Pieter Keuneman, Communist Party Vice-President, has stated that despite the accusation that the Communists were at the bottom of the alleged assassination plot, not a single member of that party had been questioned.[29] And despite the President's assertion that it was this plot and this alone that made him 'decide against a general election and go for a referendum',[30] no one has yet been charged in connection with it. On 20 December, a Colombo magistrate discharged 15 SLFP members from the Kolonnawa electorate who had been remanded since early November in connection with this 'conspiracy', saying that the police had not submitted sufficient evidence against them.[31]

The report of the CID investigation into the alleged conspiracy to assassinate the President and 'create a blood bath' was finally presented in Parliament on 21 July 1983. Even the state-controlled *Daily News* conceded that 'the 33-page report has not set out any concrete findings but has set out a tale of political intrigue full of juicy tidbits . . .'[32] An SLFP MP argued that it did not contain any 'material for a criminal charge even of a trivial nature' and the entire investigation was an 'abuse of power and unwarranted manipulation of the legal process . . . for a political purpose . . . to undermine the main opposition party.'[33]

Those questioned or detained also included the Party Treasurer, Kingsley Wickremaratne; another Assistant Secretary and leading campaign speaker, Indrapala Abeywira; the Vice President of the SLFP Youth League, Ossie Abeygunasekera; and the Secretary of the SLFP All-Island Women's League, Kamala Ranatunga. The Treasurer was questioned on a number of occasions and asked to produce various vital party documents, such as books of account, particulars of donations, etc., thus obstructing his work of collecting and organising funds for the campaign. On 19 November, Abeywira was taken to the SLFP headquarters where police removed all the 'party files, membership lists, lists of office-bearers of the various party organisations from the centre to the village level, confidential files, files relating to disciplinary inquiries and minute books of the Central Committee'.[34] This disrupted the SLFP's All-Island Executive Committee Meeting which occurred on that day and at which several hundred area organisers were to discuss the plan of campaign for the referendum.

On 30 October, Youth League Vice-President Abeygunasekera was arrested and later detained in connection with the alleged printing and distribution of 'rice ration books', a reference to a rather harmless, if ingenious, election gimmick — a leaflet based on the format of the old ration book which had entitled one to obtain free rice. This provided the excuse for a series of interrogations and detentions of many SLFP party workers. It was not until 20 June 1983 that the trial of 34 persons for having distributed these 'books' was fixed. Informed legal opinion is of the view that the indictment, if successful, would only constitute a minor infringement of the law. On 10 November, Kamala Ranatunga was assaulted in public by two men, one of them carrying bombs. Her assailants were caught and handed over to the police. On reporting at the police station to lodge a complaint, it was *she* who was remanded on a charge of being in possession of offensive weapons — the police claiming to have found bombs in her handbag.[35] In this way, a considerable number of SLFP district and electorate organisers, leading speakers and sympathisers, as well as many workers at village level, were taken into custody or regularly questioned on one pretext or another, or on none at all. Mrs Bandaranaike and her son Anura, an MP, were also questioned on several occasions. Apparently, the latter was once questioned for seven hours, a considerable part of which was concerned with internal party matters and family relationships and conflicts, possibly in an attempt to obtain material which could be used to aggravate divisions in the party.

On 26 November, the Communist MP for Kalawana drew attention in Parliament to the climate of fear that was being created by detentions and regular police interrogation of SLFP organisers at central and district levels:

. . . a climate of terror because general secretaries, leaders of parties, provincial leaders, when they go back how can you expect them to start working? . . . They do not know whether they are on trial or whether there is going to be a case against them. So, they are not in a position to put their heart and soul into a campaign on the referendum.[36]

The raid on the SLFP headquarters and the investigations into the workings of the party must have elicited considerable information of use to the ruling party. Indeed, the government-owned press ran a series of articles revealing the 'inside story' of the SLFP, to back up the President's claim that it was unfit to run the country.

This attack on the SLFP indicates that the referendum was not seen by the government as an occasion on which the people could freely express their confidence in the existing regime and their wish that representative elections be dispensed with for a further six years. Rather, it was a desperate party political struggle in which extreme means were to be used to ensure a victory for the 'lamp'.

The Right to Hold Meetings

Under the emergency, permits for meetings had to be obtained from the police. The total number of participants had to be limited to that stated in the permit and the meeting had to commence and disperse within the period stated. The opposition in many areas were only able to have small gatherings, in private houses. Sometimes permission was simply refused by the police as, for example, for the joint opposition meeting at Moneragala on 17 December. Elsewhere it was withdrawn after being granted, as happened at Galewela, in early December.[37] In Kesbewa, the UNP booked every place normally used for public meetings. The MP for Ratnapura boasted that he had booked the Ratnapura esplanade until after the referendum.[38] This situation pertained in several places.[39]

On many occasions, meetings were broken up by groups of government supporters, with the police watching but taking no action, or even protecting the disruptive elements. Apparently, when a meeting in Kurunegala was disturbed by hooligans led by a UNP MP, the police intervened only to protect the MP when the crowd tried to eject the troublemakers. Similarly, the police 'discreetly vanished when a UNP gang arrived with stones and led by the son of the MP for Matale, turned up to disrupt a ('pot') meeting there'.[40] The Lanka Sama Samaja Party reported the disruption of meetings in Dambulla. One, finally held on 17 December at Galewela after an earlier postponement due to political pressure on the police, was stopped by armed thugs who announced that the opposition would not be allowed to function in that electorate. They also informed the crowd that voters would have to show their ballot papers before putting them into the box. Another meeting in the same electorate on the same day was similarly disrupted by armed men who also assaulted and robbed two of the organisers.[41] The SLFP District Agent for Puttalam complained that prior to a meeting planned to be held in Anamaduwa, his organisers had been 'threatened and vehicles used for publicising the meeting smashed up'. Just before the meeting, they discovered that the loud speaker wires had been cut and when Mrs Bandaranaike was addressing the rally, the platform suddenly collapsed; sabotage was suspected. Apparently, the only people taken into custody in connection with this were the SLFP and CP organisers of the meeting.[42]

In this context, an editorial in the government-owned *Daily Mirror* 12 days before polling day appears particularly cynical and dishonest:

The silence if not the low profile of the Opposition lends itself to interpretation. There are some who suspect they are working underground . . . The lack of any public manifestation by the Opposition against the referendum (is) ominous.[43]

Banning of Newspapers and Sealing of Presses

An integral part of this heavy-handed campaign was the banning of newspapers and the sealing of presses. A number of presses which had printed literature for the SLFP candidate in the presidential election were sealed under the emergency on one pretext or another. This had the effect of deterring other presses from printing any material opposing the government's proposal. While the large state-owned newspaper concerns and printing establishments were flooding the country with letters from the President, circulars, hand-bills and posters, the opposition had tremendous difficulty in getting anything printed at all.

On 18 December, police sealed a press (and arrested the proprietor) where legal literature advocating a 'no' vote was being printed. They also arrested the person who carried the copy to the press. He was remanded and only released on bail two weeks later.[44] Also seized was the composed matter for the Tamil language text of Mrs Bandaranaike's message to Tamil voters. *Suthanthiran*, a Tamil language opposition newspaper produced in Jaffna, was sealed as soon as the emergency was declared. This paper would have carried the arguments against the extension of Parliament to a readership which was otherwise reached only by pro-extension papers. It was closed because 'inflammatory articles which would rouse communal feelings were being published'.[45] However, no closure was imposed on a number of other publications which clearly came into this category.[46] One of the more 'restrained' of these — *Diabolical Conspiracy* — carried the photograph of the Minister of Industries and contained allegations by him of corruption among Tamil examiners in the interests of Tamil university entrants. It was sent at public expense from the ministry and could have inflammed relations between Sinhalese and Tamil intellectuals at a time when many of them might have been united on the referendum issue.

The *Aththa* newspaper, published by the CP, enjoys a wide readership among the Sinhalese-reading public as a whole, has an island-wide circulation, and is a major opposition daily. During the presidential campaign, it was the main Sinhalese daily to promote the principal opposition candidate. It is reported that its circulation trebled during that period, so it must have had a significant impact.

Soon after it was indicated that a referendum would be held, *Aththa* carried strong criticism of the proposal. On 2 November, the Secretary to the Ministry of State and Competent Authority departed from established emergency practice which was to impose pre-censorship and closed the paper because, he stated:

there is and is likely to be in the *Aththa* publication of matter which in his opinion is calculated to be prejudicial to the interests of national security and the preservation of public order, and the maintenance of supplies and services essential to the life of the community and matter inciting or encouraging persons to mutiny, riot, or civil commotion.[47]

The press which prints the *Aththa* and other newspapers was also sealed. It was therefore extremely difficult to publicise arguments against the proposed extension of Parliament, since few presses were willing to risk undertaking such work. The fact that in early December an old CP weekly, *Mawbima*, was revived, in no way made up for the closure of the well-established *Aththa*.

The State-controlled Media

The opposition's acute problems in publicising its views were matched by the tremendous advantages which the government enjoyed thanks to the state-controlled media (radio, television and most newspapers). The major dailies of Associated Newspapers of Ceylon Ltd, like the *Daily News*, were totally committed to the government's stand and do not appear to have carried a single article or letter opposing the referendum.[48] Reports of opposition meetings and speeches were minimal and those who opposed the referendum were subjected to serious abuse. The *Daily News* carried an editorial full of slanderous and unfounded innuendoes about the moral conduct of Catholic priests who had taken a stand against the referendum, though the same paper did not print the priests' own statements.[49] Papers of the state-owned Times Group, like the *Daily Mirror*, resorted to the most hysterical abuse against the opposition, carrying blatantly distorted headlines and publicising the communal life that surfaced during the government's campaign (about which the Competent Authority did not seem to be concerned).[50]

The two major privately-owned groups, Independent Newspapers and Upali Newspapers, did give fair coverage to both sides of the question, with the latter running a forum for all views.[51] This group carried more articles on the opposition point of view than any other paper, and while including a number of speeches by ministers in its forum, was the group most critical of the government's stand (although its owner finally associated himself with the government line).

Under the Referendum Act, a recognised political party is entitled to 45 minutes of radio and 45 minutes of television broadcasting time for which it has to pay a very high price. Not all parties campaigning in the referendum were able to take full advantage of this, however. After an expensive presidential campaign, they could not afford to do so, and the cost of broadcasting time was increased considerably between the presidential poll and the referendum. Broadcasting posed no problem for the ruling party, however. It not only had 45 minutes paid time over radio and television, but many other hours of what was in effect *free* time at its sole disposal. In addition to existing propaganda-type programmes and the state-controlled news, several new programme series were launched, 'to acquaint the masses with the performance of each Minister in the interests of the common man', or 'to discuss development activity'.[52] The programmes were conducted in such a way as to promote the campaign for the extension of the incumbent Parliament. In this context, the minimal statutory time afforded to the opposition was negligible. Nor was the right to broadcast extended to other independent organisations. The Civil Rights Movement's appeal to the President that this be done met with no response.[53] The state-controlled radio and television did not conduct any interviews or panel discussions on the pros and cons of the referendum, as would be the normal practice in most democratic countries.

On the day of Mrs Bandaranaike's referendum broadcast, the government-controlled press failed to follow its usual practice and did not announce her speech in advance. And in several parts of the country, timely power cuts resulted in a total blackout of her speech.[54] Considerable advance publicity was given, however, in mid-November to the televising of an extremely popular Sinhalese film. The publicity ensured maximum viewers throughout the country, and at peak-viewing time. What was actually televised, however, was a specially-made propaganda film, thinly-disguised as a feature film, depicting oppression and deprivation suffered by the people under the last government. The same film was screened at a popular Colombo cinema, offering a special cheap rate for all seats.

The Government Film Unit, the largest film-producing body in the country, was also at the service of the UNP's campaign. The day before the referendum was promulgated, army personnel were on duty at the Times Group building because a film was being shot there about the harassment of journalists under the previous government.[55] On 21 November, a state-produced film praising the government's development effort was screened at a well-known central cinema. On 17 December, the National Film Exhibitors Guild presented the President with a copy of *Towards the Dharmishta Society* which was to be screened that day in Sinhalese and English in cinemas in every district in the country.[56]

It was in this context of partisan interference with all forms of media that the President was to claim that:

democracy was being practised in Sri Lanka at its best. Government had allowed all opposition leaders to speak against it even through television and that type of freedom and democracy did not exist even in the USA.[57]

Atmosphere of Recrimination

In the aftermath of the presidential election, the government went to great lengths to create an atmosphere of recrimination against citizens who had backed opposition candidates and against public officials who had behaved even-handedly. This generated severe tension and intimidated people from repeating such actions during the referendum.

This began with the Prime Minister who, for example, accused certain television personnel of 'blowing up Vijaya Kumaranatunga'. The basis of this seems to be that one of Kumaranatunga's films was shown during the presidential campaign and that he was greeted in a civil manner by officials on one occasion. One of the officials named failed to have his contract renewed. On 1 November, the *Sun* reported that there was to be a probe into television's coverage of the presidential election.[58] The Prime Minister also accused a well-known businessman of having made his wealth during the period of the UNP liberalised trade policy, but helping the SLFP with funds in the recent campaign. Another minister asked publicly whether the businessman's tax affairs were in order.[59] On 31 October, the *Weekend* carried headlines 'Govt. Dragnet for Fifth Columnists: Probe to Unearth "Moles" in the Public Service'. It reported that 'all bureaucrats who worked against the government during the presidential poll would face inquiry and subsequent expulsion'. Another Minister told the press that:

> the purpose of this . . . is not to carry out acts of political vengeance, but merely to eliminate the 'moles' who were within these institutions waiting merely to emerge at opportune moments to carry out acts of sabotage.

The government-owned *Sunday Times* spoke of the

> shocking but enlightening exposure of the existence of fifth-columnists and traitors in its [the public service] ranks . . . Premier R. Premadasa rattled off the names of the brood of vipers in the public service, who were poised to bite the hand that fed them . . .[60]

An *Island* editorial, 'No McCarthyism Please', argued that 'Public Servants of certain categories have been given political rights and can engage in legitimate political activity', and 'it is a known fact that under any government a blind eye is turned to those who engage in political work on behalf of the ruling party'.[61] But the atmosphere of distrust escalated. 'Spectator' in the *Sunday Times* of 14 November wrote that the President had asked one minister

> to weed out subversive elements in the Public Service. The Minister has accordingly set afoot a probe on *the behavioural pattern of public servants* during the presidential elections . . . The Minister will doubtless widen his net beyond the presidential election to bring to book *those who are by nature or political ideologies, saboteurs*. This would prevent recurrence of such activity during the referendum. (italics added)

Such was the atmosphere in which 'pot' campaigners and supporters endeavoured to carry out peaceful and legal activity. The fact that many who had campaigned for an opposition candidate in the presidential election were being victimised must have deterred others from working during the referendum, at the end of which, whatever the result, the same government would be in power.

Possible Illegalities Concerning Religious Assemblies

The Referendum Act states that once a referendum has been proclaimed, no person shall, at any procession held for religious purposes 'do any act or thing calculated to affect the result of the Referendum', and that such an act will constitute an offence.[62] It also says that in this period, anyone who

(a) utters at any religious assembly any words for the purpose of influencing the result of such Referendum or inducing any elector to vote or refrain from voting in favour of or against the proposal at such Referendum, . . .

or (b) holds or causes to be held a public meeting at a place of worship for the purpose of promoting the Referendum or the Referendum campaign in favour of or against the proposal,

shall be guilty of the offence of undue influence.[63]

In the light of this, a huge meeting held in the shadow of one such 'place of worship' two weeks after the referendum was promulgated appears to violate the spirit, if not the letter, of the law. On 29 November, the President, the Prime Minister and Industries Minister inaugurated the second stage of the Kelaniya Sacred City Restoration Scheme. The occasion was a mingling of religious ritual and political campaigning. Flowers were offered at the great Kelaniya temple, 'the President was blessed by the chief incumbent by placing the sacred relics casket on his head'[64] and 'a prayer of thanks given for the success achieved in the presidential election'.[65]

In this intensely religious setting, the President addressed a massive gathering, declaring that 'the UNP was the only political party in the country whose leaders and whose supporters had been in the forefront of Buddhist restoration work in the country'. He spoke about the history 'of the ancient shrine and said it had been hallowed by the presence of Lord Buddha'. He then called upon the people to 'give him the assistance of the same Parliament to go ahead with his development works'. 'I am asking you,' said the President, '. . . to vote "YES" at the referendum by voting for the Lamp.'[66]

Intimidation of Opposition Workers and Voters

Opposition campaigners and polling observers faced threats, intimidation and thuggery throughout the campaign. People were threatened with bodily harm, with their homes being burnt down and with reprisals against their families, if they continued to work 'against the government'. The number and location of such reports indicate a deliberate, organised and widespread campaign of intimidation. The situation became so bad in Attanagalla (Mrs Bandaranaike's former electorate), for instance, that on the eve of the poll, the Attanagalla SLFP Central Committee decided to withdraw all its polling observers from the 47 stations in the electorate because of the 'prevailing reign of terror'.[67] It appears that the IGP rushed commando units there to deal with the situation. It is alleged, however, that they were quickly pulled out when, being unfamiliar with the local situation and therefore non-partisan, they began arresting government supporters.

Many opposition polling observers were taken into custody on false complaints, and were usually released two or three days after the poll. (Police interrogations in this period particularly sought to elicit the identity of polling and counting observers.) It is alleged that the SLFP observers in Yatinuwara (Kandy District) were taken into custody and remanded on 19 December on a false complaint that they had thrown mud at the photograph of the President. In Wellawaya, the LSSP reports two 'activists' were taken into custody by the police, the day before the poll. When asked the reason for their arrest, the inspector is alleged to have stated that he had simply acted on orders from his superior. They were released on bail on the 24th. In Colombo, a CP observer was arrested on the eve of the poll. It was admitted that there was no evidence against him, but as the charge had been made by a minister's supporters, the police had to keep him in custody a while, for fear of incurring the minister's disfavour.[68]

In Kekirawa (Anuradhapura District), UNP supporters visited all the SLFP polling observers allocated to the 34 polling stations and warned them to keep away from the poll. Those who defied this threat were subsequently robbed of their documents and electoral lists by armed gangs, and chased away. On 21 December, a vehicle containing workers for the 'pot' in Hatton, including an LSSP Referendum Agent, was stopped by a jeep supporting large pictures of the President and Minister Gamini Dissanayake. They were assaulted by the jeep's occupants, and taken to Hatton police station where they were detained. Only the speedy intervention of lawyers and the Bishop of Colombo obtained their release the next day. As a result of his experience, the Agent collapsed and was rushed to hospital, so that he was thus unable to be present for the counting of the votes at Nuwara Eliya.[69] Even in the metropolis — Colombo West, for example — polling observers were threatened with dire consequences if they went to their stations.

Several independent reports, long before polling day, indicated that there was to be a widespread campaign to prevent opposition voters from going to the polls. According to one report, a Deputy Minister and MP for Yapahuwa exhorted his supporters to prevent SLFP voters from leaving their homes on polling day.[70] It is also reported that when one senior government official was told that the government could lose the referendum, as quite a few UNP supporters were unhappy about it, he retorted: 'Nonsense, the pot can't get more than 100,000 votes. To get more votes, they have to first *get* to the polls!'

The rumour was put about that people's votes could later be checked by comparing the ballot paper number with that on the electoral lists. More serious were the threats of bodily harm or loss of jobs if people did not prove that they had cast their vote for the 'lamp'. This was to be done by displaying marked ballot papers before putting them into the box. This instruction was conveyed to voters in a number of places. Reports appeared in the press of robberies of polling cards from post offices.[71] In certain areas, government supporters received their cards, while opposition supporters did not. In some places, government supporters visited opposition voters to extract cards under duress — particularly in Kekirawa and Attanagalla, where whole families were forced to surrender their cards. In Attanagalla, the cards of the entire staff and inmates of a home for the aged (over 50 people) were obtained by subterfuge. In other areas, this took a more polite form, with visits to homes where people were known to be abroad, the polite requests for *their* cards. Known opposition voters were also threatened with assault or other reprisals if they went to vote.

Part Three: Polling Day

The entire weight of the high-pressure campaign to ensure a victory for the 'lamp', the symbol of a 'yes' vote, to the postponement of elections, reached its climax on the day of the referendum itself. This involved the dramatic and ubiquitous presence of large numbers of government party supporters in green shirts and green caps, threats and assaults against opposition polling observers so that many polling stations were left completely unmanned by the opposition, intimidation of individuals, households and groups who were known to be opposition supporters, and the extension of this intimidation in several recorded instances to the public servants administering the poll. All of this was combined with what clearly appeared to be organised mass impersonation. Political thuggery has never been wholly absent from Sri Lankan elections, but the nature and scale of this operation were unprecedented. The removal of opposition polling observers and the intimidation of public servants were entirely new phenomena. Indeed, so serious were the malpractices at the referendum that they represented a virtual dismantling of the electoral machinery and the subversion of the democratic process.[72]

Continuing Illegalities and Intimidation

The illegal symbol display persisted and polling station walls were plastered with 'lamp' posters and portraits of the President or Prime Minister. People wearing green hats and 'lamp' or 'President' badges congregated illegally at the entrance to polling stations and even inside them.[73] Similarly identifiable 'pot' supporters were noticeably absent. From Dambulla District it was reported that gangs moving about in the vicinity of polling stations were pinning badges on voters — in the presence of police officers.

We have already seen that in Attanagalla the SLFP announced the withdrawal of all its observers for their own safety. Elsewhere, in Kekirawa and Matale, for instance, threats achieved similar success. Two SLFP observers who were bold enough to go on duty at Raniswala polling station, Attanagalla, despite the party's position there, were driven out shortly afterwards, along with the other opposition observers. Two other SLFP observers at Attanagalla were taken into custody only a few hours before the poll commenced, for no stated reason. In many other areas, SLFP observers — those who had not been arrested before polling day — were often expelled or excluded from polling stations on referendum day.

Many observers were intercepted on their way to the poll and their letters of authorisation seized, so that they could not prove their credentials. Reports of this came from Kolupitiya and Wellawatte (Colombo District), Kekirawa (Anuradhapura District), Bibile (Moneragala District), and Dompe (Gampaha District). In Dompe, an LSSP observer died soon after being assaulted when he tried to assume duties.[74] Elsewhere, threats to family and home or even physical assault forced others to leave polling stations. Such reports came from Wellawaya (Moneragala District), Kekirawa and Katana

(Gampaha District). An affidavit filed in the Supreme Court also refers to such incidents.[75] At a polling station at Colombo University (Colombo West), the only opposition observer present (in spite of previous threats) was compelled to leave at gun point by a UNP MP. He was also assaulted in the MP's presence. He recorded a complaint with the Senior Presiding Officer and at a police station. The MP was identified as Anura Bastian, MP for Colombo West.[76] The LSSP reported that most of its observers were turned away and that, in Colombo, the matter had been reported to the Colombo Government Agent, but the situation had not been rectified.[77] The Communist Party reported that 'many dozens of agents . . . were physically assaulted, threatened and driven out of polling stations'.[78] There were even reports of similar incidents after the poll, as in Peradeniya where thugs broke into the station and threatened the SLFP observer.

Many reports from Attanagalla, especially, and from Matale, complained of opposition voters being prevented from leaving their houses, or being waylaid *en route* to the poll, threatened and even assaulted, and their polling cards seized or destroyed. Several people from Nittambuwa, Attanagalla, said that this was done in the presence of a highly-placed government supporter.[79] Patrolling by government supporters, or thugs, to ensure that opposition voters did not leave their homes took place on a large scale in the rural areas, where isolation and the known political affiliation of the villagers facilitated the process. Cards were seized or voters were prevented from entering stations in many districts, including Gampaha, Anuradhapura, Matale and Kurunegala.[80]

In Jaffna District, where a high poll against the government's proposal was expected,

the presence of armed soldiers in polling stations and on roads leading to polling stations had made a quite a large number of women voters keep away from the polls, particularly in Jaffna (electorate).[81]

Only a week earlier, it was reported that a peaceful protest gathering inside a church in the north had been tear-gassed and people assaulted.[82] In fact, the poll in the north was considerably lower than expected being less than 60 per cent — the lowest in the country, although the initial call for a boycott there may also have had some effect.

Reports that marked ballots had to be shown to UNP observers before being put in the boxes came from Matale, Dambulla, Kalawewa, Mirigama (Gampaha) and Attanagalla, among other places. Reports from Mihintale and Kekirawa indicate that in numerous stations, unauthorised personnel positioned themselves near the voting enclosure and observed the marking of ballot papers by voters. The MP for Attanagalla personally observed someone seated outside the Veyangoda Roman Catholic School polling station, on a 'motor cycle with a gun fixed on to it'.[83]

Impersonation

Outside many polling stations, groups of people (usually with green caps and 'lamp' badges) congregated from very early in the morning, with electoral lists and large bundles of polling cards, which they distributed to 'voters'. These 'voters' were invariably ferried in cars or jeeps (an illegal practice) from one polling station to another. They were clearly impersonators and generally recognised as such, particularly when they returned time after time to vote in the same place.[84] Not only did police turn a blind eye to this practice, they also refused to act on complaints made to them.

Reports of particularly heavy impersonation with some individuals voting 15 or 20 times and more, came from Katana, Dambulla, Mawatagama, Yapahuwa and Polgahawela electorates, among others.[85] In Kuliyapitiya, the LSSP reported UNP supporters voting 30 to 40 times. In Dambulla, an official noted that one man had voted 72 times. The official informed more senior officers who later visited the station, but they said that nothing could be done in the absence of any opposition polling observers. Individual reports of impersonation were numerous: many people turned up only to find that their vote had already been cast for them. Elsewhere, it was discovered that persons known to be abroad and even the dead had voted. Well-known local and even national figures were impersonated, the most blatant example of which was at Colombo West, where SLFP presidential candidate, Hector Kobbekaduwa who had appeared so much in the media and on public platforms only two months earlier, found his vote already cast when he arrived.[86] Impersonation was aided by the fact that the ink used for marking a voter's finger was not indelible, but easily removed with soap and water. In some areas, cleansing agents were provided close to the polling stations. Cases were also reported of ink not having been used at all. The absence of opposition observers from many polling stations was clearly conducive to massive impersonation. The heavy voting and extraordinarily high swings in Matale District and electorates like Kekirawa and Attanagalla lend credence to this.

The Conduct of Public Servants

A distinctive feature of Sri Lanka's electoral system has been the efficiency, impartially and objectivity with which thousands of public servants, temporarily assigned to the Commissioner of Elections, carried out their duties. The referendum, however, generated a large number of reports relating to the intimidation and obstruction of polling officials resulting, for the first time, in their being compelled to condone or collaborate in malpractices by, for example, not detaining impersonators detected by opposition observers. From Kekirawa, it was reported that they actually supported impersonations, reading out names from the electoral lists to visiting impersonators.[87]

Over all, however, the impression is that the majority of polling officers were helpless in situations they had never before experienced or anticipated. Moreover, on occasions when they attempted to intervene, they were rarely supported by the police. A Senior Presiding Officer in Attanagalla reported that there were impersonations from the commencement of the poll, but he was threatened when he tried to take action. Appeals to the Area Returning Officer proved fruitless and police assigned to his station worked hand-in-glove with the impersonators.[88] Moreover, the fact that opposition observers were kept out of many polling stations rendered the usual procedure of the identification of impersonators largely inoperative.

It is alleged that in Colombo West when a Senior Presiding Officer tried to turn out an impersonator, thugs stormed the station and assaulted him. When the policemen on duty attempted to go to his aid, he in turn was threatened with a revolver by a UNP politician. *The Island* newspaper, whose photographer was present, published a report the next day, but did not name the politician, and later accounts stated that no witnesses had been present. However, Pieter Keuneman, a former Colombo MP and Vice President of the CP, asserts that when he went to cast his vote at this same polling station he was told of the incident by the policeman and the press photographer, who identified the politician as Anura Bastian, MP for the area. Subsequently, Bastian denied this in Parliament, offering protection to any witness who wanted to come forward to give evidence against him.[89]

Reports of interference with the count or the ballot boxes are relatively rare. A letter was sent to the President and the IGP from an opposition counting observer complaining of assault by a UNP politician in the presence of the police at Matale. Another report from this district stated that 'the majority of the counting observers of the opposition parties who went to the Matale Kachcheri (government office) were assaulted in the presence of the police'.[90] An opposition agent in Nuwara Eliya District was excluded from the count.[91] In a counting centre at Ratnapura, the local MP of the ruling party is reported to have threatened to dash the Assistant Government Agent to the ground.[92]

The conduct of the police on polling day, as during the whole referendum period, appears to have left much to be desired. Some attempted to carry out their duties in spite of intimidation, but many reports indicate that they continued to permit violations of the law, including criminal assault, and that they sometimes actively colluded in this.

Despite a warning by the IGP that 'anybody found carrying lethal or dangerous weapons (would) be detained under emergency law',[93] it was possible, even in metropolitan Colombo, for an armed politician to intimidate polling observers, policemen and ordinary citizens, and not be apprehended, as two incidents mentioned above indicate. A third such encounter was on one of Colombo's main thoroughfares. According to newspaper reports and a letter sent to the President, the son of a former Deputy Speaker, his family, a senior Queen's Counsel and another person were threatened by the same politician brandishing his gun, and the Deputy Speaker's son assaulted. Apparently, the politician was angry because someone in the group had photographed the impersonation at one of his polling stations and obtained a list of the people who were to be impersonated. A police inspector who came on the scene watched the proceedings, but took no action.[94] The politician in question was subsequently promoted to the post of Deputy Minister for Internal Security (Home Guards).[95] It was in this period that police developed the tendency to spring a charge upon someone who had gone to the police to lodge a complaint against a government activist. Citizens, therefore, became reluctant to approach the police.

In defence of the police, it should be stressed that by December 1982 it had become evident that it simply did not pay to enforce the law against ruling politicians, their thugs or supporters.[96] It was to become even more evident that, on the contrary, the opposite paid.

Political interference within the police is not a new phenomenon, restricted to the UNP regime But it assumed such serious proportions during the referendum that many observers felt it augured ill for the maintenance of genuine law and order in the country in future.

Part Four: The Results

In the context of the intensive and widespread manipulation of the electoral process, which the government indulged in with such a heavy hand in the five weeks of the campaign and on polling day itself, and especially its use of well-organised and well-coordinated thuggery, it is possible seriously to ask whether, in the light of this interference, the UNP government received a genuine popular endorsement at the referendum. The opposition clearly believed that this had not happened. Mrs Bandaranaike described the referendum as 'the biggest fraud perpetrated on the people',[97] and a joint statement of eight opposition parties called it

> an extended fraud . . . (attended by) a cynical abuse of state power, blatant deceit, widespread intimidation and physical violence against opponents, with massive intimidation . . .[98]

Those who argue that the referendum result was a true expression of the popular will must account for the markedly uneven pattern of voter response. Very large decreases in the government's share of the vote took place in many areas while very large increases occurred in others. M.P. Moore has offered one explanation for this in his contribution to this book, but it is arguable that intimidation and impersonation provide a more plausible explanation.

Consider for example that in the nine rural districts in Table 5.1 where at the presidential election Jayewardene polled less than the UNP's share of the vote in 1977, the vote for the 'lamp' and thus for the UNP proposal increased, often dramatically. And in the districts marked with asterisks, every single electorate showed an increase in the government's share of the vote. The change in Anuradhapura is partly understandable, since the pre-eminent figure in the district's politics, Maithripala Senanayake, changed sides and supported the government at the referendum. (Although, as we shall see presently, the dramatic change in voting pattern in at least one electorate in this district — Kekirawa — is partly explained by more sinister doings.) But the turn-round in several of the other districts is very curious, particularly when we recall that reports suggest that intimidation and violence were especially widespread in such rural areas. Indeed there is considerable evidence — as, in some cases, we have already shown in this essay — of chicanery and law-breaking in several of these specific districts. In the limited space available here, we will present a necessarily brief survey of several districts where results seem open to question, including some of those on the list above.

Table 5.1:   UNP Share of the Referendum Vote

District	% increase since presidential election
Gampaha	5.05
Matale*	15.66
Matara	1.38
Kurunegala	6.30
Anuradhapura*	18.65
Polonnaruwa*	2.41
Badulla*	11.62
Moneragala*	15.27
Ratnapura	7.07

Kekirawa was one part of Anuradhapura District where Maithripala Senanayake's support for the referendum does not appear to be the only explanation for the high 'yes' vote. It was here that the 'lamp' gained the biggest positive swing since the presidential election — 30.29 per cent. Polling was heavy — 20 per cent above the national average — despite a severe drought in the area which was thought by some observers to prevent many peasants from voting because they had to search out food each day.[99] Suspicions that the high poll and the large majority for the 'lamp' there resulted from impersonation gain credence from reports of widespread thuggery and intimidation which compelled opposition observers to stay away from many, indeed nearly all, polling stations in the electorate.

In Nuwara Eliya-Maskeliya District, the government increased not only its share of the vote but also its actual vote, on a reduced poll, obtaining an overall majority of 74,214 (28,949 higher than in October). The 'lamp' won over 12 per cent more votes than the President. This seems dubious, partly because of reports of the intimidation and arrest of opposition workers there, but also because of a strange discrepancy in reports from the district. The Government Agent (or chief civil servant of the district) stated that the turnout in Nuwara Eliya town was only about 50 per cent,[100] and yet according to the returns, the turnout for Nuwara Eliya electorate (including both the town and surrounding areas) was no less than 79.48 per cent. Is it possible that the Government Agent was broadly correct, and that a low poll (partly the result of intimidation of opposition voters) lent itself to substantial rigging?

In Matale District, the 'lamp' received its largest majority, 73.77 per cent, against only 58.11 per cent of the vote for the President in October. This is distinctly curious, partly because many of the reports cited earlier in this essay came from that district, including accounts of the break-up of opposition meetings, the absence of polling observers and interference with the secrecy of the ballot. Instances of heavy impersonation, like the man who voted 72 times at Dambulla, and the requirement that voters display marked ballots are mentioned in these reports. The result is also curious because voter turnout there was given as 80.45 per cent which is ten per cent higher than the national average despite severe flooding. On 20 December it was officially reported that '1,875 families were affected and 9,000 people were stranded'.[101] In Laggala, the area worst affected by floods, the poll was fully 87.40 per cent. The MP for Laggala had stated that as 'most roads were badly damaged on Referendum Day . . . ballot boxes (would) have to be carried with tremendous difficulty'.[102] On polling day itself:

> heavy rains in the catchment area swelled the Amban Ganga and as voters set out to their polling booths at approximately 7.00 a.m. the causeway went under. *Voters in Laggala and Pallegama* were cut off from their polling and *were unable to cast their votes.*[103] (italics added)

Yapahuwa electorate in Kurunegala District witnessed a dramatic rise in the pro-government vote, from 54.41 per cent for the President in October to 68.14 per cent for the 'lamp' in December. This appears to be partly explained by the instructions issued by the local ruling party MP to his supporters to intimidate the opposition. This led to violence which continued after polling day.

The heavy swings in favour of the 'lamp' in Gampaha District were also quite remarkable. Attanagalla and Dompe electorates in this district have returned members of the Bandaranaike family to

Parliament since their creation. Even amid the island-wide landslide against her government in 1977, Mrs Bandaranaike held Attanagalla by over 10,000 votes. At the presidential election, her party's candidate won in both of these electorates, carrying Attanagalla by 11,259 votes. Yet two months later, both produced huge swings to the 'lamp': yielding at Dompe a majority of 10,699 and at Attanagalla, 18,305. To accept this latter result as genuine, we must believe that the government's popularity increased by nearly 60 per cent in two months.

These swings may be better explained by considering that Dompe was the electorate in which an LSSP polling observer died after being assaulted when he went to take up his duties. And in Attanagalla the campaign conducted by the UNP against opposition workers, which Mrs Bandaranaike described as a 'reign of terror' in a letter to the President, necessitated the withdrawal of all SLFP polling observers. This area witnessed the detention of important SLFP organisers, assaults on campaigners and voters, countless complaints of stolen cards, the prevention of people leaving their homes and threats to life and property. Given all of this, it is difficult to believe that such startling majorities for the 'lamp' were honestly obtained.

If we are to accept the sizeable swings and increases in several of the districts listed earlier and in numerous electorates elsewhere, it is necessary to draw one further implausible conclusion. This is that President Jayewardene was less popular than his party in Parliament and less popular than his individual MPs in these electorates, since they were the ones being given a further six years in office by people voting 'yes' at the referendum. This is implausible because so many MPs in widely scattered areas were either suspected of lawless behaviour or regarded with open hostility by constituents. This was plainly acknowledged by no less a person than Jayewardene himself during the presidential election campaign when he repeatedly asked people to set aside their feelings about corrupt and unpopular MPs, and to put their trust in *him*.

The referendum bodes ill for the future of parliamentary democracy in Sri Lanka where it had hitherto flourished. But its implications and repercussions went far beyond the simple extension of the life of a spent Parliament. The steady undermining of respect for law and order and the feeling that illegality may be resorted to with impunity by those having the right political connections reached an unprecedented height during the referendum.[104] The Civil Rights Movement has said that in assessing the reasons behind the holocaust that engulfed Sri Lanka in mid-1983, the alarming erosion in recent years of respect for the law and for the rights of persons, often manifested by a resort to violence, should be seriously considered. It continued:

> The fact that violence has been used to meet criticism and political dissent in the country as a whole, including the Sinhala areas, may well have encouraged the belief among certain sections of the population that the ethnic problem could be dealt with in a similar manner . . . The possibility cannot be discounted that the mobs which assaulted and killed Tamils in the days following July 23rd, burnt their homes and possessions and places of business, and terrorised the general public in many cases, and the looters who followed in their wake, may well have been encouraged by the knowledge that many earlier instances of lawbreaking have gone unpunished.[105]

Historians may some day see the referendum as a watershed in the life of this small but politically sophisticated island nation.

Notes

1. Prime Minister in *Parliamentary Debates*, 24 November 1982, col. 2251.
2. *Daily News*, 23 October 1982.
3. *Daily Mirror*, 3 November 1982.
4. See references elsewhere in this article.
5. The government vote includes the vote for the Ceylon Workers Congress (CWC).
6. Cases were pending against certain MPs. For example, the MP for Wellawaya has had an alleged charge of rape against him put off for many months (for which he is on bail), but he was 'grilled by CID for four hours' in connection with it (*Island*, 28 February 1982). The case in which the MP for Polgahawela was charged with attempted murder on 17 July 1981 was committed to trial in High Court (*Sun*, 5 March 1983).
7. *Weekend*, 5 September 1982.
8. Ibid., 24 October 1982.
9. Three million was, in fact, the *total opposition* vote. The SLFP polled 2,548,438 votes.
10. Interview, *Asian Digest Magazine*, reproduced in *Daily News*, 5 January 1983.
11. The President, speaking to government parliamentary group. *Daily News*, 29 October 1982.
12. *Sessional Paper No. III — 1983*. When the report was debated in the House

on 7 September 1983, Maithripala Senanayake, former SLFP Deputy Leader (who had supported the government at the referendum) dismissed it as 'gossip' and 'hearsay', as part of a 'strategy of diversion', an attempt to 'split the SLFP by pitting one side against the other'.

SLFP MP for Attanagalla, Lakshman Jayakody, remarked: 'It was unfortunate that the government should utilise its intelligence resources in search of a non-existing plot, whereas (it) was totally unprepared for the coming catastrophe of July 1983. This reveals a remarkable deficiency on the part of the intelligence services for which the government is responsible. This is the price the country has to pay when a government is more anxious to harass political opponents than maintain law and order.' *Sun*, 8 September 1983.

13. For example, *Weekend*, 24 October 1982 refers to the MPs for Polgahawela, Ratnapura and Bibile engaging in 'unbecoming conduct during the post poll period'. See also *Island*, 24 October; *Daily News*, 25 October; *Forward*, 1 November; and letter by M.J.M. Jiffry in *Island*, 8 November 1982. *Saturday Review*, 1 January 1983, published extracts from letters sent to the President and the IGP regarding the alleged intimidation and assault on opposition supporters organised and carried out by a Deputy Minister, the MP for Yapahuwa, H.B. Abeyratne. *Daily Mirror*, 10 November 1982 reported that the MP for Passara appeared in chambers before a Badulla magistrate in connection with allegations of intimidation after the presidential election.

14. See Mrs Bandaranaike's letter to the IGP on 23 November 1982, published in *Island*, 3 December 1982: 'Public Security Ordinance used to harass SLFP supporters'. See also, *Island* editorial in 10 November 1982.

15. Ibid. See also *Emergency (Miscellaneous Provisions and Powers) Regulations No. 2 of 1982*, Sections 11–22.

16. So durable were these banners, in fact, that some of them survive to this day, despite tropical rains and civil commotion.

17. *Referendum Act, No. 7 of 1981*, Section 50.

18. *Emergency . . . Regulations No. 2 of 1982*, Section 28(1).

19. *Island*, 26 November 1982.

20. *Daily News*, 3 December 1982.

21. *Island* editorial, 12 December 1982: 'Though the IGP had reportedly instructed his men to remove these symbols nothing has been done obviously because the police are afraid of reprisals.' See also *Island* cartoon, 20 December 1982, in which a policeman is addressing his superior officer; 'I will fight the tigers in the north — I will carry out any dangerous mission — but please, please don't ask me to remove those lamps, sir!'

22. *Island*, 28 December: '. . . three LSSPers arrested in Gampaha . . . for allegedly displaying the symbol "pot" at a public place'. *Daily News*, 16 December 1982: 'Mr. Mahinda Wijesekera, Chief SLFP organiser for Devinuwara . . . remanded till December 28 . . . for allegedly attacking some UNP supporters who were putting up posters.' See also Leader of the Opposition's statement in Parliament, *Sun*, 27 November 1982.

23. For example, *Sun*, 14 December 1982: 'The UNP's publicity campaign in the display of symbols for the Referendum has been very conspicuous. Voters are yet to see the negative symbol — Pot — as far as Kurunegala is concerned.'

24. See the protests raised in a letter to the President: Civil Rights Movement (CRM) E03/12/82 of 19 December 1982.

25. See the Civil Rights Movement's protest in a letter to the President; CRM E07/11/82 of 27 November 1982.

26. Daughter of former premier, Mrs Bandaranaike.

27. *Daily News*, 3 November 1982.

28. *Daily Mirror*, 3 November 1982.

29. *Forward,* 1 December 1982. See also 'Island Politics' in *Island,* 21 November 1982.

30. *Sun,* 3 November 1982.

31. *Island,* 21 December 1982.

32. *Daily News,* 22 July 1983.

33. *Sun,* 8 September 1983.

34. *Aththa case,* S.C. Application No. 120/82.

35. Ibid.

36. *Parliamentary Debates,* 26 November 1982, col. 1986.

37. Where the police had given permission for a meeting on 5 December, but tried to take back the permit on the 3rd saying that the local Village Reawakening Committee were against it. Subsequent threats to the owner of the land and the person who was providing the public address system forced the LSSP organisers to cancel the meeting. (Information of this nature and many of the incidents reported hereafter have come from a variety of sources, including written complaints made to party and trade union organisations and human rights groups. In the interests of the people concerned it is not always possible to identify sources.)

38. *Parliamentary Debates,* 26 November 1982, cols. 1986, 1987.

39. Letter in *Forward,* 15 December 1982.

40. *Island,* 13 December and *Forward,* 15 December 1982.

41. The leaders of the gang were identified and their vehicle numbers recorded (LSSP source).

42. *Island,* 12 December and *Forward,* 15 December 1982.

43. *Daily Mirror,* 10 December 1982.

44. Up to June 1983, no charges had been preferred against him, though he has to report regularly to the police.

45. Prime Minister in Parliament, as reported in *Island,* 28 November 1982.

46. For example, a number of books associated with the Minister of Industries and Scientific Affairs, Cyril Matthew. These champion the cause of Sinhala Buddhism and the Sinhalese people by portraying the Tamil people as destroyers of the Sinhalese people and nation. The cover of one such book, *Sinhaluni budu sasuna beraganiv* (Sinhalese! Save the Buddha Sasana!) depicts a Buddhist religious edifice being destroyed by Tamils. Matthew demands that modern Buddhist temples be re-established at all sites in predominantly Tamil areas where temples once stood and that a Sinhalese community be settled around each. See also *Kavuda Kotiya? (Who is a Tiger?).* A letter in the *Daily News,* 17 July 1981, drew attention to the circulation of this shocking book 'purposely got up to incite communal tension'. A week later a government MP requested that the whole of the first of these two books be reproduced in Hansard, declaring that every word in the book was important! So it is unlikely that the authorities were unaware of what was being distributed.

47. Order of 2 November 1982. Referred to in *Aththa case,* S.C. Application No. 120/82, Annex 13.

48. They did not, for instance, carry the appeal signed by 145 university teachers to reject the extension of Parliament. See *Island,* 17 December and *Sun,* 18 December 1982.

49. See memorandum on the referendum, Centre for Society and Religion to the President (*Lanka Guardian,* 15 November 1982).

50. See for example the state-funded supplement, *Daily News,* 15 December and the *Daily News,* 19 December 1982. The *Sunday Observer* headline on 19 December 1982 was: 'A Vote for the Pot is a Vote for Eelam — Amirthalingam', but the text below contained nothing to this effect. The sister Sinhala newspaper, *Silumina* did likewise. This kind of dishonest journalism was cited by the CP MP for Kalawana (*Parliamentary Debates,* 24 December 1982).

51. The *Sun* (English) and the *Davasa* (Sinhala) are published by Independent Newspapers. Upali Newspapers publish the *Island* (English) and the *Divaina* (Sinhala).

52. Some of the new programmes and programme series were: 'National Awakening' and 'Let Us Develop', on radio: 'Development and You' and 'New Thinking in Politics', on television.

53. CRM E07/11/82 on 27 November 1982.

54. *Island*, 9 December and letter in *Forward*, 15 December 1982.

55. *Sunday Observer*, 14 November 1982.

56. *Daily News* and *Sun*, 17 December 1982. The epithet 'Dharmishta' — used by the President of his government — carries associations of justice, righteousness and rule according to law.

57. *Island*, 9 December 1982: 'We are more democratic than USA — President.'

58. *Sun*, 1 November 1982.

59. In Parliament on 28 October 1982. See *Sunday Times*, 7 November and *Sunday Observer*, 21 November 1982.

60. *Sunday Times*, 7 November 1982.

61. *Island*, 1 November 1982.

62. *Referendum Act No. 7 of 1981*, Section 45.

63. Ibid., Section 54(1).

64. *Island*, 30 November 1982.

65. *Daily News*, 30 November 1982.

66. Ibid.

67. Letter from Mrs Bandaranaike to President, 21 December 1982. See *Parliamentary Debates*, 24 December 1982, cols. 2137–9; also *Island*, 22 December 1982.

68. *Forward*, 5 January 1983.

69. *Christian Worker*, first quarter, 1983, pp. 7, 24.

70. See specific complaints cited in note 13.

71. *Sun*, 15 December 1982: 'Imposter takes 639 poll cards', from a post office in Attanagalla. *Island*, 27 December 1982 refers to another such attempt.

72. Reference must be made here to the allegation of serious malpractices during the District Development Council Elections in Jaffna in June 1981, which were spoken of as a 'dress-rehearsal' for the next general election. See for example, CRM letter to Commissioner of Elections, E02/6/81, 8 June 1981 and *What Happened in Jaffna: Days of Terror* (Colombo, Movement for Interracial Justice & Equality, nd).

73. This constitutes an offence under the Referendum Act, Section 44(1).

74. *Island*, 24 December 1982 and LSSP statement of 27 December 1982; extracts in *Christian Worker*, first quarter 1983, p. 5.

75. *Forward*, 15 January 1982 and *Aththa case*, S.C. Application No. 120/82.

76. Ibid.

77. *Island*, 23 December 1982.

78. *Sun*, 31 December 1982.

79. See references earlier in the text of this paper.

80. For example, the LSSP reported cards seized and torn at Dhamunumulla polling station in Kekirawa.

81. Leader of the Opposition, A. Amirthalingam, *Parliamentary Debates*, 24 December 1982, col. 2122.

82. Ibid., cols. 2123, 2124.

83. Ibid., col. 2148.

84. Ibid., col. 2149, and *Referendum Act No. 7 of 1981*, Sections 57(5) and 61(1).

85. *Island*, 23 December 1982. Also unofficial LSSP report on malpractices.

86. *Island*, 23 December 1982.

87. Unofficial LSSP report. This is not to say that the majority of public servants did not attempt to carry out their duties as correctly as possible in the face of general intimidation and inadequate support.

88. Letter sent to SLFP.

89. *Island*, 23 and 25 December 1982; *Forward*, 15 January and *Island*, 7 January 1983.

90. Complaint sent to SLFP.

91. See references earlier in the text.

92. Unofficial LSSP report.

93. *Daily News*, 24 December 1982.

94. Letter from M.S. Cader to President, 22 December 1982, published in *Forward*, 5 January 1983.

95. *Sun*, 5 April 1983.

96. According to an LSSP report, a polling observer at Kekirawa Muslim Maha Vidyalaya (probably the only polling station in this electorate to have had any opposition observers), was ejected by a mob about 9 a.m. When he asked police to intervene, the Officer-in-Charge said that he would be 'transferred to Jaffna' if he took any action and advised the complainant to look to his own safety.

97. *Island*, 24 December 1982.

98. *Forward*, 15 January 1983.

99. *Daily News*, 30 June 1983.

100. *Island*, 23 Decemeber 1982.

101. *Daily Mirror*, 22 December 1982.

102. Ibid.

103. *Sun*, 23 December 1982.

104. For an earlier analysis of the issues and conduct of the referendum, see 'Referendum '82: Eclipse of Parliamentary Democracy in Sri Lanka', *Logos*, xxii, 1 (March 1983), Centre for Society and Religion, Colombo.

105. *Communal Violence — July 1983*, Civil Rights Movement, E 01/8/83.

6 PROPORTIONAL REPRESENTATION AND ELECTORAL SYSTEM CHANGE IN SRI LANKA

Robert Oberst

The rules of politics are rarely neutral. A change in the way elections are conducted can alter the balance of power between competing parties in a democratic system. This study will examine a change in the electoral system of a Third World democracy, Sri Lanka, and the impact that this change may have on the nature of electoral politics in that country. Specifically, it will argue that the change from a system of single-member electoral constituencies to proportional representation could lead to a change in the balance of power among the political parties of Sri Lanka, the demise of several smaller parties, no increase in the fractionalisation of the party system, and a significant change in the nature of the legislator–constituent relationship.

For many years, Maurice Duverger's *Political Parties* and Douglas Rae's *The Political Consequences of Electoral Laws* have set the tone for the analysis of the impact of electoral laws on political systems.[1] They both argued that proportional representation tended to increase the number of political parties in a political system and fractionalise the party system. This thesis has been disputed by some later scholars such as Declan O'Connell who has criticised Rae and Duverger for their methodology — the use of a mathematical approach to study electoral laws.[2] This paper will argue that the mathematical approach may not be an invalid method when applied to an actual situation rather than the hypothetical situation used by Rae and Duverger. We will also examine the impact of proportional representation on the style of legislative representation or what O'Connell calls the 'style of politics'.[3] This analysis of the Sri Lankan system of proportional representation indicates that Rae and Duverger's thesis may be incorrect.

In 1978, Sri Lanka promulgated a new constitution which changed the electoral system to one of proportional representation. The first section of this paper will examine the nature of different electoral systems. This will be followed by an in-depth study of the impact of the electoral changes in Sri Lanka.

Electoral systems may be divided into two general classes: (i) proportional representation and (ii) single-member electoral constituencies or Anglo-American electoral systems.[4] The Anglo-American systems all have single-member districts with either a plurality or majority formula. The proportional representation systems have multi-member electoral constituencies and distribute legislative seats on the basis of the percentage of the votes received by each party contesting the election. Until the Constitution of 1978, Sri Lanka had an Anglo-American electoral system with a plurality formula. The new Constitution of 1978 created an electoral system based on proportional representation.

Each of these classes of electoral systems has a different impact on politics. The Anglo-American systems result in a strong tendency for a two-party system. The reasoning behind this is that the system favours strong parties. The only parties able to return candidates to the Parliament are those strong enough to obtain a plurality in an electoral constituency. Although smaller parties can occasionally gain enough support in a district to win, they cannot do it often enough to control the Parliament. Thus, it is to the advantage of voters in any district to cast their vote for those parties which may be able to control the Parliament and government. This control can result in patronage benefits that otherwise might not be available to a smaller party.

A second impact of the Anglo-American electoral system is a potential distortion in the distribution of legislative seats. Because the system is based on the principle of winner takes all, it is possible for great disparities to exist between the percentage of the vote received by a party and the percentage of the seats in Parliament won by that party. The ultimate disparity would be a party receiving 49.9 per cent of the vote in every electoral constituency and losing every seat in the Parliament to a party winning 50.1 per cent of the vote in each constituency. As we shall see, the tendency for unrepresentativeness among the Anglo-American systems is one of the reasons why Sri Lanka changed its electoral system.

There are several systems of proportional representation. All of these involve dividing the country up into one or more electoral constituencies, each returning more than one candidate to the Parliament. Each party contesting the election then presents a list of candidates to the voters of each constituency. The voters then face the option of voting for a list of party candidates all from one party. Thus, after the polling of votes, each party receives a percentage of seats commensurate with the percentage of votes they polled in the electoral constituency.[5] In Sri Lanka, there is a single list for each party with the party determining the order of the candidates on the list. When the seats are allocated to the parties, the names at the top of the list are the first to receive seats. The process continues on down the list until the party has run out of seats for its candidates. Other variations of this system allow the voters to cast a vote for the name on the list they prefer. The name with the highest number of votes then becomes the first name on the list.

The main advantage of the system is that the unrepresentativeness described under the single-member plurality system does not occur. Each party receives a percentage of seats almost equal to the percentage of votes it gained in the election. The only disparities result from randomness, or from several features that can be built into the system. These features will be discussed in a moment. The main disadvantage of proportion representation is its impact on the party system. Because each party receives a percentage of as many seats as it does votes, small parties can receive representation in the Parliament. This may result in the fractionalisation of the party system. For example, in a 200-seat Parliament, a party would only have to receive one-half of one per cent of the vote in order to receive a seat in Parliament. A situation where there were many small parties winning seats could lead to no party being able to obtain a majority in the Parliament, and even more importantly make it difficult for a coalition government to be formed. The solution to this problem is the restriction of party access to the ballot, or to a seat in Parliament. The latter method is used by most countries. Under this method, there is a cut-off point at which a party can no longer win a seat. For instance, if the cut-off point is 5 per cent and a party fails to receive 5 per cent of the vote in that district, they will not receive seats in Parliament.

Sri Lanka has been one of the world's most politically competitive democracies. Following independence in 1948, two blocs of parties emerged as the dominant forces in Sri Lankan politics. One bloc was centred around the United National Party (UNP). The UNP has relied in the past on the support of several smaller parties. These have included several of the political parties of the Tamil minority and splinter groups that have broken away from the second dominant bloc of parties. The UNP has been the party of the 'right' in Sri Lanka and is responsible for the promulgation of the Constitution of 1978. The second bloc of parties is centred around the Sri Lanka Freedom Party (SLFP). The SLFP was formed by dissident members of the UNP in the early 1950s and emerged as an important force in the 1956 elections. Its electoral allies have on occasion included two Marxist parties: the Communist Party (CP) which is a pro-Moscow party and the Lanka Sama Samaja Party (LSSP) which is ideologically associated with the writings of Leon Trotsky. In addition to these parties there have been a relatively large number of small parties that have emerged for one or two elections. These parties have usually been organised around a single prominent individual and then disappeared or been absorbed by one of the two major blocs of parties.

Several of these smaller parties are of importance. These are the political parties representing Sri Lanka's largest ethnic minority — the Sri Lanka Tamils. They have always supported their own parties at the ballot box and not one of the dominant blocs of parties in the country. As a result, the Sri Lanka Tamils, who are geographically concentrated in the north and east of the island, have almost exclusively returned candidates to Parliament from either the Federal Party (now known as the Tamil United Liberation Front or TULF) or the Tamil Congress (TC). This has resulted in the separation of the country into two different regions. Each of these regions has its own party system. The Tamil areas support the TULF and TC, while the Sinhalese areas support the UNP or the SLFP bloc of parties. In addition, one other Tamil party emerged in the 1977 elections. This was the Ceylon Workers Congress (CWC) which is the political wing of a union with the same name. This party represents estate Tamil tea plantation workers who consider themselves and are treated by the government as culturally and historically different from the Sri Lanka Tamils in the north and east.

The results of the 1970 and 1977 elections were an important factor in the decision of the UNP government of J.R. Jayewardene to introduce a system of proportional representation for parliamentary elections in the Constitution of 1978. In both elections there was a large disparity between the percentage of the votes polled by the major parties and the seats in Parliament received by the parties. Table 6.1 reports the election results. This gross disparity between the parties' strength at the polls and their seats in Parliament led to pressure to make the distribution of seats more equitable.

Table 6.1:   Election Results, 1970 and 1977

Parties	1970				1977			
	Votes	%	Seats	%	Votes	%	Seats	%
UNP	1,892,525	37.9	17	11.3	3,179,221	50.9	140	83.3
SLFP	1,839,979	36.9	91	60.3	1,855,331	29.7	8	4.8
CP	169,199	3.4	6	4.0	123,856	2.0	0	0.0
LSSP	433,224	8.7	19	12.6	225,317	3.6	0	0.0
FP/TULF	245,727	4.9	13	8.6	421,488	6.4	18	10.7
TC	115,567	2.3	3	2.0	Did not contest			
Others	295,527	5.9	2	1.3	375,653	6.0	2	1.2

Source: H.B.W. Abeynaike, *Parliament of Sri Lanka 1977* (Colombo, 1979), pp. 211–12.

The particular system of proportional representation adopted in Sri Lanka involves several specific features. Under this system the country will be divided into at least 20 and no more than 24 electoral constituencies (Constitution of the Democratic Socialist Republic of Sri Lanka, Article 96, Section 1). These electoral constituencies must comprise a province or part of one (Article 96, Section 2). There are a total of nine provinces in Sri Lanka, which are divided up into 24 administrative districts. When a province is divided into more than one electoral district, the Delimitation Commission is expected to attempt to make the division on the basis of the administrative districts (Article 96, Section 3). The number of seats in each electoral constituency will be determined by both population and geography.[6] The Parliament will have 196 seats. There will be 160 seats divided up between the electoral constituencies on the basis of population (Article 98, Section 3) and four seats for each of the nine provinces to be divided 'equitably among' the electoral constituencies (Article 98, Section 2).

The seats will be allocated according to the following procedures. The party receiving the most votes in any electoral constituency will automatically receive a seat in Parliament from that constituency (Article 99, Section 4). The remaining seats in that electoral constituency will then be apportioned on the basis of proportional representation. The only parties to qualify for the remaining seats must be those which polled at least one-eighth of the total votes cast in that constituency (Article, 99 Section 5a). The votes cast for those parties failing to receive one-eighth of the votes polled in that constituency will then be ignored in the division of the seats.

Thus the system has three crucial features: (1) a new method of apportioning seats between the districts; (2) a cut-off point of one-eighth of the votes cast in any electoral district; and (3) a bonus plan where the party finishing first in the electoral district receives one seat not distributed on the basis of proportional representation. This analysis will address three sets of questions all of which deal with the impact of the change to proportional representation on the political system:

(1) Will the Sri Lankan system of proportional representation lead to greater equality in the distribution of parliamentary seats than existed under the old system of single-member electoral constituencies? In addition, is the Sri Lankan system the most egalitarian system that might have been adopted by the Sri Lankan government?

(2) What impact will the changes have on the party system in Sri Lanka? Will this system of proportional representation lead to an increase in the number of political parties? Will it benefit one party over another? What impact will the high cut-off point and bonus seats have on the parties contesting elections?

(3) What impact will the changes have on the quality of representation provided by the legislators elected under proportional representation? Will they be able to provide the same kind of representation as is provided under the present system and be responsive to constituent needs?

Three elections will be examined. These are the general elections of 1970 and 1977, and the municipal and urban council elections of 1979. The two general elections were held under an electoral system of single-member electoral districts while the 1979 elections were held using proportional representation.[7] For the two elections held under the old system, the actual results will be compared with projections of what the results would have looked like if proportional representation had been used. It will not be possible to project what the results in the 1979 elections would have looked like under a system of single-member electoral constituencies. There is no way accurately to project the results. In each of these elections the impact of the various provisions of the proportional representation system will be compared with the impact of the single-member electoral constituencies. The specific provisions to be examined will be a 5 per cent cut-off provision; a 12.5 per cent cut-off provision; the bonus seat. A word of caution is in order here. The strategies that any party adopts in an election will depend on the electoral system used to distribute legislative seats. By making estimates of how the seats might have been distributed if a different system were used, this study ignores the fact that a different strategy might have been used. Therefore, the results of projections for the various formulae in most cases are not to be thought of as predictions of what *would* have happened if Sri Lanka had used a different electoral system.

In order to analyse the 1970 and 1977 elections, the results of both were transformed into multi-member constituencies along the guidelines specified in the 1978 Constitution. The votes polled in each of the single-member electoral districts that fell into the geographic confines of each of the constituencies under proportional representation were then combined. In combining these single-member constituencies a problem arose over the existence of several multi-member constituencies. In three of these constituencies, each voter received two votes to elect two candidates to Parliament. In the other two constituencies, the voters received three votes to elect three candidates to Parliament. The final results would have been distorted if votes from multi-member and single-member constituencies had been added together since voters from multi-member constituencies would have carried greater weight. Because of this, the results in each of the multi-member constituencies were divided by the number of candidates returned to Parliament by that constituency before being added into the constituencies created by proportional representation.

The first question to be addressed is the fairness in the distribution of legislative seats under the Sri Lankan system of proportional representation. The deviation from proportionality in the election results will be measured by the following formula:[8]

$$D = \tfrac{1}{2} \sum_{i-1}^{n} \left| S_i - V_i \right|$$

Where n = the number of parties in elections
      S_i = the seat share of the i-th party
      V_i = the vote share of the i-th party

Perfect proportionality will be reached when all of the parties (i) receive a proportion of seats equal to the proportion of the votes polled in the election. If this occurs, D will be equal to 0. If all of the parties receiving votes fail to receive any seats in Parliament and all of the seats in Parliament go to parties which did not receive any votes, then D will be equal to 1. Thus, the lower the value of D, the more equitable the distribution of the seats.

The examination of the D-scores for the 1970 and 1977 elections indicates a very sharp difference between the single-member electoral constituencies (SMEC) and the various systems of proportional representation (see Table 6.2). As would be expected, proportional representation is considerably more representative in its distribution of seats than is the single-member electoral constituency. The Sri Lankan system of proportional representation with its 12.5 per cent cut-off point and its bonus seat is not as equitable in distributing seats in Parliament as are the other systems of proportional representation with lower cut-off points and no bonus seats. Thus, although the Sri Lankan system of proportional representation provides for a more equitable distribution of seats in Parliament than the old system, it is not as equitable as more commonly used systems of proportional representation.[9]

Table 6.2: Deviation from Perfect Proportionality as Measured by 'D'-scores for Various Electoral Systems

Election	SMEC	Electoral formulae Proportional representation				
		No Cut-off	5% Cut-off	12.5% Cut-off	12.5% Cut-off 1 bonus seat	12.5% Cut-off 2 bonus seats
1970	.31	.05	.05	.08	.09	—
1977	.35	.04	.04	.08	.08	—
1979	—	.03	.04	.09	.10	.13

Note:

$$D = \frac{1}{2} \sum_{i=1}^{n} \left| S_i - V_i \right|$$

The second question to be addressed is the impact that proportional representation might have on the party system in Sri Lanka. As already noted, proportional representation is expected to increase the number of parties in the Parliament. However, a cut-off point will minimise the fractionalisation of the party system. In order to provide a measure of fractionalisation, the following index of fractionalisation will be used:[10]

$$F = 1 - \left(\sum_{i=1}^{n} T_i^2 \right)$$

Where F = index of fractionalisation

 T_i = percentage of the votes polled for the i-th party

The index ranges from a low of 0 to a high of 1. The lower the score, the greater the fractionalisation of the party system. Table 6.3 reports the fractionalisation scores for the electoral systems in each of the elections under study. The results are inconsistent. The level of fractionalisation resulting from the single-member electoral constituencies in the 1970 election is about the same as the fractionalisation resulting from the proportional representation systems in each of the elections. However, the overwhelming victory by the UNP in the 1977 elections resulted in a very high 'F'-score indicating a low level of fractionalisation. Thus, proportional representation will not necessarily lead to a greater fractionalisation of the party system in Sri Lanka. In at least one earlier election under the Anglo-American system, the fractionalisation of the party system was about the same as it would have been under proportional representation.

Table 6.3:   Party System Fractionalisation under Various Electoral Systems

Election	SMEC	Electoral formulae Proportional representation				
		No Cut-off	5% Cut-off	12.5% Cut-off	12.5% Cut-off 1 bonus seat	12.5% Cut-off 2 bonus seats
1970	.40	.31	.32	.33	.34	—
1977	.71	.38	.38	.42	.43	—
1979	—	.35	.36	.40	.42	.44

What is notable in this analysis is the small increase in the fractionalisation index as the cut-off point under proportional representation becomes larger. The increase in the index between the no cut-off point level and the 12.5 per cent cut-off with no bonus seat was only

.03 in 1970, and .05 in 1977 and 1979. An increase in the cut-off point does not appear to reduce the level of fractionalisation significantly. The reason for this becomes readily apparent when one looks at the size of most of the Sri Lankan electoral districts under the system of proportional representation. All but one has less than 20 seats, while 17 districts have less than ten seats (16 districts in 1977). The impact of the relatively small district size is to limit the fractionalisation of parties. In general, a party in a district with ten seats would have to poll about 10 per cent of the votes to obtain a seat in Parliament.[11] This finding raises the question of why a cut-off point is even needed, or at least one as high as the 12.5 per cent cut-off used in Sri Lanka.

A second issue is the impact that proportional representation will have on the individual parties in the system. In order to assess this, parties were divided into four classes: those in an electoral constituency that obtained first place, second place, third place and others. In order to examine the impact of the various electoral systems on these four classes of parties, the number of votes lost or gained for each party because of the cut-off points and the bonus seats was measured. This was done, in the case of the cut-off points, by the following method. Each time that a party was denied consideration for seats in excess of the cut-off point, those votes were deducted from the nationwide vote total of that party. These votes were then divided among the remaining parties on the basis of the percentage of the votes polled in that constituency by the remaining parties.

The vote increase due to the bonus seats posed a slightly more difficult problem. In this case, actual vote totals were not used. However, if the leading party received an extra seat that would not have been due them under a system with no bonus seats then the percentage of total votes in that constituency equal to the percentage of extra seats received was used as the increase in votes due to the bonus system. The party losing the seat due them under a system with no bonus seat had these votes deducted from their nationwide vote totals.

Table 6.4 reports the percentage of the total votes, polled by each class of parties, that were either gained or lost by the various provisions of proportional representation. It becomes very apparent from the results that the first and second place parties tend to gain votes from the 5 per cent and 12.5 per cent cut-off points while the other parties lose votes. The gain for the first and second place parties is about equal with no bias for either party. The bonus seat, however, removes whatever gain the second place party received from the cut-off points. The winner here is the winning party which gains a very large percentage of votes almost exclusively at the expense of the second place party. Parties finishing lower than second place are seriously hurt by the cut-off points and bonus seat provisions. This is especially the case with the parties finishing lower than third place. In each of the elections, almost all of the votes polled by these parties would have been ignored when the seats in Parliament were distributed. The third place parties would not have been seriously hurt by the 5 per cent cut-off provision. However, the increase in the cut-off point to 12.5 per cent would have had a very serious effect on the parties finishing in third place in any constituency.

Table 6.4:   Percentage of Total Votes Lost or Gained due to Bonus Seat and Cut-off Point Provisions of Proportional Representation

		First place	Second place	Third place	Others
1970	5%	3.5	3.3	1.3	− 67.5
	12.5%	3.5	3.2	− 9.9	− 32.4
	Bonus	16.1	− 17.4	− 5.4	0.0
	Total	23.1	− 10.9	− 13.9	− 100.0
1977	5%	3.9	4.2	− 5.4	− 80.9
	12.5%	4.2	4.4	− 37.1	− 12.7
	Bonus	3.9	− 7.3	0.0	0.0
	Total	12.0	1.3	− 42.5	− 93.6
1979	5%	1.6	1.6	− 1.5	− 27.0
	12.5%	11.5	11.1	− 71.8	− 73.0
	Bonus	4.0	− 5.8	− 8.9	0.0
	Total	17.1	6.9	− 82.2	− 100.0

Table 6.5 reports the impact of the cut-off points and bonus seat on the individual parties. It can be seen that the only parties to gain from the cut-off points and bonus seats are the UNP and SLFP in the Sinhalese areas and the TULF and TC in the Tamil areas. The LSSP, CP and other parties would be severely hurt by the 12.5 per cent cut-off point and the bonus seat. These parties have traditionally been the also-rans in Sri Lankan politics. In most cases these were the parties which made up the third place and 'others' categories in Table 6.4.

The Sri Lanka system of proportional representation would tend to create a two-party system in each of the Tamil and Sinhalese areas. The smaller parties would be faced with ephemeral status, occasionally receiving a seat in Parliament, or uniting with other

Table 6.5: Percentage of Votes Lost or Gained due to Bonus Seat and Cut-off Provisions of Proportional Representation for Individual Parties

		UNP	SLFP	LSSP	CP	FP/TULF	TC	Others
1970	5%	3.0	3.3	3.8	−23.9	5.0	6.7	−50.7
	12.5%	2.8	2.2	−2.7	−41.2	9.3	10.7	−32.3
	Bonus	−5.4	7.2	−7.9	−	22.9	−43.1	−
	Total	0.4	12.7	−6.8	−65.1	37.2	−25.7	−83.0
1977	5%	3.5	4.1	−6.8		4.4		−58.0
	12.5%	3.8	4.1	−36.8		7.7		−23.7
	Bonus	4.2	−7.7	−		−		−
	Total	11.5	0.5	−43.6		12.1		−81.7
1979	5%	1.5	1.5	−6.7		2.3	1.8	−12.3
	12.5%	10.2	6.8	−62.2		8.8	7.8	−44.4
	Bonus	4.1	−7.9	−		3.3	−17.7	−4.4
	Total	15.8	0.4	−68.9		14.4	−8.1	−61.1

parties to provide a viable alternative to the two major parties. This becomes very important for the leftist parties (the CP and LSSP) which have always been marked by ideological differences. In the 1970 elections they contested the elections as a single unit, in an electoral pact. In 1977, they contested each other and lost. It would be likely that the Communist Party and the Lanka Sama Samaja Party would never be a force in Sri Lankan politics unless they united with the Sri Lanka Freedom Party. The advantage of uniting can be seen in the following analysis. Up until this point, each of the parties has been treated separately except for the union of the CP and the LSSP in the 1977 and 1979 elections. If the three parties of the left had united under a single party label and polled the same number of votes as they did poll separately, the sum of their seats would have been greater than the sum of their seats if they had contested the elections separately. Table 6.6 reports the gain in seats in each election, if the parties had run as a united party.

Table 6.6: Seats Won by UNP and Left Parties if the Left Ran as a United Party

	1970		1977		1979	
	Seats won	Gain/loss	Seats won	Gain/loss	Seats won	Gain/loss
Left	84	+5	56	+2	140	+22
UNP	49	−5	95	−2	291	−22

A united front by the leftist parties would not have changed the election results in any of the three elections. However, it would have increased the left's seat totals by approximately 6 per cent in 1970, 4 per cent in 1977, and 16 per cent in 1979. Thus, the Sri Lankan system of proportional representation with its high cut-off point and bonus seat provision would create pressures for a two-party system in Sri Lanka. This would place a great deal of pressure on the parties of the left *to unite or risk the possibility of never again being competitive with the UNP.*

The final question to be addressed is the effect that proportional representation will have on the nature of legislator – constituent relationships in Sri Lanka. Under proportional representation, there will be no single-member electoral constituencies. Each legislator would represent a part of a constituency with several other legislators. Since the voters would be voting for party lists, they would have no say over who their individual legislators were. They would only be able to choose the party of their legislators. Political parties would have limited impetus to include candidates on their lists from the district where the seats were being contested.

This would be a radical departure from the old system of parliamentary representation. Under that system, representation is carried out on a very personal basis with legislators meeting with several hundred constituents per week.[12] The constituents come to the legislators seeking help with problems. Usually these problems are of a personal nature — jobs for themselves or their children, settling family disputes, etc. The constituents consider it the responsibility of the legislator to listen and try to help them with their complaint. The consequence of this system has been a very heavy work load on the legislators. Many of the legislators queried in an earlier study[13] expressed great frustration at their inability to do more productive work as a legislator.

The implications of this change are great. Once legislators are elected from multi-member districts under proportional representation, how will the voters respond? The constituents obviously saw a need being met by going to their legislator. In what way will their energies be channelled under proportional representation? Sri Lanka has instituted an Ombudsman, but this office cannot yet handle the volume of demands. If the constituents' demands go unanswered, will they resort to illegal activities, protest or insurrection? Obviously these questions cannot be answered here; however, the changes in the electoral system will have a massive impact on the system of representation in Sri Lanka. Unfortunately the nature of these changes is hard to predict. Several conclusions can be drawn from the preceding analysis:

1. The new system of proportional representation in Sri Lanka is much more equitable in the distribution of seats than was the old system of single-member electoral constituencies, but the new system is not as equitable as other systems of proportional representation utilising lower cut-off points and not using the bonus seat for the party which comes in first in each constituency.

2. The new system of proportional representation does not appear to increase the level of party fractionalisation in Sri Lanka in a significant way, thus contradicting Rae and Duverger's thesis. Nor would the other systems of proportional representation which were shown to be more equitable in the distribution of seats significantly increase fractionalisation. Increases in fractionalisation would be relatively minor.

3. The new system of proportional representation would have a significant impact on the party system in Sri Lanka. The high cut-off point and the bonus seat provisions under the Sri Lankan system would help the party that finishes first in each constituency. The second place finisher gains as much as the first place finisher due to the high cut-off point but loses most of these gains under the bonus seat provision. The real losers are the third and fourth place parties. Both provisions damage the distribution of seats to them. In most cases, in all three elections, the two Marxist parties were the third or fourth place party in each constituency. There is a very strong possibility that these two parties would be seriously hurt by the new electoral system. The system is heavily skewed towards two-party dominance.

4. The new system places serious constraints on those parties relying on electoral coalitions to win elections. This is because of the tendency of the system to create two-party dominance. The UNP has been the one party in Sri Lanka which has not had to rely on other parties to control Parliament in every election. The SLFP has never won an election unless it has made an electoral agreement with other parties of the left. Thus, the SLFP bloc would be seriously harmed by the new system unless it is able to unite under a single banner to contest future elections, a prospect which must be considered exceedingly unlikely.

5. The impact that the new system would have on representation

is unknown. However, serious questions were raised concerning the nature of the Sri Lankan electorate and the relationship that they have with their elected representatives. The new system will seriously disrupt that relationship. The question that remains to be answered is whether this disruption will have a detrimental effect on the political system. It would appear that the close legislator–constituent relationship acts as a safety valve for discontent arising from the high unemployment rate among young people and general level of poverty in rural areas.[14] If the relationship is removed and not replaced by some other institution that functions in the same manner and provides the security and personal touch that the present system of representation provides, the possibility of violence or protest exists.

In summary, proportional representation would provide Sri Lanka with a more equitable system of distributing seats in Parliament to the parties contesting future elections. However, its most important impact would be in its effect on the party system. The Sri Lankan system of proportional representation would create pressures leading to a two-party system in Sri Lanka. Third and fourth place parties in the various constituencies would be placed at a comparative disadvantage to the dominant parties in the political system. The high cut-off points and bonus seat provision of proportional representation in Sri Lanka would place a heavy burden on the leftist parties. If the leftist parties continue to contest the future elections separately, they may seriously damage their chances of ever regaining control of the government. There is nothing in the proportional representation system that inherently damages th SLFP's electoral chances; however, their electoral successes in the past have always come with the support of other parties. The Sri Lankan system of proportional representation demands that these parties contest elections as one party or risk defeat in the future.

Notes

1. M. Duverger, *Political Parties* (New York, 1963); and D. Rae, *The Political Consequences of Electoral Laws* (New Haven, 1967). For similar approaches, see J. Loosemore and V.J. Hanby, 'The Theoretical Limits of Maximum Distortion', *British Journal of Political Science*, i (1971), pp. 467–77; G. Grudgin and P.J. Taylor, 'The Decomposition of Electoral Bias in a Plurality Election', *British Journal of Political Science*, x (1980), pp. 515–27; H. Thiel, 'The Desired Poli-

tical Entrophy', *American Political Science Review*, lxix (1975), pp. 521–5; and G. Doron, 'The Hare Voting System is Inconsistent', *Political Studies*, xxvii (1979), pp. 283–6.

2. D. O'Connell, 'Proportional Representation and Intraparty Competition in Tasmania and the Republic of Ireland', *Journal of Commonwealth and Comparative Politics*, xxi (1983), pp. 45–58.

3. Ibid., p. 46.

4. Rae, *Political Consequences*, p. 40.

5. The actual distribution of seats varies from country to country depending on the formula used. The formula used in Sri Lanka will be discussed later in this paper.

6. Under the present system of single-member electoral constituencies, the number of seats in each administrative district is also determined by population and geography. However, the number of seats determined by geography is based on land area. Under the new system, each province receives an equal number of seats. In both systems, the overwhelming number of seats are distributed on the basis of population.

7. The system of proportional representation used in 1979 was the same as described earlier in this paper with one exception. This exception is that there were two bonus seats going to the party with the largest vote total in each constituency, instead of one bonus seat.

8. Loosemore and Hanby, 'Theoretical Limits', p. 168.

9. D-scores were computed for three European democracies using proportional representation. The results were: Netherlands (1974) D = .02; Sweden (1976) D = .01; Norway (1977) D = .09.

10. Rae, *Political Consequences*, p. 56.

11. In actuality it would be possible to receive a seat with less than 10 per cent if enough parties split the vote.

12. Robert Oberst, 'Constituent Control of Parliament: The Case of a Third World Democracy, Sri Lanka', PhD dissertation, Syracuse University.

13. Ibid.

14. Ibid.

PART TWO:
SRI LANKA IN CRISIS — MID 1983

7 SEEKING THE ROOTS OF THE TRAGEDY[1*]

Eric Meyer

The suddenness and violence of the dramatic days of July and August 1983 took by surprise those who were familiar only with the tourist stereotype of Sri Lanka, and the image of stability which had been fostered by a regime anxious for foreign investments. Hasty conclusions have been drawn attributing the catastrophic events both to the continued existence of long-standing religious hatred and to the rehashing of easy explanations regarding the oppression of minorities. Without denying that there is some truth in these interpretations I must emphasise that they provide a most inadequate explanation of the events which I observed over a period of two months and that they are, in the last analysis, even misleading.

The Warning Signs

After the presidential election in 1982, the political climate deteriorated in the island. Having been returned to power with an absolute majority President Jayewardene decided, amidst general astonishment, to hold a referendum, the aim of which was to prolong by six years the mandate of the MPs elected in 1977. This consultation of the popular will, the purpose of which was to consolidate governmental authority, represented yet another departure from democratic tradition by a political system whose authoritarian drift had been discernible since 1977, or even 1971. Far from reinforcing the government's stability, however, it revealed disaffection with the party in power, not only in the Tamil regions of the north and east, which were attracted by separatist claims, but also in the urban areas with a Sinhalese majority in the south-west of the island. The campaign, moreover, had been marred by trickery and violence, indicating a clear deterioration in political morality. At the beginning of 1983 a *malaise* set in, whose seriousness the President, locked away as he was in de Gaulle-like isolation, did not perhaps fully appreciate.

* translated from the French by Sheila Berridge

137

During June and the first weeks of July symptomatic incidents occurred. Above all, the cycle of provocation and repression in the Tamil regions broke out afresh. There were attacks on soldiers and policemen by Tamil terrorists and unchecked reprisals by the forces of law and order. Two incidents stand out from the rest: the deliberate attack on Tamil shops in the harbour town of Trinco-malee (an especially sensitive area) by groups of Sinhalese — backed, it seems, by Sinhalese merchants — during which some witnesses recognised members of the armed forces amongst the attackers; and the burning by Tamil terrorists, in a station close to Jaffna, of the train which provides the rail connection between Colombo and the north of the island. This was followed by the inter-ruption of all rail traffic between the Sinhalese and Tamil areas, an interruption desired by the authorities in order to prove to the inhabitants of Jaffna that separation would be an economic catastrophe.

The deteriorating situation was not, however, confined to the Tamil regions. Thus one saw a Sinhalese ringleader, a deserter from the leftist revolt of 1971 now working for the authorities, organising demonstrations against the supreme court judges who had found a policeman guilty of violating basic rights in his dealings with a leftist militant.

Faced with the rising tide of danger President Jayewardene decided to call a conference which would bring together his own party, the United National Party (UNP) and representatives of the following parties: the principal opposition party, the Sri Lanka Freedom Party (SLFP) of Mrs Bandaranaike; the Tamil plantation workers' union, the Ceylon Workers Congress (CWC); the Tamil separatist party, the Tamil United Liberation Front (TULF); the left-wing parties represented in Parliament, the pro-Soviet Com-munist Party (CP) and Mahajana Eksath Peramuna (MEP). Only the UNP and CWC attended the first meeting. The other organisa-tions took the view that the discussions should not be limited to the problem of Tamil terrorism, but should encompass the whole ques-tion of minority rights. This demand was finally accepted by the Pre-sident after pressure from the CWC and a meeting was arranged for the week in which the troubles broke out. At the same time, the TULF met to decide on the possibility of withdrawing its MPs from Parliament.

The Explosion

It was at this precise moment that the Tamil terrorists struck, mounting an ambush on the night of 23 July in which 13 soldiers, all Sinhalese, perished. On Sunday, 24 July, the bodies were brought to the central cemetery in Colombo for funeral rites, which the army wished to celebrate with ceremony and the government with discretion. That night a hysterical crowd gathered around the cemetery and overran the police. Later breakaway groups attacked Tamil shops in the area, only a few hundred metres from the presidential residence. Despite the violence no curfew was proclaimed. Late next morning the business districts of the capital caught fire one after another and the burning and looting then spread to the residential areas in the south of Colombo where large numbers of Tamils live. Many factories on the outskirts were attacked in their turn. During the following days, despite a curfew which the armed forces did not effectively enforce, the violence continued in Colombo and spread to all those provincial towns where Tamil businessmen lived, as well as to many plantation areas with an immigrant Tamil population.

During these days violence was aimed at property rather than persons. The operations that I witnessed were methodically organised. Their leaders often dressed in European clothes and had written instructions and lists of places to attack. Groups of five or six youths in sarongs armed with Molotov cocktails and clubs would empty houses and shops of a part of their contents and set fire to them, continuing on their way forthwith, often by car. The looters from the nearest shanty town would then arrive whilst the generous distribution of arrack would help to maintain the excitement.

Three days of the most singular silence was broken by a television address in which the despondent President seemed above all preoccupied with convincing the Sinhalese that he would make no concessions to the separatists. This did not help to restore calm. On the following day, 29 July, the rumour of an attack by Tamil terrorists spread like wildfire in the capital, creating an unprecedented panic, under cover of which hysterical groups of rioters attacked and savagely massacred hundreds of innocent people. That same evening the Prime Minister, and the following evening, the Minister of State, attempted to put an end to the violence by denouncing the action of provocateurs and developing a conspiracy theory. Many Sinhalese felt distressed and guilty as a result of these events. Many welcomed Tamil neighbours into their homes. The rumour that the violence had been organised for political reasons and was not the product of spontaneous racist reflexes had the effect of restoring a minimum of confidence and facilitating a return to order. The measures taken to ensure supplies to towns and to provide shelter for the refugees demonstrated the ability of the civil servants to master a critical situation better than the military could do.

During the next few weeks the violence became less frequent and a majority of the refugees left the camps, moving, for the most part, to areas where Tamils were in the majority. The crisis, however, developed an international dimension, for in order to satisfy Tamil public opinion in the south of the sub-continent, India imposed its good offices on the Sri Lankan government, intending to push it towards a compromise with the TULF. After spending some time trying to placate Sinhalese chauvinists — a ban on separatism was presented to Parliament — the government took a more moderate line. The official press stressed reconciliation, and the possibility of a coalition government which might include representatives of the SLFP was raised.

Several months later, at this writing, it is still difficult to analyse and measure the significance of the tragedy, especially as information only filters through with difficulty and we are dealing with many-faceted and complex events. There are two levels of inquiry: one is concerned with the play of political forces, and in this area lack of evidence ensures that probability, and even the sort of speculation which would not be out of place in a spy novel, take the place of certainty; the other is concerned with social forces and here it would seem an easier task to analyse the impact of separatist Tamil sentiment, Sinhalese chauvinism and the effects of the upheavals undergone since 1977.

The Official Theory and the JVP Plot: 1983 = 1958 + 1971

In the light of the information received by its agencies, the government laid the whole blame for the riots on three extreme left-wing parties whose activities it banned and whose leaders it attempted to arrest: the Janatha Vimukthi Peramuna (JVP) which was responsible for launching the leftist rebellion of 1971; the Nava Sama Samaja Party (NSSP), a small organisation which emerged from a split in the Trotskyist LSSP; and the pro-Soviet CP. This explanation convinced the government's own supporters, who had been bewildered by its long silence, but it immediately fell foul of the scepticism of the government's opponents and a certain number of independent observers. They stressed the improbability of co-operation between parties who had never before followed a common line; the paradox of an attack directed against the Tamils by the JVP and the NSSP, whose recent writings revealed the desire for a *rapprochement* with the terrorists and an attempt to analyse the minorities problem; and finally the unlikelihood of such an action, on so vast a scale, being prepared in secret without the intelligence services becoming aware of it, or of its being carried out without the armed forces immediately putting a stop to it.

Nevertheless, the official theory should not be rejected out of hand. It only becomes plausible, however, if one takes it to its logical extremes. Its implications are that the organiser of the 1971 revolt, the JVP, had a considerable reserve of power at its disposal, as well as superior strategic skills, and that it played a double game with the skill of a master. Failing in its 1971 bid to gain power from the outside, it infiltrated the armed services and certain sections of the UNP but at the same time operated a double *rapprochement* with the Tamil separatists, co-ordinating its actions with those of the terrorists (the contacts could have been made in the Middle East where some Tamils were trained) and forming ties with the politicians. (A recently banned Jaffna weekly used to open its columns to Tamil separatists and left-wing Sinhalese intellectuals.) The leader of the NSSP had frequent contacts with the Tamils in Jaffna and it is thought by some that he took refuge there to escape arrest.

This machiavellian strategy, consisting of allying with the Tamils on the one hand and attacking them on the other, is not totally implausible if one remembers that the victims of the attacks were the wealthy Tamils of Colombo and that they are the group most attached to the unity of the country. Their withdrawal to Jaffna created conditions which were most favourable to a partition. This would cause the UNP to lose face, create chaos in the army and make possible the seizure of power by leftist officers. Then again, careful observation of the Middle East and other trouble spots suggests that the exploitation of communal tension is the most effective means of destabilisation, and this has led some to accuse the eastern bloc of having had a hand in the plot.

The Other Hypothesis: Hawks versus Doves

The presence amongst the rioters of several hired men who had sold their services during the election, the evident passivity, to say the least, of the forces of law and order during the first days, the constant propaganda of the most chauvinistic elements of the UNP who were keen to 'teach the Tamils a lesson' and finally the precedent of 1981 — all of these factors encouraged many observers to lay the responsibility for the disorders on the governing party itself. But such an interpretation is scarcely credible if the *whole* of the ruling party is supposed to have been involved, as the leftist parties and the TULF have alleged. If, on the other hand, one admits the existence of a serious internal crisis in the ruling party, the mechanisms become more intelligible. The course of events in 1981 allows us to see this more clearly.

In that year, the President used his personal authority to set up district assemblies (District Development Councils or DDCs) which were to initiate a process of autonomous development in the regions to respond to one of the Tamil claims. During the elections for these councils, which were held in Jaffna at the beginning of the summer of 1981, the terrorists assassinated candidates and policemen in order to intimidate the moderates. Police reaction was extremely violent. They set fire to the market, to the public library and to the houses of several separatist leaders. Shortly afterwards some Sinhalese politicians, amongst them the Minister of Industries who had been in Jaffna with the Minister of Lands when these events took place, launched into violent diatribes in Parliament. Taking them at their word, gangs attacked Tamil shops and houses in Colombo and in the plantation district of Ratnapura, setting fire to 200 buildings and killing at least seven people. President Jayewardene, throwing all his prestige into the balance, was able to put a rapid end to the violence, expelling the most compromised members of the UNP and telling his Minister of Industries to keep out of the limelight for a while.

The following question must, therefore, be asked: why was the President unable to repeat in 1983 what he had achieved in 1981? The only possible answer is that, despite appearances, he had lost control of his party and his armed forces. It is certain that at the heart of the UNP there was a latent crisis between those favouring opposing strategies to deal with Tamil terrorism, the Prime Minister being, amongst the president's entourage, more favourable to negotiations, and the Minister for Industries taking a hard line. A second cause of dissension began to emerge, however, without its ever being discussed openly: the question of a successor to an ageing president who had just been re-elected without any real obstacle. The only non-politician capable of taking over, the businessman, Upali Wijewardene, had disappeared in an aeroplane accident at the beginning of the year, and the Prime Minister, R. Premadasa, who had acquired a large following in the rural areas by a programme of improvements in housing and the standard of living, whilst keeping his urban following, seemed well placed. However, his plebeian origins counted against him in the eyes of many people, who preferred the young bloods of the UNP, notably Gamini Dissanayake. He had benefited from the prestige of the hydro-electric and land development scheme of the Mahaweli Ganga of which he was in charge. Finally, the beginning of a *rapprochement* between the President and Mrs Bandaranaike's party, which Jayewardene saw as a means of freeing his hands to settle the Tamil problem without being outdone in the electoral bidding by the SLFP, also fuelled dissension within the UNP (and in the SLFP as well, where it caused a serious internal crisis).

Developments within the Armed Forces

In the face of a new situation, the character of the Sri Lankan police and armed forces has changed completely over the last twelve years. Whilst before 1971 they were simply a force for the maintenance of law and order, they later found themselves engaged in military operations, firstly in 1971 with the JVP revolt and then, after 1974, with the increase in Tamil terrorist activity. They thus found themselves acting as an army of occupation in Tamil areas, a role for which they were ill-prepared. Recruitment to these services, as to other public sector employment has also been transformed, giving a predominant place to patronage. (Under the 'chit system' one needs a recommendation from one's constituency MP in order to obtain a post.) The recruitment of Tamils has ceased because of this and also as a result of the constant threat to them posed by terrorists. Between 1977 and June 1983, out of 37 soldiers or policemen attacked, 17 were Tamils. The result is that the Sri Lankan armed forces have been gradually transformed into Sinhalese armed forces at the grass roots, although Tamils have maintained their increasingly uncomfortable positions in the higher echelons of command. Within these troubled, sometimes ill-disciplined forces often confined to their barracks in order to avoid incidents, unrest has grown and Jayewardene has more than once been compared to de Gaulle. It is easy to see that soldiers or junior officers, who reproach the President for wanting to give away Jaffna or Trincomalee and are intolerant of the tutelage excercised over them by a high command in which his relatives and followers hold high positions, could be tempted by a putsch in the style of the OAS. The security forces, which lack the professional standards of the Indian army, have also been penetrated by unhelpful outside influences. Witness the influence of anti-Tamil shopkeepers as seen at Trincomalee, but also the influence of politicians. It is not impossible that the JVP made use of this in order to infiltrate the armed forces, dreaming of making the army into a political resource of the left one day, as it is in many Third World countries.

If we view the two theories alongside one another, the armed forces appear as the only common denominator between the hardliners of the UNP and those of the JVP. Their role in the creation of the tragedy was certainly decisive. It is possible that President Jayewardene and Prime Minister Premadasa, confronted by an intensification of Tamil terrorism, growing indiscipline in the army and an increasingly hard line by the hawks in the UNP, decided to call a last chance conference to cement the *rapprochement* with the SLFP. This — if the TULF decided not to participate — would throw the ball into the separatist court. The announcement in the press on the eve of the tragedy of an imminent Cabinet reshuffle and an interview with the President, broadcast on the BBC, which ended with a solemn promise to protect lives and property, seem to provide evidence of a desire to outflank the hawks. The terrorist ambush came at just the right moment to spark off the crisis, and the Tamils who perpetrated it also had an interest in preventing a dialogue from taking place. At this stage the JVP could have tried to exploit the situation for its own ends,the paralysis of the police force making possible spectacular operations such as the burning of factories, which seem incomprehensible if one attributes them to hired men close to those in power. However, one could also point out that among the businesses that suffered damage, there figured prominently the Jaffna Tamil Maharajah Group with which the Prime Minister enjoyed close relations, and which may have been attacked by the Premier's rivals within the ruling party. It is also true that the followers of the Industries Minister were especially sensitive to gains made by Indians, Tamils and Muslims within the liberalised economy.

Tamil Separatism

The conjectures above should not make us lose sight of the essential fact: the terrorist activity of a section of the Tamil separatists which is at the root of the whole affair. There can be no question here of dealing with the Tamil problem in its entirety. My purpose here is, rather, to sketch an outline history of the relations between the Tamils and the central government and to gauge, as far as possible, the depth of separatist sentiment within the different groups which make up the Tamil minority.

It has been said that the history of relations between the Tamils and central government has been a succession of missed opportunities. Even before Independence, under the regime of self-government allowed by the British since 1931, communalist attitudes dominated political life, culminating in the Tamil claim for parity of parliamentary representation between the Sinhalese majority (about 70 per cent of the population) and the minorities. From 1948 until 1977, despite the fact that successive Sinhalese governments toyed with the idea of concessions, all promises came to nothing since the opposition party of the moment, either UNP or SLFP, constantly raised the communalist bidding, whilst the constant attitude of the Tamil leaders was to turn in on themselves.

When J.R. Jayewardene took power in 1977, it seemed that things would change. The government did not have to fear the criticism of an opposition whose numbers had been greatly reduced. Almost all of the plantation Tamils had voted for him as well as a large proportion of the east coast Tamils and the minorities of the north-west. In 1978 the new constitution recognised Tamil as a national language along with Sinhalese, although the latter remained the only official tongue. The government, however, waited until 1981 to set up the organisations (the District Development Councils or DDCs) to put the promises of decentralisation into force. These councils, which were elected, but controlled by a district minister appointed by the central government, were intended to replace in time the traditional system of administration and make possible a gentle evolution towards a certain amount of autonomy.

Tamil leaders assert that the Tamil language is still not employed in government and that the DDCs have done nothing in their two years of existence to free the district ministers from central tutelage. Another objection is that these bodies were established at district rather than at regional level, and therefore foster local particularism instead of contributing to the formation of an autonomous Tamil region which would take in the provinces of the north and east — something the government does not want at any price.

It is true that separatist sentiment is far from general in all the Tamil areas, or at least this was true before the events of summer 1983. Tamils who lived in areas with a Sinhalese majority were naturally the least receptive to separatism, knowing that they would be the first to be exposed to reprisals. Most of them, however, kept their links with their home areas which would allow them to return there if need be; they were, therefore, no strangers to separatist claims. Any member of the family might be a separatist supporter. The majority of them voted for the UNP whose economic policy promised a free rein to their spirit of enterprise. (A large proportion of these Tamils settled in Sinhalese areas are merchants, small-time industrialists, employees in the private sector and members of the liberal professions.) Recently, however, some have had no hesitation in saying that the SLFP might, after all, be a better defender of their interests.

The Tamils who migrated to Sri Lanka in the last century and settled mainly in the plantation areas constitute a separate group whose numbers relative to the population as a whole have continually declined since the 1950s; this is a result of a policy of repatriation to India pursued by successive Sri Lankan governments and acts of violence continually perpetrated against them, notably in 1977. Despite some attempts, however, they have never identified their interests with those of the indigenous Tamils. And given their geographical situation in the high country where they form a pocket of alien population, separatist claims have no meaning for them. Their leaders have always, therefore, sought an alliance with the party in power. The fact that they have again been the victims of violence can only increase the despair of the most humiliated and exploited community on the island, a community which includes hundreds of thousands of stateless persons whose only way out seems to be emigration to India.

The situation of the Tamils in the Eastern Province is also special. They do not represent an absolute majority there, the Muslim and

Sinhalese communities being strongly represented. They harbour a certain resentment towards the Sinhalese, large numbers of whom came to settle on the outskirts of the Tamil areas in the wake of the great irrigation schemes. The separatists have been able to exploit this hostility by promising to make Trincomalee (incidentally one of the best natural harbours in southern Asia and the object of foreign cupidity since the seventeenth century) the capital of the independent state they are seeking. However, the Tamils on the east coast do not feel any special affinity with those of Jaffna, from whom they are separated by history (the great families of the area were vassals of the Sinhalese kings), the caste system and the favours bestowed upon them by the present government (two of their number are ministers). Their area is the stumbling block in any plan for a negotiated settlement of the Tamil question and would become a battlefield if the country were partitioned. It was not a matter of mere chance that Trincomalee served as the theatre for the dress rehearsal in the tragedy of 1983.

It is in the Northern Province, more precisely in the Jaffna peninsula, which is like an island within an island, that separatist claims find the most sympathetic reception. The Vellala caste, which makes up about half of the population, but dominates all the social life of the area, has a very strong sense of its own unique nature. It considers itself the guardian of Tamil orthodoxy, free of the contacts which transformed Tamil society in southern India, whence it emigrated eight or ten centuries ago. The ideology of purity and hierarchy which is at the root of the caste system greatly influences the behaviour of this social group. They provide one of the most perfect examples of what M.N. Srinivas calls Sanskritisation (the adoption of Brahmin values by a caste situated below them in the caste system) and dominate a great mass of 25–30 per cent untouchables in its service. In a traditional Indian context the idea of the state is inseparable from the presence of a dominating caste, occupying a fixed territory. Jaffna did indeed remain a small independent kingdom until the Portuguese conquest at the beginning of the seventeenth century and maintained an autonomous existence until the dramatic improvement in communications during the nineteenth century.

The recent history of Jaffna is intimately connected with the phenomenon of emigration. The peninsula is overpopulated and its resources limited. Since the nineteenth century, many young Vellalas, having benefited from an excellent English education at the hands of American missionaries, have found employment in the colonial administration, the transport services and the liberal professions in the Sinhalese areas of the island and overseas, notably in Malaysia and East Africa. Also Tamil merchants, who had been active long before throughout the island, found that the take-off in domestic trade gave them the opportunity to develop their businesses. At the time of independence they were a privileged minority.

The politics of Sinhalisation pursued by governments since Bandaranaike (1956), and the similar measures taken after the independence of Malaysia, had the effect of drying up one of the principal sources of employment to the youth of Jaffna. All that remained open to them was entry into the liberal professions, skilled employment in the private sector, or emigration. During the 1970s, the Sri Lankan government established a quota system for access to universities, the effect of which was to restrict the chances of higher education for the young Tamils of Jaffna, notably in law, sciences and technology, in which up until then they had been more than proportionately represented. The resulting unemployment and frustration became, and remains, the principal stimulus to separatism. The young who remained in Jaffna were attracted by the separatist movement. Those, increasingly numerous, who found the means to emigrate towards the countries of the Persian Gulf, Europe and North America, naturally became the propagandists of separatism and its source of money — a 'classical' process. If the Tamils of Colombo do not find a home again in the south and leave the island, the ranks of Tamil moderates will be depleted and the influence of the advocates of partition will grow decisively.

Sinhalese Chauvinism

It is very significant that the Sinhalese Buddhist majority *also sees itself as a minority whose identity is threatened.* The community of 11 million is practically the only one in the Indian world (of nearly 900 million) which has remained faithful to Buddhism which originated in India. Moreover, the language spoken in this community belongs to the north Indian group of languages, from which it is separated by the Dravidian bloc. To this latter group belongs Tamil, spoken by more than 50 million inhabitants of India itself.

The evolution of the Sinhalese community since the beginning of the last century is characterised by the emergence of a national movement closely connected with the renaissance of Buddhism in the face of the political and cultural challenge posed by colonisation, as Gananath Obeyesekere shows in the essay which follows. After Mr Bandaranaike's election victory in 1956, Buddhist militance penetrated all Sinhalese institutions without exception and found in education and the media an influential vehicle. With the spread of primary and secondary schooling (Sri Lanka has one of the highest school attendance rates in all Asia) and the abandonment of English as the medium of instruction in the large private schools where the children of the middle classes are educated, physical separation and the identification of the pupils according to linguistic criteria resulted in a widening gap between the Sinhalese and the Tamils, without a serious effort ever being made to promote bilingualism.

Sinhalese chauvinism feeds on a distorted vision of ancient history, which emphasises the destructive effects of invasions coming from southern India and omits to mention that the Sinhalese have more than once called upon Tamil princes to govern them. Above all it ignores the fact that a great number of southern Indians have intermingled with the Sinhalese community in the course of history, as Obeyesekere again explains in detail. Sinhalese–Tamil integration ended with the arrival in Sri Lanka of the British, from whom the Sinhalese borrowed the idea of race.

However, this chauvinism contradicts the universalist principles of Buddhism and it has by no means gained the support of the whole population. Racial hatred between the two communities is not pervasive and many Sinhalese in 1983, as before, rescued threatened Tamils in both towns and villages. Many remained passive, but in this respect European commentators are in no position to lecture anyone. Nevertheless, many of the latter have wondered, with a certain amount of naïveté or hypocrisy, how such violence could break out in a Buddhist society. Formulated in these terms the question has no meaning. Societies claiming to be Christian demonstrate similar contradictions. However, the particular form taken by violence in this sort of culture is a matter worthy of investigation.

Sri Lanka has one of the highest murder and suicide rates in Asia. This violence, far from being racial in origin, is carried out within communities, even within families. It is generally unforeseen, sudden and of short duration. It has been interpreted in two ways: first, as a traditional phenomenon, peculiar to a society in which accumulated passions, long repressed by a system of values which favours non-violence, suddenly explode; secondly, as a recent phenomenon, linked to alcoholism, which became widespread during the colonial period but continued to be regarded as an asocial form of behaviour. (Even today villagers turn aside when they gulp down their glasses of arrack.) This view also connects the violence with the decline of Buddhist morality and the rituals which channel aggression and with changes in the education and recruitment of monks who often study at university, acquiring there a militance which is alien to tradition. One could also add that the cinema helps to glorify violence amongst the young. The success of Hong Kong films, which are beginning to offer serious competition to the sentimental big Indian productions, is a sign of this change, which affects both Tamils and Sinhalese.

The Other Side of Economic Liberalism

During the six years of the Jayewardene government, the country's economy has undergone a profound change. Reversing the protectionist policies of its predecessors, the government chose the Singapore path towards development. Despite an unfavourable world economic climate, a high rate of growth was achieved, but only at the price of very high foreign debts and inflation which most affected the petty bourgeoisie and the urban working class. In addition, the tertiary sector developed more quickly than the rest and the import of consumer goods created more needs than there were means to satisfy. The display of luxury goods such as audio-visual appliances in shop windows contrasted sharply with the austerity of ten years before and created insupportable frustration amongst a youthful population which was still largely under-employed.

Such a situation became explosive when chauvinist propaganda made it seem that businessmen from the minorities — Tamils, Muslims, Bombay Indians — had benefited more than their Sinhalese counterparts from the liberalisation of the economy. The phenomenon took on a flavour akin to anti-semitism, as had happened once before, in the 1930s, with the Tamil Chettiar financiers. Now, for about 15 years the influence on public life of the Sinhalese *mudalalis* (shopkeepers, carriers, small businessmen) had increased steadily. They had assumed a predominant role in the majority of local institutions and had become the agents and political backers of political parties in provincial towns and villages. The connections of a number of these *mudalalis* with members of the underworld who were engaged in illicit distilling or the traffic of Indian hemp were an open secret, as was the corruption that they fostered in the lower echelons of the police and armed forces, as the events at Trincomalee were to demonstrate. The rise of this new middle class which was unconnected with the anglicised bourgeoisie in Colombo, which had enjoyed until then a monopoly on political activity, upset the rules of the game. Indifferent to the subtle principles of parliamentary democracy, seeking to impose their new authority by any means possible, these parvenus constituted a class which was particularly receptive to chauvinist propaganda, which, recognising it to be in their own interest, they propagated and amplified.

In fact the liberalisation of the economy had brought on the one hand an increase in the volume of trade, but on the other hand a narrowing of profit margins. In many sectors the proliferation of small businesses led to bitter competition, the most obvious example being the multiplication of rival bus companies after the abolition of the state monopoly. With the reduction in the flow of foreign capital upon which this, in many respects artificial, expansion directly depended, many financially insecure businesses were threatened by bankruptcy. In such a financial situation it became tempting to eliminate dangerous, often more efficient, rivals. In addition, a call to loot one's competitor, whom one could characterise as an exploiter or race enemy was a cheap way of making a reputation amongst the lower classes, and there was always the possibility of making an easy financial killing by buying in at low prices the booty which had become burdensome to the looters. The activities of the *mudalalis* do not in themselves explain the organised manner in which the riots began, but they were in large measure responsible for their extension.

The Conditions for Survival

As a result of the violence of mid-1983, the prestige of the President has suffered and his room for manoeuvre has been reduced in the face of a coalition of extremists, his undisciplined army and party, and pressure from India. After the violence of 1981, he threatened the UNP with resignation if he ceased to be able to feel proud of the party that he led, and this temptation has probably occurred to him in the last few months. He still holds, however, several trump cards: an efficient administration; an economic potential little affected by the riots (the destruction was by all accounts limited, but its direct impact will be felt sooner or later and is likely to affect the island's financial position very seriously); and the confidence of the population. He is obviously trying to restart the political process which the riots interrupted by drawing closer to the opposition SLFP in order to obtain a consensus of Sinhalese parties which will enable negotiations with the separatists to take place. But does he still have sufficient power at his disposal to impose a solution on the army and his own party? On their side, do the moderate elements among the Tamils still have sufficient influence on their activist youth to persuade them to accept concessions? Nothing is less certain.

Whether or not President Jayewardene finishes his term of office, it is possible that the succession question will be posed in terms of the capacity for survival of a stale but still effective civil regime, which faces an inconsistent but adventurous military — in other words the classical right versus the temptations of fascism. The Jayewardene government which itself delivered the first blows against the liberal order, is now perhaps the last rampart of one of the last Third World democracies. But the crisis has revealed more dramatically than before the growing inability of the Colombo-based political class to channel and control the new political forces in both the north and the south of the country.

Note

1. An earlier version of this paper appeared, in French, in *Le Monde Diplomatique* (November 1983), pp. 16–17. The author is grateful to numerous Sri Lankan colleagues, particularly Dr Sarath Amunugama.

8 THE ORIGINS AND INSTITUTIONALISATION OF POLITICAL VIOLENCE

Gananath Obeyesekere

In Colombo on 26 July Air Lanka, the country's only airline, put out its usual television advertisement, 'Visit Sri Lanka: A Taste of Paradise'. This commercial, with pictures of brand new hotels with expanses of beach and ocean and tables overflowing with lobsters and tropical fruits, routinely appears, but on this occasion the advertisement was not in the best taste. The paradise isle was in flames, the houses and business establishments of the minority Tamil community were being systematically burnt and looted by well-organised mobs belonging largely to the lumpen proletariats of the cities and small towns of Sri Lanka. The brutality was unbelievable: homes and shops were set alight, cars were doused with petrol and lit, sometimes with the occupants inside; some people were hacked to death, others burnt alive. Thirty-five political prisoners were killed by irate regulars in the country's maximum security prison. The next day, 17 more were slaughtered in the same manner. There was a total breakdown of law and order in the nation that had been touted by foreign governments as the model of stability, the apogee of free enterprise. A few days and the illusion was shattered: the house of cards had crumbled.

The antagonism between Tamils and Sinhalese is rooted in the country's history but has been exacerbated into inter-ethnic violence only since 1956. Sporadic riots, characterised by extreme brutality, occurred periodically thereafter, but what was striking about the events of 1983 was their scale, which was beyond anything that had ever occurred before, and the fact that the marauders were not uncontrolled mobs on the rampage (this occurred later) but, at least on the first day (25 July), well-organised groups who had electoral lists of Tamil houses and enterprises and systematically went about destroying them. The purpose of this paper is to examine the historical and cultural origins of this violence and its institutionalisation since 1977, and particularly during 1983. Before 1983, violence had been practised by both sides, but its systematic organisation was characteristic only of the Tamil extremists (terrorists) of the north, and they for the most part targeted their attacks on police and military personnel and occasionally on Tamil politicians who supported the government of President J.R. Jayewardene. When violent acts were committed, the brutality on both sides was extreme. Tamil terrorists who killed service personnel were not content with killing *per se*, but they also disfigured the bodies and desecrated the corpses. This time, however, the Sinhalese outdid all others in the scale and brutality of their violence. Their attacks, like those of the Tamil terrorists, had a planned, systematic character. The political organisation of violence goes beyond the problem of Tamil – Sinhalese ethnic conflicts and has larger political implications for the future of democracy in the island.

What, then, is the background to this violence, unprecedented in the recent history of a country designated by the people themselves as *dhamma dipa*, 'the land of the Buddha's *dharma*', a doctrine of non-violence and compassion? I am a Sinhalese and a Buddhist and this is the troubling question that I ask myself. Even to attempt an answer one must focus on the historical and cultural background to the conflict and, most crucially, on the recent erosion of the law and the institutions of justice and with it the political institutionalisation of violence in Sri Lanka.

The Historical and Cultural Background to the Communal Conflict

Underlying the linguistic and religious differences which have been explained in the introduction to this book are strong cultural and racial similarities. Physically the Sinhalese and Tamils cannot be differentiated. Though the initial Sinhalese migrants were probably Indo – European language speakers who arrived over 2,500 years ago, practically all later arrivals were South Indians (mostly Tamil speakers) who were assimilated into the Sinhalese – Buddhist community. The South Indian influence is omnipresent among Buddhists. On a level of popular religiosity Buddhists propitiate Hindu gods like Vishnu, and Skanda, the son of Shiva. However, the Buddhists view these gods as totally subservient to the Buddha while the Tamils view the Buddha as an avatar of Vishnu. Kinship and marriage patterns among the Sinhalese are also part of a larger Dravidian pattern. It is these cultural and subdoctrinal similarities that permitted the assimilation of South Indians over centuries into the Sinhalese Buddhist social structure.

The core of the Sinhalese identity was Buddhist: the destiny of the ethnic group and that of the religion were inseparable. Myths and historical events confirmed the twin facets of this identity. Historically, almost all the invasions of Sri Lanka came from South Indian kingdoms. Thus opposing the Sinhalese – Buddhist identity was the Tamil – Hindu identity. In times of stress, these identities were reaffirmed to mobilise popular support.

When the Portuguese arrived in Sri Lanka in 1505 there were several contending kingdoms in the country among which was a Tamil Hindu kingdom in Jaffna, the northern peninsula of the island. No king was content to see himself as ruler of a *part* of the island since the island was always considered a single entity. The call for a separate state of Tamil-speaking peoples is thus a contemporary historical phenomenon. In so far as it is the current reality, we must enquire how it came about.

The Tamil kingdom of Jaffna had ceased to be an independent unit in the sixteenth century when it was captured by the Portuguese and then by the Dutch. The Sinhalese Buddhist kingdom in the interior of the island remained independent till 1815 when it was taken by the British. The Tamils of the east coast and parts of the North Central Province traditionally owed suzerainty to the Sinhalese kings of Kandy and trade routes connected the east coast with the kingdom of Kandy. Sinhalese – Tamil intermarriage, exceptional in the north, was accepted and practised on the east coast until recent times. When the British took over Sri Lanka, they introduced yet another complexity. They brought in large numbers of South Indian tribal and often low status groups as coolie labour on the tea plantations of the central highlands. Thus there were three Tamil – Hindu zones well established by the end of the nineteenth century: in the north, in the east and in the central highlands. Though outsiders (as well as some Sinhalese) see the Tamil problem as one, the internal reality is very different. The northern Tamils were much more orthodox Hindus than Tamils elsewhere and were strongly patrilineal. The east coast Tamils came from Kerala and were divided into matrilineal clans, while the Tamils of the central provinces were recently introduced groups from South India, alienated from both the other groups. They were thrust into the midst of a surrounding Sinhalese population from whom they were also alienated.

During the early twentieth century when constitutional agitation against British rule gathered momentum, Sinhalese and Tamils at first presented a united position. In 1919 the Ceylon National Congress was founded by both Tamils and Sinhalese. But political parties soon began to polarise along communal lines. The Sinhalese increasingly felt threatened by Tamil control of business and the professions while the Tamils became increasingly self-conscious of their minority identity. The political democratisation of the state exacerbated these tendencies. Universal adult suffrage was introduced in the 1931 elections and this brought communal issues into public voting patterns. When Independence was declared in 1948, there were several Tamil political parties with an exclusively ethnic base, while the ruling United National Party (UNP), the main Sinhalese party, though formally non-ethnic, was in reality committed to Sinhalese nationalism.

A further escalation of Sinhalese – Tamil tension occurred after 1956 which saw the massive electoral success of Mr Bandaranaike's Sri Lanka Freedom Party (SLFP) over the UNP. Much of Mr Bandaranaike's success depended on the slogan 'Sinhala Only': there was to be one language for the nation — the language of the majority — Sinhala. This led to Tamil demands for equality of status for both languages and for greater autonomy for Tamil areas which generated Sinhalese anxieties about a Tamil separatist movement with South Indian support which might threaten the very integrity of the state. In the 1970s, economic hardship, unemployment and the rise of discontented youth groups created new problems. The abortive insurrection of 1971, based on Sinhalese youth, was one example. In the Tamil north, similar bands of young militants demanded a separate Tamil state. As a result of their pressure, the Tamil Federal Party changed its name and manifesto, becoming the Tamil United Liberation Front (TULF), committed to an independent Tamil state. This fanned Sinhalese fears which increased further when Tamil youths in the late 1970s, funded by expatriates, adopted terrorism to achieve their goal. Terrorism in turn forced the government to send an ill-disciplined and poorly trained army into the Tamil areas of the north, further exacerbating the pattern of violence and reprisals.

The Religious Dimensions of the Ethnic Conflict

It is against the backdrop of this complicated situation that one must understand the importance of the religious revivals of the late nineteenth century and their impact on Tamil and Sinhalese identities. Briefly stated, the trauma of imperial conquest and the disestablishment of the two major religions produced in the north a Tamil – Hindu revival movement headed by Armugam Navalar and in the south a Sinhalese – Buddhist revival headed by Anagarika Dharmapala. Both reformers were educated in Protestant Mission schools and brought a kind of 'this-worldly ascetism' (very like the Protestant ethic) into Hinduism and Buddhism. Both rationalised their respective religions, scorned folk beliefs and rituals, affirmed their respective great traditions. Navalar gave contemporary Hinduism a philosophical base in Saiva Siddantha while Dharmapala affirmed the ascetic and abstract values of doctrinal Buddhism largely influenced by Western commentators on Buddhism. Both provided a philosophy and an ethic for classes that had practically no historical parallel in the past — a bourgeoisie and a proletariat that emerged in the colonial and post-colonial periods. Dharmapala not only affirmed the traditional Sinhalese – Buddhist identity but opposed it to other identities — Muslim, Hindu, Christian.

The victory of Mr Bandaranaike in 1956 was spearheaded by those who were directly or indirectly influenced by Dharmapala. Thus the post-1956 era saw the introduction of a new fundamentalist and militant Buddhism advocating the takeover of denominational schools to reduce the power of the Christian missions; the compulsory teaching of religion in schools; the propagation of the intellectualist view of Buddhism as being not a religion but a philosophy consonant with the spirit of science; and above all the use of Buddhism for political purposes. As a result, in our time, Buddhism had effectively become the political and civil religion of the state, the implications of which are further explained in R.L. Stirrat's paper in this volume.

In popular as well as doctrinal Buddhism, the Buddha was not a conventional deity that could either grant favours or affect the movement of history. He had achieved *nirvana*, the state of final bliss and consequently had no intercessionary role in the affairs of the world. The internalisation of this figure in the socialisation of children was radically different from that which occurs in monotheistic religions or in Hinduism where the deity is an active figure issuing punishments and rewards for the transgression of religious morals. People worshipped the Buddha as the embodiment of Buddhist values, but demanded nothing from him and expected nothing.

Abstract Buddhist values such as *karuna* (universal kindness), *metta* (compassion), *mudita* (tenderness), etc., and the complex Buddhist philosophy (such as the theory of dependent origination) were never inculcated as abstractions. Abstract Buddhist ideas were concretised through the Buddha legend and the *Jataka* tales in which the Buddha's exemplary life, his self-sacrifice, his compassion for others, etc., were described. The values embodied in these tales were disseminated in various ways: through sermons, religious gatherings at temples and through popular books. Villages also staged many ritual dramas where these themes were enacted or sung. The opposed values of greed and hatred were embodied in demonic figures of evil which also formed a part of folk beliefs and rituals.

Thus what I have called Buddhist identity — the idea that Sinhalese equals Buddhist and that the nation is a Buddhist one — was tempered by a Buddhist conscience which concretised the abstract values of the doctrinal tradition and gave a Buddhist humanism to traditional culture. With the reforms of the nineteenth century, Buddhist folk traditions were rejected by the Sinhalese bourgeoisie. The *Jataka* tales were underplayed or rationalised. The emphasis shifted to the abstractions of the textual traditions highlighted by Western scholars. Buddhism was a compulsory school subject and parents left the onus of teaching Buddhist values to the school curriculum. The socialisation of the conscience, to be effective, must start in infancy and early childhood. Today, this is rarely done. As for the ritual dramas they are non-existent in urban society and are dying out even in the villages. An absence or gap thus exists in the Buddhist conscience. People attempt to fill this gap in a variety of ways, through the inculcation of bourgeois moral values imparted through a secular idiom or through meditation. But what happens with a lumpen proletariat in a city like that of Colombo, where half of the people live in crowded slums and only a quarter of its children go to school? The gap must surely be wide. To continue the metaphor, the empty space in the Buddhist conscience is then filled with the predominant identity, Sinhalese equals Buddhist, reinforced by the hatreds and frustrations that slum dwelling breeds everywhere.

The Institutionalisation of Political Violence

One of the fascinating problems of population growth in Sri Lanka is the relative absence of huge cities on the scale of other Asian nations (excluding Burma). People seemed to prefer to migrate into villages, and up to the 1940s this was the dominant pattern. Through time, however, this had the unfortunate effect of destroying the homogeneous kin-based nature of village society, and producing a variety of social groups in village life competing for scarce resources. The spillover from increasingly large and heterogeneous villages moved into the little market towns scattered all over Sri Lanka, and of course into Colombo, the nation's one large city. The trade in these market towns is controlled by Sinhalese, Tamil and Muslim merchants. Racial violence was often sparked by business competition. Merchants employ the dispossessed proletarians of these towns to eliminate business rivals, especially during periods of post-election political violence.

In addition to these anomic market towns, colonisation schemes where surplus villagers were siphoned off to new irrigation projects generally in the north central and southern dry zones became increasingly important after Independence. The recruitment to the colonisation schemes took place from crowded village areas. Settlers were often chosen by local MPs, from among party supporters. As a result settlements but not communities were created. Often, in more recent projects, total outsiders have come in and taken over the political control of colonies. In addition, outsiders from Colombo and its suburbs have begun to infiltrate old villages as small-time merchants and entrepreneurs. Practically all civil disturbances — post-election riots (endemic after the 1960s) and race riots — have occurred primarily in these lumpen colonisation schemes, in the anomic market towns and in Colombo. These civil disturbances have never been a village problem — though it will soon become one as the villages change their character.

One of the features of the politics of Sri Lanka since the 1960s is the use made by politicians of all parties of these dissatisfied urban people. Nowadays it is routine to use them to intimidate opponents or voters. Since the 1960s it has been commonplace for ordinary citizens to use phrases like 'so-and-so's (politician's) thugs'. Furthermore, increasingly disturbing trends have occurred in the use of these elements for political 'thuggery' (as it is called in Sri Lanka). These trends are not my inventions — they have been widely reported in the local press. Here are three examples.

First, thugs who are at the service of politicians in power are linked on the local level to merchants, some of them genuine businessmen but others involved in a variety of illegal activities, the most common of which are *kassippu* (moonshine) distillation, *ganja* (cannabis) cultivation and distribution, and the felling of timber from forest reserves. In recent visits to villages in Sri Lanka I have come across MPs serving remote areas actively involved in these activities, especially the latter two.

Second, police who oppose these activities or prosecute these people can be, and often are, transferred out of the area or cowed into acquiescence in illegal activity. Several newspaper editorials over the last few years have underscored this trend. The result has been the demoralisation and corruption of the police force. Village people whom I interviewed in many parts of the nation often mentioned that the police are in the hands of the local MP or local undesirable. The view is widespread that some of the institutions of justice have become an alienating force turned against the people themselves.

The third and most disturbing trend in the institutionalisation of violence occurred after the massive election victory of the ruling UNP in 1977, in its relations with the trade union known as the Jatika Sevaka Sangamaya (National Workers Organisation), hereafter referred to as the JSS. Prior to the 1977 election, the JSS was a minuscule working-class trade union (most unions being controlled by the Marxist parties of Sri Lanka). Today the JSS is the single largest union in the country and has an effective say in the working of government offices and corporations. Its president is Cyril Matthew, the Minister of Industries, whose name has been explicitly mentioned by several foreign correspondents as an inveterate enemy of the Tamil minority.

How did the JSS come into prominence? The answer is simple but one that has frightening implications. Traditionally the leftist unions provided a Trotskyite or Marxist ideology for the working classes. Whatever one may think of these ideologies, they had the effect of filling the empty space in the conscience of people with a specifically working-class ideology. After the massive election victory of the UNP, several political leaders emerged who had access to, and control over, the slums and anomic areas of the city. Prominent among them were R. Premadasa, the Prime Minister and Minister for Housing, whose power base was Central Colombo, one of the most crowded areas in the city; and M.H. Mohammed, Minister of Transport, who was MP for Borella (which also contains one of the largest slums in the city). With the expansion of the economy, produced by the free enterprise policy of the government, jobs in the working-class sector were increasingly given to members of this lumpen proletariat who swelled the ranks of the JSS. Soon members of other unions were intimidated into joining it. The JSS was without a working-class ideology; its leadership owed personal allegiances to party bosses. It is in a sense an exaggerated version of what I noted in the smaller market towns where culturally dispossessed people serve as small bands of thugs for local merchants and politicians. However, before 1977 these bands of thugs served their masters but had no institutionalised authority. The JSS changed this. They were now organised and they effectively controlled government offices and corporations and wielded enough power to transfer and intimidate even high officials. It also adopted and promoted the Sinhalese – Buddhist political ideology. The precarious identity of marginal people was thus given a new reality and meaning: a political and nationalist ideology. The nature of this ideology was spelled out by their president, Cyril Matthew, in a speech in Parliament on 4 August, soon after the recent riots.

Matthew's thesis was that Sri Lanka should follow the Malaysian example as set out by Mahathir Bin Mohammed in his book, *The Malay Dilemma.* In this book Mahathir states, says Matthew, that while the Malays are for a free enterprise system, they should not allow other racial groups to compete with Malays. Protection must be initially afforded the Malay community and Islam (their religion) should be upheld and propagated. Malays have no place else to go, whereas the Chinese can go to China and the Indians to India. The Malays are the original or indigenous people of Malaya and the only people who can claim Malaya as their one and only country. In accordance with the practice all over the world (*sic*), this confers on the Malays certain inalienable rights over the forms and obligations of citizenship which can be imposed on citizens of non-indigenous origin.

This thesis can be applied, says Matthew, even better to the Sri Lanka situation. Malaysia has 53 per cent Malays and 35 per cent Chinese, Sri Lanka has 74 per cent Sinhalese and 17 per cent Tamils. In spite of this disproportion, Tamils dominate every aspect of professional and economic life. You do not have to go to Madras, he says. Come to Colombo and you will see the Pettah (market district) dominated by South Indians. (This is no longer so, since the Pettah was burnt down in the summer violence.) The Sinhalese also have nowhere to go, but Tamils can go to India. The Sinhalese have been extraordinarily patient. In Malaysia, there was a political rally by

Chinese in May 1969 when they jeered at Malay policemen. The Malay government squashed it, 'killing all the Chinese who were there'. We, however, says Matthew, have been patient for ten years and now 'what had happened there has occurred in Sri Lanka also'. Earlier in his speech Matthew quoted from another speech he made in Parliament: 'By non-violent methods or violent ones the Sinhala people are ready' to prevent the division of the country.[1]

Such an ideology has a great deal of appeal to the Sinhalese, but it is also fostered by the Tamil elites who self-consciously identify with the Tamils of South India. The Sinhalese identity nowadays is predicated on the view that since they speak an Indo-European language, they are of North Indian origin whereas the Dravidian-speaking Tamils are from the South. The historical reality, however, is totally different. Except perhaps for the oldest stratum of settlers prior to 500 BC, almost all subsequent settlers in Sri Lanka came from South India, mostly from Tamil Nadu, Orissa, and Kerala and quickly became Sinhalised. In fact, some of the most vociferously anti-Tamil castes among the Sinhalese were post-fifteenth century migrants from South India. By contrast, the Tamils of Jaffna and the East Coast have been in Sri Lanka from at least the tenth to the fourteenth centuries AD, if not earlier. They also came from diverse parts of South India though the Jaffna (Northern) Tamils now claim that they came from Tamil Nadu. The only group of recent Tamil immigrants are the estate populations of the hill country brought over by the British in the middle and late nineteenth century. Both sides share antagonistic myths that are opposed to historical reality, and, like human beings everywhere, they act in terms of the former — with tragic consequences.

Matthew's ideology is doubtlessly shared by a vast number of Sinhalese, but the JSS has given it an unprecedented militancy. Moreover, the union has spread its tentacles into other areas of the country. Thus today, MPs have created through the JSS and through other local groups in small market towns a complex, powerful network of organisations that can be put to political use. At the same time there has occurred a remarkable change in the composition of political power brokers in the country, even in village areas. Traditionally the vote, and especially the village vote, was delivered or controlled by an educated village elite, coming generally from 'respectable' families. This was true of all parties but especially the UNP, the country's most important conservative party. Today this has changed or is fast changing; political power on the village level is in the hands of those who can control the unemployed and the discontented, primarily the youth.

It is in this context that one must examine specific examples of political violence in recent times. A large number of these events have been documented by the Civil Rights Movement (CRM) of Sri Lanka whose chairman until his recent death was a highly regarded Anglican bishop, the Rt. Rev. Lakshman Wickramasingha. Here are a few cases from the CRM files and my own notes.

(1) A series of violent acts occurred in Jaffna in late May and early June 1981, of which the most serious was the burning of the Public Library by thugs from outside while the security forces did nothing to stop the arson. This was a profoundly symbolic act: the library contained priceless manuscripts pertaining to the identity of the Tamils of Jaffna. On the Buddhist side it was an unparalleled act of barbarism, since rarely in Sri Lanka's recorded history (and perhaps even in the larger history of Buddhism) was there an example of book burning of this magnitude. The people of Jaffna identified the outsiders as the thugs of a prominent cabinet minister. The rumour in the Sinhalese areas was the same. Yet no action was taken by the President.

(2) A second event pertained to a gathering of artists and writers protesting against being refused work at the government-owned Broadcasting Corporation. A gang of thugs brandishing clubs and knives broke up this meeting, tore up the microphones, and chased away the participants. They shouted, 'What kind of artists are you! We are Premadasa's boys.' It is of course unlikely that Prime Minister Premadasa had any hand in this matter, but the thugs chose to make the claim. Even more disconcerting was a disruption of a meeting of a Sinhalese–Buddhist middle-class organisation where Ediriweera Sarachchandra, Sri Lanka's best-known dramatist, was beaten up. Sarachchandra had written a satirical book called *Dharmishta Samajaya* (A Just Society) where he highlighted the decay of cultural values brought about by the social and economic policies of the government. The thugs came in buses belonging to the state-owned bus corporation, and the Communist newspaper even carried the licence numbers of the buses. Sarachchandra himself made a complaint to the police. As in previous cases, no police action was taken.

(3) On 15 June 1978,[2] 9.30 a.m., about 400 thugs, members of the JSS, threatened six section heads at the Thulhiriya Textile Mills and

drove them off the premises. The six were forced to resign. The management was warned by the thugs not to allow the six people back. It appeared that only JSS members and those who accepted their terms were allowed to stay in the Mills.

(4) On 4 July 1980, teachers at Maharagama Teachers Training College were picketing peacefully when Government Transport Board bus No. 23 Sri 2549 came through the college gates, carrying 27 people including a leader of the JSS. Thugs got out and began to assault the teacher trainees with rubber belts, stones, bicycle chains, etc. Women were thrown to the ground and waste oil was poured over their clothes and into their eyes and ears. The toughs tried to run over one girl with the bus. Police arrived after the incident and took a statement. Two hours later people were taken to Colombo South Hospital. Four female teachers were seriously injured.

(5) On 3 January 1980, the Personnel Manager of the Peoples' Bank was abused and assaulted in his office by JSS officers, in the presence of several members of staff. The police were informed and the four assailants were arrested. However, they were shortly released on minimal bail of Rs. 250 each. The next day, a JSS official threatened certain staff members near the head office entrance over this matter. The management suspended four people from their jobs as a result of this incident. Then on 1 September, a mob roamed the building, abusing and threatening officers. Eventually, the police were sent for and the Staff Department was put under police guard. The mob then looted the canteen. On 1 November 1980 the interdicted JSS members were reinstated as a result of pressure exerted on the Personnel Manager to withdraw his complaint. He was later transferred.

The pattern in these activities is clear: the gangs were organised, they came in government vehicles, they were sometimes accompanied by MPs and for the most part they belonged to the JSS, the trade union arm of the party in power. This almost certainly accounts for police inaction. These activities received little public comment in the press largely owing to the fact that the newspapers were either directly owned by the government or by supporters of the government. The exception was *Aththa*, the Sinhalese newspaper of the Communist Party, but its circulation was limited and its offices closed and sealed by the government for various periods of time.

The greatest shock to public opinion, however, occurred as a result of two recent events whereby Supreme Court decisions seemed to have been openly flouted by the government. In a public meeting held in 1982 by an interreligious organisation, a police officer seized leaflets that were being distributed. A Buddhist clergyman filed suit against the police officer. The court held that the police officer had violated the fundamental rights of the petitioner and decreed that damages and costs be directly paid by him. The Cabinet, however, promoted this police officer and ordered that the costs and damages be paid out of public funds. The government stated that 'public officers should do their jobs without fear of consequences from adverse court decisions'.

The second event followed a similar pattern but received full publicity in all newspapers and outraged the middle class, which had been generally favourable to a government that supported their class interests. In this case a senior left politician, Mrs Vivienne Gunawardene, complained of assault and unlawful arrest by the police during a march to the American embassy in Colombo in protest against the nuclearisation of the military base at Diego Garcia. The Supreme Court presided over by three judges held that her arrest was unlawful and unconstitutional and ordered that the state pay her compensation. On the very day the judgement was issued, the Cabinet presided over by the President promoted one police officer involved in the case. A few days later practically all newspapers headlined the sensational news that thugs in government-owned buses paraded outside the homes of the three judges and shouted obscenities at them. The police were conveniently not available when the judges tried to contact them.

I was then in Sri Lanka and it was commonplace for people gathered at bus stops and in other public places to speculate whether it was X Minister's thugs or Y Minister's thugs that did it. Prime Minister Premadasa, however, made a strong statement saying that the government took a very serious view of the matter and that 'appropriate action will be taken in consultation with the Attorney-General'. Thus far nothing has emerged from police inquiries. It should be remembered, however, that this open scoffing at the judgement of the Supreme Court on these two occasions is part of a long conflict between the government and judiciary which commenced under the previous government of Mrs Bandaranaike, particularly during the period 1970–7. The present government with its political slogan of a 'Just Society' promised to rectify these abuses, but in the last few years the rift between the executive and the judiciary seems again to have widened.

Virtually every Tamil I met in mid-1983 was of the opinion that the violence against them was organised by the government, and especially by the JSS and the influential politicians who controlled this union. Given the pattern of political intimidation, this view has considerable plausibility, as the following example suggests.

One of the most shameful aspects of the troubles of 1983 was the refusal of the minor staff of several hospitals to tend or care for wounded Tamils. I know of an upper-class Tamil woman who broke her leg jumping from a balcony as her house was burning. She was removed to a hospital, but was refused admission because the minor staff (orderlies and labourers) threatened to strike if she was taken in. I know of another instance where a Tamil was actually stabbed to death in a hospital bed, allegedly by a minor employee. In these and many other instances, the JSS may be culpable since the hospital system is almost totally controlled by it. Indeed, five months earlier the Government Medical Officers Association complained of indiscipline in the hospital system and appealed to the government to protect the medical profession from union thugs. In an editorial of 4 January 1983, the government-owned newspaper, *The Daily News*, commented on the situation thus:

> The issue brings into focus again the part of trade unions in the medical profession, no matter at what level . . . Union leaders, no matter where, must not be encouraged to get away through some show of force . . .
>
> Sadly, the Government Medical Officers Association is not the only organisation that has protested against the extension of political patronage to hoodlums. Sadly, there is nothing new in this malady . . . it is to be seen in other state-controlled organisations where again the management apparently lacks the strength to enforce discipline on favoured sections or individuals on their staff.
>
> One thing is clear enough. No state, no government, no party that condemns Naxalite (leftist insurgents that operate in Bengal) methods can condone equally outrageous behaviour in any institution under its control.
>
> It is futile to denounce thuggery on the one hand and resort to it or let it go unpunished on the other . . .

Political Rhetoric and the Violence

The racial riots started on the night of 24 July. Many of us who were witnesses felt that the government would impose an immediate curfew. I know of several senior government officials and politicians who said that they telephoned the President on the seriousness of the situation, which he must surely have realised anyway, since mobs demonstrated near his private residence. Yet no curfew was imposed until 5.00 p.m. the next day, and by that time most of the damage to property and looting had already taken place. One thing must be clearly stated: President Jayewardene is not a racist. It is likely, therefore, that his inaction was due to bad advice from groups within his own party. Even more incredible is that neither the President nor any member of the government appeared on national television or radio to exhort people to calm down, or to condemn the violence. The President made his speech five days later with practically no sympathy extended to those who suffered most — the Tamils of Colombo. The tone of the speeches of other government leaders was the same: these speeches were designed to placate the Sinhalese community — not a word of compassion for the Tamils. Lalith Athulathmudali, the young Minister of Trade, opened his speech to the nation thus: 'A few days ago, my friends, I saw a sight which neither you nor I thought that we should live to see again. We saw many people looking for food, standing in line, greatly inconvenienced, seriously inconvenienced.' Here was the leading intellectual in the government speaking of the hardship faced by Sinhalese people queuing for food when 70,000 Tamils were in refugee camps. Equally astonishing is the fact that neither the President nor any minister of the government made an official visit to a single refugee camp to console the dispossessed.

The public utterances of government leaders seemed to be carefully orchestrated. It was as if they viewed the racial violence not as a product of urban mobs but as a mass movement of Sinhalese people in general. Hence, perhaps, the refusal to extend compassion to those who actually suffered. This came out clearly in the President's own speech on 28 July where he promised to introduce legislation to ban separatism or even the talk of it. He said, furthermore, that because of the violence initiated by Tamil terrorists, 'the Sinhalese people themselves have reacted'. Prime Minister Premadasa was even more explicit:

We have now taken a decision to include in the Constitution that even advocating a division of the country is illegal. No one would be able to even talk about it. Such a campaign will be made illegal. We would not only deprive those advocating any division of the country of their civic rights, we would even bring legislation to confiscate their properties. Those advocating any division of the country will not be able to talk about it even in a foreign land. Because we would punish them on their return to Sri Lanka. The President yesterday promised you that such actions would be ordered by the government. He said so to dispel any doubts that you may have had in your minds.

But see what was happened today. Today they have heard rumours that tigers [Tamil terrorists] have come to Colombo and invaded Colombo. Just imagine the great destruction and the crimes committed based on such wild rumours. Our people not only were aroused but also engaged themselves in violent acts. They have taken clubs and other weapons and engaged in violent acts. As a result even our Sinhala and Muslim brethren have been subjected to harassment.

It is true that the greatest destruction of property occurred in the areas represented by Prime Minister Premadasa (Colombo Central) yet the phrase 'our people' in his speech does not refer to those specific elements of the city population. According to the government scenario, those committing acts of violence were the generality of Sinhalese people. This is certainly not the case: most middle-class people, as well as ordinary villagers whom I know, have a strong Sinhalese – Buddhist identity, but they did not engage in violence against Tamils and were for the most part shocked by the brutality and suddenness of these events. It is true that some connived in acts of violence, but others gave Tamil refugees shelter in their homes at great personal risk. They were not without a profound ambivalence, but this was not a mass movement of the Sinhalese people against the Tamils. If this were so, one would have to give up any hope for the future not just of the Tamils, who could flee to the north and east of the island or to South India, but for the Buddhists entrapped in their own violence. What a fate for a nation subscribing to a religion of non-violence!

The Tamils who suffered, many Sinhalese and the foreign press openly stated either that the violence was condoned by the government or that it was the work of factions within the government. The government responded with its own theory of an international and local Communist conspiracy. This time it was not a Naxalite plot as was claimed after the presidential election, but an internationally aided Communist plot to take over the country. The President even implied that the killing of the army personnel in the north on 23 July may also have been part of the plan. According to this scenario, the Muslims and Christians were to be massacred next. The parties who allegedly planned this were proscribed. Dark doings by foreign embassies were also hinted at by the local newspapers.

For once the public was skeptical of these 'complots', as Richard III would have said. All three of the proscribed parties were sympathetic with Tamil language aspirations. Two were supposedly in cahoots with the terrorists, while one openly sided with the Tamil demand for a separate state. It was difficult to believe that the very groups sympathetic to the Tamils would systematically plunder, loot and destroy Tamil homes and gruesomely murder men and women. It also seems unlikely that a government so promptly informed of a Naxalite plot by the CID a day after the presidential election could have been ignorant of a more serious plot by Marxist groups to create race riots. We are asked to believe that the government was forewarned in late 1982 of a plot that did not occur, but not warned in mid-1983 of one that did! Finally if the racial riots were caused by Marxists, why did the government imply that it was a popular uprising by the Sinhalese and why in heaven's name did no one offer sympathy for the dispossessed or visit refugee camps? The rhetoric of plots was obviously less for local consumption than for the Thatcher and Reagan governments whose co-operation was necessary to rebuild the economy. It is also obvious that the proscriptions would further eliminate political opposition to the ruling party.[3]

Prospects for the Future: The Political Issue

The future for Sri Lanka is bleak. Behind the rioting is the spectre of increasing authoritarian rule. The prestigious Indian newspaper, *The Hindu*, commenting on President Jayewardene's 'victory' at the referendum, stated in an editorial of 25 December 1982: 'Mr. Jayewardene will be leading the country towards one-party rule with all its menacing implications — and, in the end, may have won nothing but a Pyrrhic victory.' In my view the riots would not have occurred — at least on the same scale — if general elections had been held, providing Parliament with a strong opposition. The very existence of an opposition creates criticism of the government and provides opportunity for public debate. The actions of the JSS would have been subject to parliamentary criticism, and so would the ultra-nationalism of government party leaders. The effect of such criticism would surely have brought about division and debate between the two major Sinhalese political parties. It is therefore sad to hear eminent Sri Lankan political scientists like A. Jeyaratnam Wilson attempting to establish that Westminister-type constitutions are of little use in Third World nations and that strong presidencies are required. Surely we are dealing here with the prison house of language, where a convenient label like 'Third World' is reified to designate a single social and political reality. It is also a mistake to assume that modern political institutions imported from the West have no parallel in tradition, since forms of voting and consensual government are not alien to traditional societies.

Introduced political processes can often thus be given traditional validation. Sri Lanka with its long history and tradition of Buddhist thought took readily to the concept of universal suffrage so that it had the largest voluntary voter turnout in the whole world. People understood the power of the vote and they used it to vote out practically every government in power since independence. There was also no attempt to tamper with the electoral process itself. Moreover, it was doubtful whether Sri Lanka ever had a Westminster-type government, except on paper. They had, through the long years of British rule and after, adapted the Westminster model to suit their own character and institutions. The one key institution they held in high regard was the free vote and free elections. The overthrow of this institution and the widespread violence and impersonation of voters that occurred during the referendum have led to serious public disillusionment and demoralisation to be seen and felt everywhere. People both in villages and cities, have told me on several recent occasions, that they will not vote hereafter because it is 'useless'. This to me heralds the impending death of the democratic process.

The pernicious myth that it needs a strong authoritarian ruler to govern 'Third World' countries is partly responsible for the present situation, providing intellectual justification for one-party rule, and not just in Sri Lanka. If Marcos uses his army to crush opposition, Sri Lanka (which has no army to speak of) has created a parallel institution in a government trade union that has a paramilitary function. In doing so she may well have created a model for other small nations to emulate. The impending development of 'Home Guards' I fear may also have a similar effect.

All of this means that one should not be deluded by words like 'Westminster-type government', 'Gaullist-type regime' or that charmingly innocent term 'Home Guards'. One has to probe the reality that lies beneath. The implications of that reality are also clear: unless the government holds a general election soon, under conditions which permit people to exercise their vote without fear and intimidation, one of the few democracies of the Third World will surely go the way of nations like the Philippines.

The erosion of political institutions has a paradoxical effect for it eventually creates a peculiar dilemma for the rulers themselves. The ruler who can no longer rely on supra-personal institutions to carry on the process of government is forced to personalise them. Increasing personalisation inevitably pushes the authoritarian ruler to balance one power group or institution against another. In doing so he gets trapped in an internal conflict that takes on a momentum of its own and undermines the very basis of his authoritarian power. This seems likely to be the fate of Sri Lanka, as it has been the fate of other Third World countries.

President Jayewardene is a man of some stature; it is possible that he may have realised the monster that has been created (perhaps unwittingly) in recent years. The monster seems now to have taken on a life of its own and must be tamed or killed if democracy is to survive in Sri Lanka and the President himself is to gain a niche in history.

Prospects for the Future: The Ethnic Issue

What about the immediate issue, that of the secession movement in the north and the Sinhalese reaction to it? One thing is clear: if the intention of the mobs was to push the Tamils out of the Sinhalese areas, they have had much success. Not all Tamils have roots in the north and east, so some will have to come back and settle in Colombo and elsewhere, but professionals will probably leave the country and anyone with alternatives will resort to them. If the intention was to stifle the secessionist movement, then surely the strategy has backfired. The Tamil moderates have been virtually eliminated in this polarisation of forces, and more people, particularly youths, who had seen or heard of the macabre nature of the riots are now likely to join the terrorist organisations.

This is a real pity for, in my view, political sovereignty on the basis of language cannot work in South Asia, especially in Sri Lanka. Underlying the language uniformity which one sees in large areas of South Asia are serious and persisting divisions on the basis of culture and social structure. In the Tamil areas of Sri Lanka these differences are especially conspicuous. We noted that there are two major sets of Tamil speakers, Hindu and Muslim. Sri Lanka Muslims do not consider themselves Tamils (in the ethnic sense) but Muslims. Prior to the language conflicts between Sinhalese and Tamils, there were endemic conflicts between Muslims and Tamil Hindus, some extremely violent, particularly on the east coast. This was to be expected, given the Hindu – Muslim conflicts on the mainland. In an independent Tamil state, one set of minority problems would be replaced by another, except that the Tamils would be in the majority *vis-à-vis* the Muslims.

There are also deep subdivisions among the Tamils living in different areas of the island. The Jaffna peninsula, where most of the political agitation takes place, is self-consciously identified with high Hinduism and a patriarchal ideology and the great tradition of Dravidian culture. By contrast the east coast Tamils are mostly matrilineal, practise Dravidian folk religion and claim origins in Kerala. Even today there is considerable suspicion and hostility between these groups, especially the resentment by east coast Tamils of the economic domination of northern merchants. The Tamils imported into the central highlands by the British are generally of low caste and remain divided, socially and spatially, from the two previous groups. These divisions between the various groups of Tamil speakers are reflected today even in the political system where the ruling party has three ministers in its Cabinet representing the Tamils of the highland regions, while Tamils of the north are represented by the TULF which is an opposition party. What the recent riots may have done is to push people from the east and highland areas into a larger Tamil movement. If so, Sinhalese extremists will have fulfilled a prophecy — not theirs but that of their opponents.

One must also mention that great divider in Hindu society — caste. The aristocratic caste of landowners or Vellalas dominate the politics and economy of the north and east and constitute about 40 per cent of the population. In recent years their hegemony has been challenged by the Karaiyar (traditionally fishermen) who have moved into professional and entrepreneurial positions. There are also other large and powerful minority castes (e.g. Koviar, Mukkuvar) who are opposed to both these groups and are not likely to welcome the perpetuation of Vellala hegemony. Finally there are untouchables and near-untouchables who are barely considered human by the rest of Hindu society and who consequently were some of the first Buddhist converts in this region. Caste is compounded by another division, that of Tamil-speaking Christians in the north, who are politically and economically powerful. As R.L. Stirrat shows elsewhere in this volume, a striking feature of recent politics in both Sinhalese and Tamil areas is the extreme linguistic chauvinism of the Christians. It is as if their marginal position in Buddhist and Hindu society has forced them to overemphasise their ethnic identity. But it is equally likely that in the event of an exclusive Tamil – Hindu domination in the north the Christians would be in an even more vulnerable position than the Muslims.

Thus, in the eventuality of the Tamils achieving political independence (or even a form of federalism), there will arise a series of 'minority problems' which will be as serious (I think even more serious) as that which prevails now between Sinhalese and Tamils. Language unity is an illusory one in Tamil Sri Lanka (as elsewhere in South Asia); the reality is internal division based on religion, caste, ethnic origins, etc. It should also be remembered that even the northern terrorist groups who are fighting to establish a separate Tamil state are not a single entity. They are also divided into at least two groups based on caste affiliations and vying for political dominance. One such group, currently very powerful, has a Karaiyar caste leadership and power base, while the other (now operating from South India) is Vellala caste based. Indeed the latter has publicly upbraided the Karaiyar organisation for killing the 13 Sinhalese servicemen in ambush on 23 July, thereby triggering the massive Sinhalese reprisal and violence.

Sri Lanka's current problems seem to defy immediate political resolution. Yet it is virtually certain that only political compromise by both Sinhalese and Tamils can bring about any lasting solution. It is to President Jayewardene's credit that he attempted to start this process well before 1983 by introducing legislation to give greater autonomy to the Tamil regions of the country. But much of this remained on paper since reactionaries in his own party would not permit the implementation of government policy. On the Tamil side terrorist organisations brooked no compromise, and moderate

Tamils did not speak up for fear of reprisals from terrorists. It is likely that when the riots broke out, the President was advised not to impose an immediate curfew, since some strong-arm tactics by Sinhalese toughs against the Tamil business community would facilitate negotiations. But it is unlikely that the President or the Prime Minister would have condoned the use of UNP unions for mass reprisals against Tamils. An analysis of events make it equally clear that elements within their own party forced the issue, and once urban mobs were roused, all sorts of pathological elements in the city population went on the rampage. Contrary to Tamil opinion, I do not believe that the government actually organised the riots; rather it was organised *for* the government by forces which the government itself had created, albeit for other purposes. Perhaps the government is still unaware that this many-headed monster which it created may destroy not only its creator but the entire democratic fabric of Sri Lankan society as well.

Notes

1. This summary of Matthew's speech and the quotations are from *Hansard (Parliamentary Debates)*, 4 August 1983, pp. 1308–24.

2. This and the following examples are drawn from 35 cases of intimidation and assault documented by the Civil Rights Movement in a publication dated 12 October 1981.

3. At this writing, the ban on one of the three parties, the Communist Party, has been lifted. Bans on the Janatha Vimukthi Peramuna and the Nava Sama Samaja Party remain.

9 SOME THOUGHTS ON SINHALESE JUSTIFICATIONS FOR THE VIOLENCE[1]

Elizabeth Nissan

I was in Anuradhapura when violence broke out in Colombo and elsewhere in late July 1983. On 26 July, curfew was extended to cover the whole island. A friend called by in the early afternoon on her way home from work to make sure that I knew that I could not go out. Being unsure about what she had told me — there had been some confusion about when the curfew started — I went out onto the road and asked a man who was passing if there was already curfew in the area. He was a labourer, also on his way home early. Enraged, he answered my question: 'Yes, there's curfew. If those Tamils want to come and live in our country they should help us. But they cause us all this trouble. Now there's curfew. How are we to work and buy food? It's those Tamils cause us problems . . .' He continued, cursing, down the street and I went inside. Tamils were being attacked, killed, driven out of their homes in thousands in areas of the island, presumably by mobs of Sinhalese. Yet here was a Sinhalese man instantly blaming Tamils for the problems this curfew could cause him. 'Those Tamils' had come to 'our country': visitors should know their place.

This was a theme I heard again and again. Even most of those I spoke to who condemned the violence would go on to say that such a backlash was hardly surprising: 'but they killed thirteen of our soldiers, so what do they expect'; 'they came here and now they are trying to divide the country; that's why it happened'. I met only a few Sinhalese who rejected such justifications for what was occurring.

As it happened, there was no violence in Anuradhapura. There are few Tamils resident in Anuradhapura town nowadays, since the violence of 1977 which drove most Tamil families out of the area. Those working in government offices or banks mostly left their quarters and went to Jaffna after the violence broke out. I was frequently assured not to worry in Anuradhapura, because there were no Tamils living there. I was relieved to find that most townspeople discounted the Tamil families who remained in the circumstances. But there was fear in Anuradhapura that the town would be attacked by Tamil Tigers, descending on this most northern Sinhalese town from the Jaffna peninsula. Several people expressed this fear to me, one which was not just local, but which had been generalised to the point where, in Colombo, panic broke out on Friday 29 July when it was believed that Tigers were attacking the city.

At times, too, I was confused by some people's assurances that Anuradhapura would not suffer violence. It was sometimes unclear whether this was because there was not a significant Tamil population to attack, or because there were not sufficient Tamils to launch an attack themselves on the Sinhalese. One person even went so far as to reinterpret the events of 1977, when Tamils in Anuradhapura suffered greatly in a wave of violence against them,[2] as disruption caused by Tamils invading the town from the north and attacking Sinhalese.

Justification for the violence was sought by many Sinhalese. An identification was made between all Tamils and those involved in violent separatist activity. Violent separatism was seen not just as an attack on the state apparatus, but as a threat to all Sinhalese personally through an attack on their state.

'They killed our soldiers'; 'they want to divide our small country'; 'we have given them a lot but they always want more': such statements were part of a common vocabulary of explanation and justification, and contained within them certain ideological assumptions concerning the nature of the state of Sri Lanka and its relation to the Sinhalese people. Implicit in all such statements is the fundamental premise that Sri Lanka is inherently and rightfully a Sinhalese state; and that this is, and must be accepted as, a fact and not a matter of opinion to be debated. For attempting to challenge this premise, Tamils have brought the wrath of the Sinhalese on their own heads; they have themselves to blame.[3]

As all Tamils came to be identified with terrorism and anti-state activity, which was inherently against Sinhalese interests, so too was any other anti-government activity interpreted as anti-state and thus also anti-Sinhalese. As I will show, this identification was made, with its inherent confusions, in the theory of the violence which the government propounded. I will set out this theory by examining ministerial speeches broadcast to the nation during and just after the worst of the violence.

Sinhalese justification for anti-Tamil violence, then, rests on the assertion of a Sinhalese identity which incorporates inherent 'natural' rights to political ascendancy in an undivided island. This argument was not just one which was implicit in the explanations that I heard on the streets of Anuradhapura, but was one which was also made explicit in various speeches broadcast to the nation by Cabinet ministers throughout this period. In the rest of this paper, I will focus on these speeches[4] and try to draw out some of the ideological themes that ran through them. Assumptions are made in these speeches about the collective identity of the Sinhalese and their relationship to the island of Lanka. Certain assumptions were also made as to who the relevant audience for this message was, as to who needed reassurance at this critical time on these points, and various appeals were made in the speeches to an implicit 'we' group. Certain omissions were as revealing in this respect as the statements themselves. For example, all speeches by Sinhalese ministers were addressed first and foremost to the Sinhalese public and not to Tamil victims of the violence. Several omitted any reference to the suffering which Tamils had undergone, but pointed instead to the hardship the violence had brought to Sinhalese themselves.

Given the limitations on space and time that I have had in preparing this paper, my treatment of these speeches will be somewhat selective. I do not believe, however, that the conclusions that I will draw out of this material would be invalidated by more comprehensive treatment. The speeches that I examine in this discussion are those of the President of Sri Lanka, J.R. Jayewardene (broadcast on 28 July); the Prime Minister, R. Premadasa (29 July); Minister of State, A. de Alwis (30 July); Minister of Lands, Land Development and Mahaveli Development, G. Dissanayake (31 July); Minister of Trade and Shipping, L. Athulathmudali (1 August); Minister of Finance and Planning, R. de Mel (2 August). As these speeches display a gradual elaboration and confusion of certain themes, I will discuss them in roughly chronological order.

The President of Sri Lanka, J.R. Jayewardene, spoke to the nation on 28 July. He had remained silent, at least to public ears, for the four days after violence broke out. His speech, like the others which followed from Cabinet ministers, was broadcast on television and radio and also published in the newspapers.[5] The speech opened with an expression of distress and sorrow about the recent violence, and about the distrustful relationship between the Sinhalese and the Tamil communities. The seeds of distrust were sown in 1956 in this account, but were encouraged in 1976 through the development of the movement for a separate state. Because this movement became violent, 'Sinhalese people themselves reacted'. Such a reaction from the Sinhalese is not condemned but presented as an understandable consequence. Early on in the speech the assertion was made that: 'The Sinhalese will never agree to the division of a country which has been a united nation for 2,500 years.'

Violence against Tamils was not in itself condemned in this speech. Instead, the President mentions that he thinks that it could be used to undermine the progress which his government has brought to the country. He outlined government's intention to declare illegal any advocation of separatism, declaring that the government 'cannot see any other way by which we can appease the natural desire and request of the Sinhala people to prevent the country being divided . . .' The speech reads as a statement of the government position, without any direct linguistic appeal being made to any particular group. Certain other themes emerged in this speech which were elaborated in later ministerial addresses.

The Prime Minister, R. Premadasa, broadcast his speech to the nation the next day. That day, Friday 29 July, had been one of renewed panic and violence in Colombo after the incidents in Gas Works Street which provoked the rumour that Tigers had invaded the city. Jayewardene had framed his statement as an address to the whole country outlining government policy to deal with the crisis. Identification of the government with a particular community was only evident in Jayewardene's address through consideration of government policy, action that the government proposed to take in keeping with the Sinhalese 'national request'. A notable shift in style was evident in Premadasa's speech. Here, direct appeal was made to a particular community, and this was explicit in the language used: 'We see that our people who have been misled by such rumours are enraged and frightened. As a result they have been led to violent acts.' 'Our people' are here clearly Sinhalese, misled to the extent that 'even our Sinhala and Muslim brethren have been subjected to harassment. You can just imagine what a catastrophe that is.' (No mention is made of 'catastrophe' befalling the Tamil victims of violence.) For those who feared that the government may not have their interests at heart the message is plain: 'If there has been any doubts in anybody's mind that the country will be divided the government has now promised you that positive action will be taken to prevent any division.' The audience had been narrowed in this speech to address and reassure those who feared Tamil independence. But the Gas Works Street incident, in which the armed forces were said to have been attacked by Sinhalese, has confused the issue of just who the enemies of the state and the Sinhalese are. A generalised explanation is given: anti-government forces, 'those who cannot come to power by the ballot', are attempting to wreak destruction on the country. 'We' who care for our country must, therefore, not allow ourselves to be misled, must not give in to false rumouring and engage in violence provoked by such rumours, which will only be to our own detriment. The appeal was repeated several times.

Minister of State, Anandatissa de Alwis, spoke the next day, following on from the theme of Premadasa's speech, appealing to people neither to believe the rumours that they hear nor to pass them on. Again there was emphasis on how Sinhalese themselves had been adversely affected by the violence, and no mention of the ills that the Tamils had suffered: 'Some of the factories that have been burned down employed thousands of people. Ninety per cent of the employees in all these establishments were Sinhalese.' The scene is thus set for the Master Plan conspiracy theory of the violence, which de Alwis unfolded, to appear credible. This was the plan which the government claimed to have uncovered, and halted at its first stage. The violence was seen to have proceeded according to certain patterns, and the plan was to have followed the three stages of Sinhalese/Tamil, Sinhalese/Muslim and Sinhalese Buddhist/Sinhalese Christian conflict, bringing the country to chaos. Unnamed 'Sinhala parties in the South' and 'Tamil parties in the North' were said to have plotted this together.[6] The stress in this and other speeches on the harm done to Sinhalese themselves seemed part of the attempt to persuade the Sinhalese public that the violence was not really communally based at all, but that communal tension was being manipulated to the detriment of all, to bring about chaos, food riots and the downfall of the elected government. Images of great danger were compounded in this speech: northern and southern plotters, aided by 'the minds of certain foreign elements'; groups of trouble makers 'unconcerned with Sinhala or Tamil or any other race or issue'; looters waiting on the side lines to benefit from the destruction. Only by refusing to be misled, and by supporting the President, could such multiple threats be averted, and majority interests ensured.

Other ministers also reiterated this theme: the violence was instigated by anti-state forces, both from the Tamil North and the Sinhalese South, to cause chaos. Unwittingly, this argument goes, people have been swept into this violent current thinking that they were engaging in anti-Tamil action in the Sinhalese national interest, without realising that they do so to their own detriment. Thus Gamini Dissanayake asserted that 'what took place last week was not merely a communal riot',[7] a point he later repeated in Parliament when commenting on the conduct of the armed forces during the rioting: 'It was only when they realised that this was not a mere communal outburst that they thought of doing their duty of maintaining law and order.'[8]

Despite the conviction with which the government repeatedly asserted the Master Plan theory of the rioting, there was still a tendency to blame lthe Tamil leadership itself for what had happened. Gamini Dissanayake, in his speech on 31 July, argued as follows:

It is true that the activities of the self-styled terrorist organisation in the North combined with the short sighted and if I might say so, unwise policies of the representatives of the Tamil community who are in the Tamil Liberation Front, created a situation in which the majority community felt terrible resentment even anger at what was going on in the North. It is our belief that what took place last week was not merely a communal riot. No one can deny that the initial flames of violence on the aftermath of incidents of the 23rd had definite communal connotations. But this incident has been cleverly utilised by those who have been rejected by the people, to destroy all the gains that this country has made during the last 6 years. What has been attacked is not merely a community, what has been attacked has been the open economy.

The two theories were conflated and the organisers remained obscure. Thus Athulathmudali, Minister of Trade and Shipping:

We now know there is a hidden hand behind these incidents . . . It is the hidden hand of those who will benefit from any kind of chaos. It may be the terrorists of the North, extremists and terrorists in the South . . . Their common objectives are by and large the same, they seek to destroy, not to build.

The Master Plan theory of the riots could not have stood independently from the explanation which said that the Sinhalese had been provoked beyond endurance by Tamil terrorist attacks on their state, for it was communal sentiment that was aroused to put the plan into action. And as the Master Plan theory was elaborated and conflated with the objectives of Tamil separatism, the identification of the Sri Lankan state with the Sinhalese people and with Buddhism was spelt out very clearly in ministerial speeches. Since 1956, successive governments have self-consciously asserted that they protect and promote the state of Sri Lanka as a Sinhalese Buddhist state.

Jayewardene's government, too, has stressed this theme. Jayewardene came into power in 1977 promising to introduce a 'dharmishta' society, a state of righteousness and justice based on Buddhist principles. As head of state, he has been extolled in the government press as a man of Bodhisatva virtues, a future Buddha himself.[9] An attack on the state, so represented, is interpreted as an attack on these very principles. These are principles which were the source of Sinhalese nationalist inspiration, and around which nationalists consolidated a sense of Sinhalese-Buddhist identity in the late nineteenth and early twentieth centuries. This sense of identity was built on a sense of historic, ancient roots,[10] which were recovered in politics when Mr Bandaranaike was elected in 1956.[11] But whilst governments have spoken of Buddhist revivalism in accordance with the fulfilment of the Sinhalese national destiny,[12] and assert Sinhalese-Buddhist hegemony over the island,[13] they have failed to persuade the Jaffna Tamil leadership that this can be compatible with united nationhood for all communities.[14] Unless all accede to this assertion, it must remain essentially fragile, the national assertion of a minority in the context of South Asia as a whole. Common but contradictory characterisations of Tamils depict them as barbarians, but with superiority in intelligence, deligence, earning power and cunning. Such images received fullest expression in the panic about Tigers, who would overrun the whole country.[15]

Against such fears, I believe, some ministers directed their speeches. Athulathmudali appealed to all those who supported the UNP to rally round government and help preserve law and order whilst building up a sense of commitment to the nation as a whole. He spelt out clearly what the foundation of this national commitment must be:

. . . in this context there are certain unalterable facts. The problems begin when we seek to change these unalterable facts. The first is that we are one land, one country. We know now if we did not know before that Sri Lanka is one. The Sinhala people, the Muslim people, and people of many other communities will never, never allow the division of this country. To put it simply, so long as there is one Sinhala man remaining on the soil of Lanka, there will be one person to oppose this division. The second unalterable fact is something which we Sinhala people tell ourselves. We have a duty to explain this to our compatriots from other communities. The Sinhala people feel that they have an important place in this country, that they have no other place to go to, and that they have a special duty here. For example in protecting the Buddhist religion, and they have done so to the admiration of the whole world. But, while that has been so, it is also a fact that throughout history, other communities, other people, have lived in Lanka . . . We must then look forward to a Sri Lanka which is *the indisputable home* of the Sinhala people and also *the home* of other people who have lived in this land. (emphasis added)

Ronnie de Mel, Minister of Finance, took up this theme with even greater emphasis the next day:

The Sinhalese people have faced many crises in their history of 2500 years. We have faced invasions from South India from the time of Senaka and Guttika the sons of horse dealers, from the time of Elara and from the time of Chola Empire. We have faced the imperialisms of the West, the Portuguese, the Dutch and the British. We lost our independence in 1815. We have faced communal riots in 1958 during the time of the SLFP government; in 1961 and 1962 again in the time of the SLFP government; in 1978 in the time of our government.[16] Despite all these crises the Sinhalese race, the Sinhalese language and Sinhalese culture have endured for the last 2500 years. We should be particularly grateful to the Maha Sangha [Buddhist monkhood] for that. Why should we be afraid that something that has endured for 2500 years will now be destroyed? This government will never allow the country to be divided . . . Are we going to jeopardise the Sinhalese nation or the Sinhalese race? Are we going to allow our country to be divided? We would prefer to die rather than to live in slavery.

Here, then, whilst asserting that government is at one with, and heir to, the heroic Sinhalese heritage of cultural, religious and national survival, de Mel actually reinforced the image in many Sinhalese people's minds that the separatist threat is a threat against their very lives and their continuation as a people. The Sinhalese race, it would appear from this speech, is to be saved through outlawing Tamil separatism, which if not halted would bring doom and destruction to Sinhalese Buddhist civilisation and the Sinhalese people.

These references to the Sinhalese people as essentially a Buddhist people in Athulathmudali's and de Mel's speeches evoke a host of allusions to key reference points in national representations of the Sinhalese, and touch on the cornerstone of the special Sinhalese claim to the island as a whole. According to Sinhalese tradition as recorded in the chronicles of the island (particularly the Mahavamsa, written in the sixth century AD by Buddhist monks), the island was consecrated by the Buddha himself before Vijaya, the founder of the Sinhalese race, arrived there. The duty of his descendants, the Sinhalese, is to protect and preserve the island as the Island of the Doctrine through the institution of righteous Buddhist kingship. Post-Bandaranaike, since an assertively nationalist style of politics gained ascendancy, these themes have been reinterpreted such that the government must be seen to promote Buddhism and the destiny of the Sinhalese in a manner allegedly continuous with that of righteous kingship.[3] Hence Jaywardene's representation as Bodhisatva, and the emphasis on religious development in government rhetoric generally.

Such themes in post-independence politics have been hard to reconcile with the democratic ideal of the nation-state operating without regard to racial or religious criteria, and no successful reconciliation has been effected. The ideal of the state has been unable to transcend the divisions of racially or religiously defined sectional communities. Government is identified by the Sinhalese majority as a defender (or otherwise) of its own rights, and by the Tamil minority as representing sectional interests opposed to its own. As Manor[18] has pointed out, whether the UNP or SLFP has been in power, each has appealed for communal reconciliation, but when in opposition, each has appealed to communal sentiment as reconciliation is seen to jeopardise Sinhalese interests. The violence of the summer, and the government response, tragically illustrate the dangers inherent in such a situation. Government, for whatever reasons, appealed to Sinhalese interests in the speeches broadcast to the nation. In the name of upholding democracy, it asserted majority sectionalism; it evoked emotive communal sentiments to justify both the banning of a large section of Tamil political opinion, and the proscription of parties opposed to the government on other grounds.

On the one hand, Tamils were themselves blamed for provoking the violence. On the other, the situation in the north was seen merely to provide an excuse for others to instigate violence designed to undermine the integrity of the state. Through this contradiction, a series of identifications were made. Any Tamil might be a terrorist or a sympathiser with separatism. Anti-state activity in this form was interpreted as inherently anti-Sinhalese, threatening the survival of the Sinhalese people, their religion and civilisation. Similarly, the 'hidden hand' of southern extremists' anti-state activity (whether it existed or not) was also identified as being opposed to the principles of Sinhalese national identity. The two sides became one. The UNP government insisted that it would not forget the special needs of the Sinhalese people in Sri Lanka. It appealed to the very sentiments that it claimed the plotters against the state were manipulating. National chauvinism and violence were implicitly endorsed through being condemned only because they were being used for the wrong ends. Anti-UNP parties could be proscribed, with no evidence produced against them, and even talk of separatism could be banned, in the name of protecting majority Sinhalese interests, equitable with the continuing power of the UNP.

I would not expect any state to treat separatists in its midst kindly. Nor do I find it useful to dismiss such ideological constructions as I have been discussing here out of hand. The government in its public broadcasts answered the fears of the Sinhalese public as I had heard them expressed. Had there been no such representations in the minds of this public to be answered, I think it unlikely that violence on the scale that occurred last summer could ever have happened. In justifying and explaining the violence in the way that it did, the government of Sri Lanka has laid yet more foundations for increased state repression of all peoples living there. The left wing plot is a common enough explanation resorted to when violence breaks out.[19] In this case, however, it has been set against all that constitutes Sinhalese identity by being linked with Tamil separatism. The thrust of the ministers' rhetoric was such that any anti-UNP activity could be held up as inherently anti-Sinhalese, or conversely that the true Sinhalese or Sinhalese sympathiser had to be pro-UNP.

Notes

1. This paper is based on material collected during a two month visit to Sri Lanka in July and August 1983. This visit was intended as a follow up to anthropological research that I had done in Sri Lanka between June 1980 and February 1982 on the Sacred City of Anuradhapura. I am grateful to R.L. Stirrat and Mark Whitaker for their comments on this paper.

2. The findings of the Sansoni Commission on the violence of 1977 are published in *Report of the Presidential Commission of Inquiry into the Incidents which took place between 13th August and 15th September, 1977*, Sessional Paper no. VII (1980). Specific attacks on Tamils in Anuradhapura Town are catalogued at pp. 154–74.

3. See the quotation from Ronnie de Mel's speech of 2 August 1983.

4. I deal here only with speeches broadcast between 28 July 1983 and 2 August 1983. A speech by a Sinhalese minister was broadcast daily in this period. The Muslim Transport Minister, M.H. Mohamed, broadcast a speech on 3 August 1983, in which he argued that Muslims in Sri Lanka do not favour division of the country; that violence was intended to undermine the government; that Muslims 'marched shoulder to shoulder with the Sinhalese' during the Portuguese invasion, and that they should rally round the leadership of the President now 'to build a united Lanka'. On 7 August 1983, the Tamil Home Minister broadcast a speech. This was the only speech directed to the Tamil population specifically from a Cabinet minister. In it, Devanayagam traces the roots of communalism to 1956, and outlines the ways in which Jayewardene's government has attempted to solve Tamil problems by guaranteeing the language rights of minorities.

5. Full texts of each speech can be found in various Sri Lankan newspapers of the period. I list only one reference for each speech here: Jayewardene, *Daily News*, 29 July 1983; Premadasa, *Sunday Observer*, 31 July 1983; de Alwis, *Daily News*, 1 August 1983; Dissanayake, *Daily News*, 3 August 1983; Athulathmudali, *Daily News*, 3 August 1983; de Mel, *Daily News*, 4 August 1983. Mohamed's speech and Devanayagam's speech are published in *Sun*, 5 and 8 August 1983, respectively.

6. The same day, although not mentioned in this speech, government had announced the proscription of three left-wing parties, the Communist Party, the Janatha Vimukthi Peramuna and the Nava Sama Samaja Party.

7. In his speech of 31 July 1983.

8. *Daily News*, 6 August 1983.

9. For example, *Ceylon Daily News*, 17 September 1980, on the President's birthday.

10. Note the references to 2,500 years of Sinhalese nationhood in both Jayewardene's and de Mel's speeches. A revisionist version of this historic past from the Tamil side is given in S. Ponnambalam, *Sri Lanka: National Conflict and the Tamil Liberation Struggle* (London, 1983), ch. 2.

11. See W.H. Wriggins, *Ceylon: Dilemmas of a New Nation* (Princeton, 1960) and H. Bechert, 'S.W.R.D. Bandaranaike and the Legitimation of Power through Buddhist Ideals' in B.L. Smith (ed.), *Religion and the Legitimation of Power in Sri Lanka* (Chambersburg, 1978).

12. This theme is repeated continually in the press and in parliamentarians' speeches. Even during the troubles last summer the papers carried such articles; for example, a *Daily News* report bore the headline 'Jayewardene Era spurred a great Buddhist revival' (30 July 1983).

13. See G. Obeyesekere, 'Religious Symbolism and Political Change in Ceylon', *Modern Ceylon Studies*, i, 1 (1970) for discussion of some symbolic expressions of this phenomenon. Many political issues are sensitive in these terms.

14. See R.L. Stirrat's contribution to this volume on the Catholic accommodation to this shift in power.

15. See also Jonathan Spencer's contribution to this volume.

16. Notably, de Mel does not mention the outbreak of communal Sinhalese/Tamil violence in 1981, nor the limited Sinhalese/Muslim violence of 1982 in Galle, both of which occurred under UNP rule.

17. Many writers have addressed this theme, e.g. M. Roberts, 'Meanderings in the Pathways of Collective Identity and Nationalism' in M. Roberts (ed.), *Collective Identities, Nationalisms and Protest in Modern Sri Lanka* (Colombo, 1979); Wriggins, *Ceylon*. For analysis of themes in the *Mahavamsa* from which such a relationship between the state and the religion derive, see R.T. Clifford, 'The *Dhammadipa* Tradition of Sri Lanka: Three Models within the Sinhalese Chronicles' and A. Greenwald, 'The Relic on the Spear: Historiography and the Saga of Dutthagamini', both in B.L. Smith (ed.), *Religion*. On contemporary state use of Buddhist ritual, see H.L. Seneviratne, 'Politics and Pageantry: Universalization of Ritual in Contemporary Sri Lanka', *Man*, xii, 1 (1977). On the recovery of a Sinhalese-Buddhist ethnicity in the late nineteenth and early twentieth centuries see K. Malalgoda, *Buddhism in Sinhalese Society 1750–1900: A Study of Religious Revival and Change* (Berkeley, 1976); G. Obeyesekere, 'The Vicissitudes of the Sinhala–Buddhist Identity through Time and Change' in M. Roberts, (ed.) *Collective Identities*.

18. J. Manor, 'Sri Lanka: Explaining the Disaster', *The World Today* (November 1983).

19. For example, a similar explanation was used in 1958. J. Manor, 'Self-inflicted Wound: Inter-Communal Violence in Ceylon, 1958' in *Political Violence*, collected papers, Institute of Commonwealth Studies (University of London, 1981).

10 POPULAR PERCEPTIONS OF THE VIOLENCE: A PROVINCIAL VIEW[1]

Jonathan Spencer

Sometime in the summer of 1983 — it must have been a month or two before the dreadful violence of late July — I had a conversation with a friend which stuck in my memory, never more so than in those later days when, like many others, I found myself desperately trying to make sense of that familiar paradox — the perpetration of evil by apparently nice, decent people. The conversation took place in a village on the southern edge of the central highlands, where I had been living for the preceding 15 months. The friend I was talking to was an educated, intelligent young man, neither especially paranoid nor in any sense a racist or communal extremist.

We had been discussing a whole string of strange events, some purely local — a man struck by lightning in his paddy field, a murder in a neighbouring village — others more national, especially, I suppose, the ever-increasing incidence of political violence. Did you hear, he asked me, about the six strangers seen near the sixteenth mile post? I replied that they were probably gem hunters wandering, like many others, through the area in search of a lucky strike. No, he said, people think they might be Tigers.

I was astonished and incredulous. The Tigers had never carried out an operation outside the northern Tamil areas, and all the evidence suggested that they had neither the resources nor the inclination to attempt such an operation, even somewhere like Colombo where there was a substantial Tamil population. The idea that they could be stupid enough to see some strategic value in such a remote rural setting struck me as fatuous.

My friend was not, however, wholly convinced by my expostulations. He reminded me of a story currently circulating in the neighbourhood: a group of men had hired a minibus from a local Sinhalese gem dealer; the bus had not been returned and the murdered body of the driver had eventually been found in the north near Mannar. This was obviously the work of the Tigers. But surely, I pointed out, large gem dealers have quite enough local enemies to account for this otherwise pointless murder; why should the Tigers come so far to

187

carry out such a risky operation? Well, he said, the merchant in question helped the government in 1981 — the killing was the Tigers' revenge.[2] And remember, too, in 1981 people say they found a machine gun in one of the burnt-out Tamil shops in town.

I have started with this story as it illustrates the main theme of this contribution. During the violence of July 1983 I was in the same village, many miles from the atrocities, and relying on the same mixture of censored news and rumour as the villagers themselves. Not being an eyewitness I have only a limited contribution to make in any discussion of what happened in specific incidents. And, lacking any privileged information on high-level political machinations, whether of left or right, Sinhalese or Tamil, I leave it to those better qualified than I to assess the various conspiracy theories which purport to account for the riots. What I do have, however, is some understanding of the mood of ordinary people before the trouble broke out and of their subsequent perception of it. While it could easily be argued that an impressionistic and local account like this can hardly justify general conclusions, I must at least point out that for every incident and conversation I mention here there were dozens of similar stories collected both by myself and by friends elsewhere in the island.[3] And while, in certain context, all manner of people could express views different from those summarised here as 'the popular mood', in other contexts there was an awful monotony to the arguments and rationalisations of Sinhalese people from all social backgrounds.

Moreover, I believe that my experience does have some limited value in discussing the causes of the violence. While no one has disagreed with the government's claim that there was a large element of organisation in the rioting, this does not mean that events can be explained solely in terms of manipulation by a few ringleaders. It may be possible to argue that the violence could have been perpetrated without widespread popular support, but it is just as valid to point out that it would have been impossible had there been any measured show of opposition from the Sinhalese population. For this reason, some gauge of the popular mood is a necessary complement to an assessment of the claims and counter-claims of rival conspiracy theorists.

Furthermore, although from the first 'patterns' were being detected in the violence, there is a quite different pattern which has, so far as I know, gone unnoticed until now. It helps if we think in terms of three kinds of violence that occurred in that week. Firstly, there was the inchoate anger at the murder of 13 members of the security forces on the night of 23 July. But the localised appearance of the violence — the complete absence of trouble in towns like Ratnapura, Balangoda, Hambantota and Tissamaharama, none of them normally thought of as havens of peace — and its gradual move outwards from Colombo, would suggest that this alone would not constitute a sufficient cause for what happened. In the village where I lived there are four or five Indian Tamil families and they suffered no harassment at all on this occasion.

The second and most common kind of violence was the calculated destruction of Tamil property by relatively small and well organised gangs; by and large the Tamil occupants of such property were given the opportunity to escape to the relative safety of the refugee camps. But the third and most disturbing kind was the horrific murder of innocent Tamils. It is likely that some of these murders occurred in that first wave of blind rage that spread out from the cemetery in Borella on Sunday, 24 July. But the best documented massacres seem to have followed in a perverse but regular way from the relative calm of systematic and 'rational' looting and burning. These massacres only begin to make sense, both to a troubled outsider and to Sinhalese people themselves, if some notice is taken of the popular fears that prevailed in the months before the violence; fears that are exemplified in my friend's detection of suspected terrorists in a poor and remote corner of Sabaragamuwa Province.

During my stay in the village I had only sporadic access to the local English language news media. For much of my day-to-day information about political events in the country I, like the villagers, relied on government-controlled or government-supporting vernacular newspapers like *Dinamina* and *Dawasa*. These were delivered by bus to a couple of shops in the village where people would stop by during the day to read them. Only a few village intellectuals would bring back from town the occasional copy of the more independent *Diwayina* (sister paper to Upali Newspapers' *Island*). During the period of tension leading up to the riots — and it should be remembered that the outbreak of large-scale violence had seemed imminent to many observers, it being only the occasion and target that surprised people — I would discuss the news almost daily with a few friends, exchanging information that I might have picked up from the English language-press and external sources like the BBC World Service, from synopses of the SLBC Sinhalese news and the leading stories in the vernacular press. While this arrangement, grounded in expediency, may disqualify me from commenting on national politics, it did have the advantage of keeping me in very close touch with both the news, and especially the interpretation of that news, available to that vast majority of Sinhalese people who have no access to the English-language media.

In late March, articles first appeared in both the English and Sinhalese press suggesting that the Tigers had started to establish themselves in the hitherto peaceful Trincomalee area. These stories coincided with the escalation of the conflict between the state and the Gandhiyam movement in the area around Vavuniya and with a growing campaign of official apprehension about Indian Tamil squatters in the north-eastern dry zone. The papers continued to be full of stories about 'terrorists' (*trastavâdi*), even during lulls in the political violence in the north, through the months of April and May. In June this reached a climax with the report of disturbances in Trincomalee, followed by a news clamp-down from that area except for the occasional brief acknowledgement of further deaths in the trouble. The fact that all those killed in that first wave of rioting were Tamil was not reported until much later in the English-language press;[4] all that was reported to the Sinhalese audience, again well after the first riots in Trincomalee had abated, was that the Leader of the Opposition, A. Amirthalingam, had *claimed* that all those killed were Tamil. For most people I know, there was only one interpretation — the earlier reports were true and the subsequent deaths were the work of Tamil terrorists. In other words the terrorists were both increasing their operations and starting to attack in areas with a substantial Sinhalese population.

This particular press campaign cannot, however, completely explain the popular panic that swept through Sinhalese areas in the build up to the riots. It is true enough that the Sinhalese press is communally slanted but, to assess properly the impact of that kind of reporting, we would first have to answer the thorny question of how much the press is able to mould popular opinion, and how much it merely reflects it. This becomes clear when we consider the supplementing of official news with hearsay and rumour and the filtering of the resulting pot-pourri through the mesh of racial stereotypes.

Thus as I was again and again reminded throughout my stay, in Sinhalese eyes, the Tamil is an inherently violent and dangerous creature whose excesses from time to time try even the saintly patience of the majority Buddhists.[5] One conversation at a friend's home on the Wednesday of the riots illustrates this. Why were people doing this, I asked. It's like this, explained a young man who was staying with my friend. This country is a good, straight Buddhist country (*niyama honda baudha rata*). Yet these Tamils are always making trouble, killing people . . . But it's the Tamils who are getting killed, I objected. They started it, burst in my friend's wife, they have done so many terrible things. For example, in 1958 in Batticaloa, they dropped a baby in a barrel of tar and set fire to it.

I have heard this baby story at least half a dozen times, located variously in Colombo, Trincomalee, Batticaloa and Tissamaharama. (I have even been told it twice by long-term European residents, at least one of whom thought it was a Tamil baby that had been killed.) I mention it here as the most popular example of a whole genre of imaginary horrors remembered from earlier bouts of communal trouble. Tarzie Vittachi, in his book on the 1958 communal riots, cites it as an unfounded rumour that was prevalent at the time, while the *Daily News*, in a reprint of an article from the 1950s lampooning the spread of rumour at times of communal tension, thought it ludicrous enough for satirical comment.[6] The author of that article can hardly have expected that the tale would linger as an accepted tenet of popular history a quarter of a century later.

Bearing in mind that the very word 'Tamil' was largely eschewed in news and speeches during the days of the rioting, people again drew their own conclusions about what was going on. One day, having just heard a news item about the numbers in refugee camps, I happened to say to my next door neighbour that there were now so many thousand *Tamils* homeless. Oh no, he said, at least half of them will be Sinhalese. And well after the violence had abated I mentioned to an old *radala*[7] lady I had been interviewing that I was intending to travel to Colombo. She looked concerned and advised me to be careful. But the trouble is over for now, I said, and besides, no Europeans were attacked even in the worst days. Ah, she said, but you know those Tamils, they'd attack anyone. In other words, for many Sinhalese people away from the centres of the trouble, the Tamils, far from being innocent victims, were assumed to be at least equal partners in, if not the main protagonists of, the rioting. The lacunae in official news had been swiftly filled by the assumptions of popular prejudice.

It is possible to view Tamil political history as a kind of doomed and unconscious acting out of the most paranoid fantasies of the majority community. In the 1950s, any suggestion of minor administrative devolution to Tamil areas was greeted with the response from

Sinhalese chauvinists that this was just the thin edge of the separatist wedge. By the 1970s, when 20 years of political frustration had finally resulted in popular support for separatism, these same chauvinists were able to say that they had been right all along. So too the emergence of the Liberation Tigers — of Tamils prepared to kill in furtherance of their aim to split up 'the island of the doctrine' — merely served, for many Sinhalese people, to confirm their own misapprehension that Tamils are inherently violent people. When, furthermore, the same Tigers appear to be able to carry out their operations with total impunity, they become, in the popular mind, blessed with superhuman cunning. By the summer of 1983, Sinhalese areas were gripped by a collective panic, with people like the friend whose conversation I reported earlier, seeing Tigers everywhere and believing them to be capable of the most extraordinary feats.

It was this collective panic that emerges as a recurring feature in the more reliable reports of murders and massacres. As I have already suggested, the greater part of the violence was directed at property and not at people. But whenever any Tamil attempted to defend himself or his property he became, by definition, a 'terrorist', and the mood of the crowd (and, in some cases, of the security forces), changed dramatically. In the death of the 'Camphor Mudalali' and his family in Badulla,[8] and also I believe in a similar incident in Nuwara Eliya, the act of firing into the air to disperse the crowd actually provoked the massacre. In one case, quoted by a member of the government in a speech some time after the riots, a Sinhalese dockworker in the crowd in the Pettah (Colombo market district) felt someone removing his wristwatch and started to fight back. His actions became, in the eyes of the crowd, proof that he too was a terrorist and he was murdered. In other words, a thread of insane logic links a number of these incidents — aggression against the crowd, even in some cases simply running away from the crowd, was, *ipso facto*, evidence of terrorism, of being a Tiger. Clearly and objectively, this was never the case; equally clearly and objectively, this was what the crowd *believed* to be the case.

This phenomenon, savagery born in terror, can be seen as a natural product of the deep-rooted Sinhalese perception of the violent Tamil. As the violence persisted so people daily expected the Tamil backlash, the Tigers' revenge. Although it never in fact came, this expectation, centred in Colombo, provoked some of the worst atrocities. The identification of 'Tamil' and 'Tiger' could be made without any other evidence than the crowd's own certainty, based on hearsay, of the terrorist threat. On the Thursday morning, a mob burst out of the Pettah and took a group of Tamils off the Kandy train at Fort railway station, then beat and burnt them to death. On the Friday, shots were heard coming from Gasworks Street in the Pettah, initiating a crazy stampede of office workers, policemen and soldiers[9] (and, it seems, foreign correspondents, some of whose reporting of this incident was astonishingly irresponsible). By the weekend, the return of students and others who had been stranded in Colombo, all of whom 'knew' someone who had seen something of the Tigers' mythical attack on Colombo, meant that the presence of terrorists in Colombo on those days became an established 'fact' in my village.[10] I suspect it remains so to this day.

I knew somewhat differently. A neutral acquaintance had been on that Kandy train. This time the crowd arrived with the 'knowledge' that terrorists were on board preparing to plant bombs. The victims of the tragedy did no more to provoke their fate than to try, quite understandably, to get out of Colombo. By now, 'knowing' as they did that the train was planted with bombs, all the crowd needed to do was find the culprits. And for the crime of being Tamil, once found, they paid the price.

But the imaginary discovery of mythical terrorists has had another longer term effect. As well as provoking terrifying brutality, it has now taken its place alongside the burning baby in the popular memory. Embarrassed and ashamed by the news of murder, many Sinhalese people were relieved to hear that those killed had been 'terrorists'. But, as well as relieving the collective conscience, the readiness to believe these stories has sown the seeds for the next time. A whole new catalogue of mythical atrocities has joined that burning baby in the memory of the community.

There is no doubt that the press and politicians alike, in their reaction to the activities of the northern Tamil youth, must take their share of responsibility for the emergence of this mood of savage paranoia. But it should also be remembered that the use of armed force against the state has provoked the Western democracies to employ some startlingly illiberal measures: in Northern Ireland we have seen the suspension of trial by jury, and of *habeas corpus*, as well as the use, at times, of institutionalised torture ('sensory deprivation'). And the press in Britain, as in West Germany and Italy, has hardly been noted for its moderate and sober response to the use of violence against the state. But where these situations differ from Sri Lanka is that not even the Birmingham bombings brought bloodthirsty mobs to the streets of Kilburn. Baader-Meinhof assassinations did not lead to the burning alive of left-wing students in Munich and Berlin. To discover the roots of the collective panic which swept Sri Lanka in the summer of 1983 we would have to look at the specific sources of social and cultural insecurity within Sinhalese society — a task too daunting to undertake here.

Lest I be misunderstood, let me restate my original argument. I am not claiming that the activities of the Tigers, even as absorbed and refracted in an impressionistically established 'popular mood', were the *cause* of the violence of July 1983. But the existence of very widespread anti-Tamil resentment made that violence possible, while the emergence of a pathological fear of 'terrorists' was probably the key factor in escalating the level of violence from looting and burning to killing. This point is especially important as there are those on the left in both major communities in Sri Lanka, but especially amongst the radicalised northern youth, who see the Tamil question being turned into a national class struggle, with the Liberation Tigers joining hands with the oppressed Sinhalese masses to fight the bourgeois state. My experience would suggest that this is not merely a pipedream; it is a very, very dangerous pipedream.

Notes

1. Research in Sri Lanka was carried out between November 1981 and October 1983 as a student attached to the University of Peradeniya and was supported by a Social Science Research Council studentship. This paper is a personal view arising from a troubled, and I would frankly admit, confused conscience. In order to forestall too much misunderstanding I must point out that I write from a sense of shared tragedy — shared, that is, with my Sri Lankan friends of all communities. My intention is not to apportion blame but to try and understand the human causes of this tragedy in a perhaps naïve belief that reaching an adequate understanding might lessen the chances of terrible events like those of July 1983 occurring again.

2. In 1981, the nearest town had been one of those affected by a smaller but, in many ways instructively similar, outbreak of anti-Tamil violence.

3. See the contributions in this volume by Stirrat and Nissan.

4. In an excellent article by the late Ranil Weerasinghe in *Weekend*, early July. This article also conclusively rebutted the earlier allegations of Tiger activity in the area.

5. Most people whom I spoke to were genuinely shocked when I revealed that, not surprisingly, there is a corresponding Tamil stereotype about the Sinhalese.

6. 'Fact and Rumour', *Daily News*, 12 September 1983; T. Vittachi, *Emergency '58* (London, 1958).

7. The highest, 'aristocratic', subcaste of the dominant *goyigama* caste.

8. *The Guardian*, 13 August 1983. A friend who had been in Badulla shortly after the troubles gave me an account of the massacre that tallied exactly with this report.

His source was a neighbour of the victims. Neither of them was aware that the story had been reported in the foreign press.

9. The best account of Friday's panic, again written by Ranil Weerasinghe, appeared in *Weekend* in August.

10. The imagined attack on Colombo by the Tigers quickly attracted a cluster of extraordinary details (one of the most absurd of these is mentioned by Stirrat in his essay in this book). In this respect, fears were fanned by the few details that were reported in the news. At one point it was announced that suspected terrorists *had* been arrested in Colombo only for this to be subsequently denied. On Friday, 29 July, it was reported that one soldier had 'succumbed to his wounds' after accidentally shooting himself in the Pettah; this tale impressed no one. Even the denial of specific rumours in official statements might be met with the response — 'if it's not true, then why are they bothering to mention it?' The President's speech on Thursday night, 28 July, with its long catalogue of Tamil *hinsaka vada* ('violent work') caused an exchange of glances amongst my fellow listeners at the time — 'the Tigers must have done something else otherwise he would be scolding the Sinhalese' was the general verdict.

11 THE RIOTS AND THE ROMAN CATHOLIC CHURCH IN HISTORICAL PERSPECTIVE[1]

R.L. Stirrat

Almost exactly a century ago one of the most serious riots of the late nineteenth century broke out in Kotahena, a suburb of Colombo. At Easter 1883 a procession of Buddhists led by the famous activist monk Migettuwatte Unnanse attempted to march past St Lucia's cathedral on its way to the local Buddhist temple. Outside the cathedral, probably with the encouragement of the cathedral priests, a mob of Catholics attacked the Buddhists killing bullocks, destroying carts and images and inflicting personal injuries from which one Buddhist died.[2]

The Kotahena riot was not an isolated incident. Throughout the last quarter of the nineteenth century and the first quarter of the twentieth century there was a series of violent clashes between Catholics and members of other religions, the incidents usually sparked off by processions passing sacred buildings. Thus to mention just a few of these outbreaks, Catholics and Buddhists came to blows in Ambalangoda in 1890, Wadduwa in 1891, Kalutara in 1897 and Anuradhapura in 1903 whilst there was violence between Catholics and Hindus in Negombo during 1899 and Neervali near Jaffna in 1902.[3] In the view of the commissioners who inquired into the Kotahena riot, 'The Roman Catholics generally appear to think that any supposed insult to their religion should be resisted by force',[4] a view that the Catholics would appear to have endorsed. As the semi-official *Catholic Messenger* put it after the Negombo riot of 1899, 'In the scuffle the Hindus fared very badly . . . They will at least think twice before they attempt such a thing again.'[5]

The period around 1900 was one in which the major schisms in the country took a religious form. As well as riots involving Catholics, there was also violence between Buddhists and Muslims and the occasional trouble between Muslims and Catholics. Both Buddhists and Hindus saw Catholics and the Catholic Church as their common enemy. Buddhist and Hindu journals such as *Sandaresa* and *The Hindu Organ* spent most of their time attacking the Church whilst societies such as the *Saiva Paribalana Sabai* in Jaffna were essentially dedicated to fighting Christian influence in Sri Lanka. Yet the Church remained highly confident. 'Nothing can check her progress' wrote the *Catholic Messenger* in 1909, 'because she is endowed with a divine vitality and a supernatural power . . ., because she is *the true religion*, and truth will always win.'[6]

A century later the picture is very different. Most conflict now takes place across ethnic and not religious boundaries. From being a unified, self-confident and assertive body, the Catholic Church as an institution today tries to keep out of politics and to avoid any actions which might offend the Sinhalese – Buddhist dominated state. Rather than stress a common religious identity, Catholics today are divided on grounds of ethnicity, a split which affects not only the laity but also the priesthood. Ethnic identity has taken over from religious identity. In the riots of 1983 Catholic Sinhalese were active in attacks on Tamils and Tamil-owned property in the west coast areas where Catholics are most numerous, and being Catholic was no defence for Tamils against such attacks. Thus even in Kotahena Tamil Catholics were attacked by Catholic as well as by Buddhist Sinhalese. The Church, one of the few bodies which straddles the ethnic divide, has been unable to find for itself a meaningful role in the present situation in Sri Lanka. To understand the position of the Church, of priests and of the Catholic laity in relation to the riots of 1983, we must examine the decline of the Church in the context of increasing racial polarisation in Sri Lanka as a whole.[7]

Conflict between Sinhalese and Tamils around the turn of the century was relatively undeveloped. At that stage the main thrust of political activity was, first, to recover (or invent) indigenous Sinhalese and Tamil culture in the face of Western colonial and cultural supremacy, and secondly, for the indigenous population of the island to gain some sort of power *vis à vis* the colonial rulers.

As Malalgoda, Obeyesekere and others have pointed out,[8] the cultural revival of the late nineteenth and early twentieth centuries was in large measure a search for an identity — cultural, linguistic and religious. These various elements became intermingled for both Tamils and Sinhalese in Sri Lanka, the most obvious case being the work of the Sinhalese–Buddhist revivalist, Anagarika Dharmapala.[9] For these revivalists, Catholics and the Catholic Church provided a useful focus for attack. Catholics were by far the largest of the Christian groups in Sri Lanka, whilst Catholicism had been introduced by a colonial power and was being promulgated by often arrogant missionaries. Yet at the same time Catholicism was never the 'official' religion of the British, and thus attacks on the Catholic Church could avoid being interpreted as direct challenges to colonial rule. Furthermore, Catholic missionaries went out of their way to create a separate Catholic identity in Sri Lanka, actively discouraging contact between Catholics and non-Catholics whilst encouraging rituals, ways of thought, traditions and even forms of language which demarcated Catholics from non-Catholics throughout the country. The efforts of the priests and the efforts of anti-Catholic cultural activists both worked to the same end: the separation of Catholics from both Buddhists and Hindus, and the creation of a Catholic identity which crosscut ethnic divisions.

The relative calm of Sinhalese – Tamil relations began to dissolve with the movement towards limited Home Rule for Sri Lanka. Just as Buddhist and Hindus were united in their opposition to alien cultural forms such as the Catholic Church, so too were the early political activists united in their demands for political power, but with the deliberations over the Donoughmore Constitution in the late 1920s, the picture began to change. Whilst the Sinhalese leaders favoured a 'one man, one vote' system, Tamil leaders objected to this on the grounds that it would give the Sinhalese majority total control over the country, and so they demanded some sort of communal representation to safeguard their position. As Jane Russell[10] has argued, this period marked the beginnings of a shift towards the domination of Sri Lankan politics by the communal divide. Furthermore, it marked the beginnings of an intensification of ideas concerning 'race' and 'language', culminating in the exclusive opposition of two groups defined in these terms. As Dharmadasa has pointed out,[11] ideologies of the 1930s such as that represented by the writings of Cumaratunga stress the unique nature of the Sinhalese people to a much greater extent than those of Dharmapala for instance, and by the 1970s such concepts had come to dominate the views of the Sinhalese concerning their place in Sri Lanka and their relationship with the island of Lanka.

None the less, during the pre-Independence period, despite the growing importance of the Sinhalese – Tamil divide, the conflict between Catholics and other religious groups continued. One of the most important organisations involved in these attacks was the All Ceylon Buddhist Congress which attacked the Church for purveying an alien religion, missionaries as being foreign interlopers and Catholics as being 'denationalised'. Compared with the self-confidence of the Catholic community in the years before the Donoughmore Constitution, the Church's response grew somewhat disorganised. To take a year at random, the *Messenger* in November 1931 ran a series of leaders extolling the benefits of colonial rule whilst at the same time indignantly denying that, 'the Christian by following western ideas becomes denationalised and loses his title to be called a "true Sinhalese" '. 'Religion', said *The Messenger*, 'is not an element of nationality.'[12] Yet the Church continued to encourage an exclusiveness and a separateness on the part of the Catholic community in Sri Lanka on both cultural and political levels. In areas where the Church was powerful priests acted as mediators between the government and the local community, and in some areas they seem to have acted as the local administration.[13] As long as the British remained in Sri Lanka, the Church could more or less maintain the separateness of the Catholic community and was protected against the more extreme attacks from the Sinhalese – Buddhist extremists. Admittedly there were isolated cases of churches being burnt and aggressive speeches from Buddhist leaders on the supposed power of the Church in politics, its control over an excellent school system, and overrepresentation of Catholics in the professions and the civil service, but it was only after Independence that these threats could be put into practice.

The Church's response to Independence itself was somewhat muted. Whilst the Archbishop ordered church bells to be rung on Independence Day there were few specifically Catholic celebrations of political freedom. In a rather half-hearted effort at indigenisation a new advocation of the Virgin Mary, 'Our Lady of Lanka', was announced, whilst any explicit praise of colonial rule was not out of fashion. Instead, an effort was made to discover the Catholic fighters against the British. Thus, somewhat hopefully, *The Messenger* tried to claim that, 'The Reform movement in Ceylon was started by Christian patriots and benefactors long before the Sinhalese Buddhists ever thought of it'[14] a claim that must have done little for Catholic – Buddhist relations.[15]

As many writers have argued, the real shift of power to the Sinhalese – Buddhist masses came in the general election of 1956 with the victory of Mr Bandaranaike.[16] UNP governments had previously generally followed a policy of non-involvement in religious affairs and had done little to attack the Church or the Catholic community. Not surprisingly the Church and the majority of the Catholic laity supported the UNP but with the victory of Mr

Bandaranaike in 1956 the Catholic community was now open to the attacks of both the Buddhists and of left-wing groups in the country.[17] These attacks were focused on a number of themes:

1. The wealth of the Church.
2. The involvement of the Church in political matters, particularly the 'advice' given by priests to the laity on how to vote.
3. The activities of *Catholic Action* which was held to be a sort of 'Mafia' ensuring preference for Catholics in both the public and private sectors.
4. The existence of a Church-controlled system of schools which gave Catholic students advantages denied to the Buddhist majority.
5. The existence of a body of Sri Lankans who were seen as owing allegiance to a foreign Pope, an allegiance epitomised by the presence of European missionaries.

In practical and symbolic terms the struggle between the Catholics and other groups in Sri Lanka centred on the schools issue. Since the late nineteenth century the Church had been remarkably successful in creating an impressive schools system which received grants-in-aid from the government. From the 1930s Church schools had been a major target for attack by the Buddhists and later by left-wing groups, and with Mr Bandaranaike's victory in 1956 the stage was set for the takeover of the Church schools. With hindsight the hierarchy could be said to have made a strategic error in choosing to fight the schools takeover, but so much stress had been placed on the right of the Church to control the education of Catholic children that it had little choice. Through the late 1950s a vigorous and often bitter debate took place between the Church and its opponents, but in 1961 the government finally took over the schools. With the encouragement of the priests large numbers of Catholics occupied the Church schools in an attempt to prevent 'the bands of thugs and political charlatans' who were being organised to 'invade Catholic schools'.[18] But the Archbishop was soon forced to climb down.

> The entire hierarchy of Ceylon have decided, in the interests of the Church and the State, to appeal to the faithful to withdraw their 'Occupation' in order to enable the schools to function in a normal manner.[19]

The defeat over the schools issue meant the effective end of the Church as a major political entity in Sri Lanka. In its wake, the government began to expel foreign nursing sisters and impose restrictions on the entry of foreign missionaries. The involvement of a number of prominent Catholics in the coup plot of 1962[20] only made things worse, and the hierarchy of the Church was forced to come to some sort of accommodation with the state. In the face of a series of pro-Sinhalese – Buddhist governments the aim of the Church was to avoid confrontation and seek a *modus vivendi* with the state.

One of the results of the defeat of the Church over the schools issue was the disillusionment of large sections of the Catholic laity with the hierarchy. Furthermore, 'being Catholic' ceased to have the pragmatic benefits it once had. With the takeover of the schools Catholics lost many of their educational advantages and with the deliberate attempt to 'Buddhicise' and 'Sinhalise' the civil service and indeed the private sector, Catholics began to feel an oppressed minority. As a result many Catholics, both Sinhalese and Tamil, began to reassert their ethnic rather than their religious identities, and attempted thereby to gain access to new channels of patronage and preferment.

This renewed stress on ethnic rather than religious identity was part of a larger process involving both national and international factors. The Church in Sri Lanka during the nineteenth century was a missionary church run by European priests who attempted to create a replica of their native brand of religiosity in Sri Lanka. Through the twentieth century, however, an increasing proportion of the priesthood was locally recruited, mainly Sinhalese or Tamil, and by the time of Independence these local priests were beginning to explore the possibilities of a more indigenised form of Catholicism. To a certain extent this was encouraged by the remaining missionaries who realised that some sort of accommodation had to be reached with the Sri Lankan context in which they worked, but the real push came during and after Vatican II which encouraged the use of the vernacular in the rites of the Church and accepted that local forms of worship and local 'customs' were not necessarily anti-Catholic. And as foreign missionaries declined in numbers, so the local Church became progressively indigenised at all levels.

This process of indigenisation eroded the barriers between the Catholics and members of other religions in Sri Lanka, whilst at the same time creating new barriers between Sinhalese and Tamil Catholics. Admittedly, sermons and hymns had always been in the two indigenous languages but now there was not even Latin in common between the two communities, and in the 1960s a number of bitter disputes developed over the language of worship in churches used by both Sinhalese and Tamil Catholics. Furthermore, the spread of the mass media, both newspapers and the radio, and the stress on *swabasha* (indigenous languages) erected further barriers between the two groups of Catholics whilst increasing the degree of contact between Catholics and non-Catholics amongst both Sinhalese and Tamil speakers.

Finally, the role of the priest changed. The missionaries of the nineteenth century saw their role as mediators both between man and God and between Catholics and the state. Over the last 30 or 40 years both roles have changed. First, the priests have lost their political role, the rise of mass politics and the power of the MP making them redundant as negotiators between parishioners and bureaucrats. Secondly, in the post-Vatican II world, the role of the priest has shifted from being a mediator between man and God to being something closer to a social worker, salvation being increasingly defined as something to be gained through the brotherhood of man rather than through spiritual activities. This has involved certain elements of the priesthood becoming involved in political and quasi-political activities where their constituencies are not defined in terms of religious affiliation but in terms of class or exploitation, the stress being on helping the 'oppressed minorities', no matter what their religious affiliation. Thus whilst the Church as an institution has attempted to move out of the political arena, priests as individuals have moved into politics, particularly left-wing politics and into activist social-work roles. Although a minority these priests are particularly vocal and articulate, and their visibility outweighs their numbers.

The result of these processes has been to erode severely the identity of the Catholic community as a distinct segment of Sri Lankan society. With the political decline of the Church, Catholics at all levels have had to come to an accommodation with the political situation in the country, and this has undermined their separate identity. With these changes, Vatican II and the impact of the press and the radio, splits have developed between Sinhalese Catholics and Tamil Catholics.

By the early 1970s, relations between the Sinhalese and Tamil sections of the Church had deteriorated to such an extent that priests commonly referred to a 'Palmyrah Curtain' dividing the diocese of the north and east from those of the south. Despite the existence of a unified hierarchy and the Sri Lankan Bishops' Conference, contacts between the Tamil and the Sinhalese areas became fewer and relations more strained. The creation of a separate Vicarate covering the North-Central Province was part of this process of separation. For historical reasons, NCP was part of Jaffna diocese despite being a predominantly Sinhalese area, and the creation of a separate, essentially Sinhalese, diocese in this area was a recognition of the deterioration of Sinhalese – Tamil relations within the Church.

Even in Sinhalese-dominated areas, tension between Catholics of the two communities grew. Priests influenced by Vatican II began to work for such groups as the estate Tamils, and individuals such as Bishop Leo of Kandy (and later of Badulla) began to alienate the Sinhalese both within and outside the Church through their outspoken comments on the situation of the Tamils on the estates. Other activists such as Father Tissa Balasuriya and Father Paul Caspersz similarly alienated not only Sinhalese chauvinists but also the government through political activities which were seen as being dangerously left wing. Frequently their socialist activities were represented by the government as being pro-Tamil.

By the time of the formation of the TULF and the elections of 1977, most Tamil Catholic priests and probably most Tamil Catholics were, to a greater or lesser extent, supporters of the separatist movement. By this stage their identity as Tamils and as members of the 'Tamil nation' had forced them into this position, and the spread of 'Liberation Theology' amongst the younger priests made armed struggle a legitimate possibility. In the riots of 1977 and in the pacification that followed the riots, the Sinhalese-dominated security forces made no distinction between Tamils on the basis of religion: all Tamils were potential enemies. As repression spread, so both laymen and priests found themselves having to take up more extreme positions. Some young Catholic laymen became involved in the 'Tiger' movement, and at least a few of the priests supported 'the boys' seeing in them a defence against the repressive measures of the army.

In reaction to the increasing militancy of the Tamils, the government introduced the 'Prevention of Terrorism' Act. Modelled in part on the laws used in Ulster, the Act put severe limitations on the rights of the individual and was strenuously opposed not just by the Tamils but also by civil rights groups and by certain groups of the clergy including left wing activists from both the Sinhalese and the Tamil Catholic communities. By challenging the official government line, these clerics drew some rather vicious criticism from the government-controlled press. The *Daily News* ran a story and a leader attacking these priests as being 'Rasputins', and accused the Church of supporting the Marxist parties. This accusation was vigorously denied by a spokesman of the Bishops' Conference who asserted the rights of individuals including priests to hold political views.[21] But the fact that individual priests were opposing the Act which was also under attack from the Tamils left the Church open to the accusation that it was supporting not just the left but also the Tamil separatist movement.[22]

Towards the end of 1982 two Catholic priests in the Jaffna peninsula were arrested by the security forces and charged with giving support to two injured 'terrorists' and being in possession of a large sum of money which the authorities suspected of belonging to the 'Tiger' movement. A few decades earlier, the arrest of a priest would have caused outrage amongst the whole Catholic community in Sri Lanka, but this time the only protest came from the Tamil areas of the country and a small number of Sinhalese priests. Three (Sinhalese) members of the Bishops' Conference met the President, and in a statement made afterwards they said little except that 'The Church does not dabble in politics', that it was not responsible for the activities of individuals, that they claimed no special privileges for priests and that they hoped for a fair trial.

The general opinion amongst Sinhalese Catholics was that these two priests had been involved in supporting the 'Tigers', and that as priests this action was doubly heinous. Amongst Sinhalese priests there was more doubt as to the actual involvement of the priests in terrorist activities. The Bishop of Jaffna claimed that the money found in the possession of the priests belonged to him and was nothing to do with the 'Tigers', whilst the priests' defence was that they would give shelter to anyone who was injured, and that this did not mean they were supporters of the 'Tigers'. Sinhalese critics of the priests claimed that a priest's first duty was loyalty to the state and that they should have handed the two injured terrorists over to the authorities. A few rather brave Sinhalese priests disagreed with the argument pointing out that if this policy had been followed by priests during the Dutch period, there would have been no missionaries in the country.[23] For them, a priest's duties towards the sick came before their duties to the state. Matters became more complicated with the involvement of the Papal Nuncio. He had already shown an interest in the problems of the Tamil community in Sri Lanka and had become unpopular with the government. When he tried to intercede on behalf of the arrested priests this gave the government the excuse they needed to ask him to leave the country.

In the months before the 1983 riots, relations between Catholics of the two communities deteriorated as did those between non-Catholics. In the Trincomalee area, riots in May which appear to have been part of a general attempt to 'Sinhalise' the area, left many Indian Tamils who had settled on government land homeless, and Catholic bodies in Trincomalee provided shelter to many of the refugees. In the riots themselves, Sinhalese Catholics were involved in attacks on Tamils and Tamil-owned property, irrespective of whether or not the Tamils were Catholic. Throughout the Catholic strip running north along the coast from Colombo, large numbers of Sinhalese Catholics were active in the riots which spread from Colombo over two or three days to such areas as North Colombo, Wattala, Negombo, Kochchikade, and to a lesser extent to the small towns towards Chilaw.[24] Negombo and Kochchikade, both towns in which Catholics are dominant, were particularly badly hit.

Eyewitnesses in both places mentioned that the security forces — particularly air force personnel — were active in the riots, and that in both towns the police did little to prevent attacks on property or people. In Chilaw, although the local police were told that a mob was gathering, no attempt was made to prevent the riot and in the violence that followed, the police failed to intervene to prevent the death of the only victim in Chilaw. These witnesses also asserted that a number of Buddhist priests were present during the riots and that in some cases these priests encouraged the rioting. It must be said straight away that no Catholic priests were involved in these incidents and many did their utmost to stop them. In places such as Kotahena and Chilaw, Church property was immediately made available as refugee camps, Church charitable bodies were among the first to provide food, shelter and medical aid for the refugees, and individual priests ran considerable risks in attempting to prevent violence. But in more than one case Sinhalese Catholic priests refused to leave their mission houses during the riots, excusing themselves on the grounds that there was little they could do in the face of the mob. As far as the laity were concerned, despite the involvement of Catholics in the mobs which killed, looted and burnt, there were many individual cases of Sinhalese Catholics giving protection to Tamil neighbours, and in the Negombo region Tamils seem to have found shelter with the staunchly Catholic fishermen, many of whom speak Tamil despite being Sinhalese.

Up-country there were attacks on a number of churches used by Tamil-speaking congregations, mainly estate workers. The worst incidents included burnings, shootings and the death of a nun from wounds after she had been attacked by a mob looking for two Tamil priests. It would appear that these attacks were primarily motivated by anti-Tamil rather than anti-Catholic sentiment, but at the same time there was a strong undercurrent of anti-Catholic feeling and a real fear amongst sections of the Sinhalese Catholic population. Two Sinhalese priests working in the North-Western Province received letters after the riots threatening that their churches would be burned and Catholics attacked unless they and their congregations returned to the coast where they belonged, and there was a certain amount of fear amongst the priests that the 'Catholics of the Diaspora' might be liable to future attack.

The situation was aggravated as far as the Catholic Church was concerned by the comments made on the riots by the World Council of Churches which was meeting at the time, and by Radio Veritas. The WCC was fast to condemn the violence in Sri Lanka and blame the government for much of the killing during the riots. Even though the Catholic Church is not a member of the WCC, the Church in Sri Lanka had to deny that it had anything to do with the decisions made by the WCC.[25] Radio Veritas is a broadcasting station based in the Philippines, and during and after the riots it reported highly critical reports of the government and the actions of the Sinhalese. As Radio Veritas is supposedly owned by the Filipino Church, critics of the Church in Sri Lanka accused the Church of feeding anti-government propaganda to Radio Veritas.[26] The Church was quick to deny these accusations,[27] but the impression remained amongst non-Catholics that the Church was in part at least in contact with anti-Sinhalese and anti-government bodies.

The fears of the Catholics that they might be the next victims of Sinhalese Buddhist violence were only made worse by the government statements that the rioting in Colombo and elsewhere was inspired by a coalition of left-wing groups. In a series of statements made just after the riots, the government claimed that the Sinhalese – Tamil riots were only the first of a planned series of violent incidents which would involve Buddhist – Muslim and then Buddhist – Catholic clashes. The aim, so it was claimed, was to create domestic chaos which the extreme left would then use to mount a revolution.[28] This somewhat unlikely story was soon dropped but it did form the basis for an attack on the left including left-wing priests, and at least one missionary was expelled from Sri Lanka for supposedly revolutionary (and pro-Tamil) activities. Furthermore, it could be interpreted as a warning to both Catholics and Muslims not to step out of line and challenge the Sinhalese – Buddhist hegemony. In this context the remark made by Lalith Athulathmudali that 'the Tamils should learn a lesson from the Catholics',[29] suggesting a more tractable attitude to the Sinhalese – Buddhist majority, is as much a warning to Catholics as an admonition to Tamils.

Amongst the Catholic laity of the Colombo – Chilaw belt, the general reaction to the riots was that 'it was all the Tamils' fault'. Whilst being genuinely horrified by the suffering and the destruction, many laymen argued that Tamils had always been the aggressors and quoted the myths of Duttugemunu and Gajabahu in support of their arguments. Whilst many admitted that Tamils in this area had not been involved in the *Eelam* movement, the fact that they were Tamils and that the Tamil community had tried the patience of the Sinhalese for so long was sufficient excuse for the violence in this area. In other words, the violence was not the fault of the Sinhalese but rather of moderate Tamils who had failed to keep their more extreme brethren under control.

Many priests accepted much the same sort of argument as the laity, and described the riots as a 'perfectly natural' reaction to the Tamil demand for a separate state and the actions of the Tigers. This attitude was quite clear at all levels of the priesthood and is obvious in the statement made by the Archbishop of Colombo soon after the riots as well as in the statement made by the Negombo priests a month later. In the latter, the Negombo priests condemned 'all sorts of violence' and in particular called 'upon our Tamil brethren to eschew violence and terrorism'. Yet no specific mention nor condemnation is made of the Sinhalese violence against Tamils. Instead stress is laid upon the 'privileges' which the Tamils and various Christian groups gained during colonial rule. Whilst admitting that there are 'due rights of the minority group', the stress throughout the statement is on the grievances of the Sinhalese.[30] The last paragraph of the statement starts with, 'We stand for a concept of a Dhamma Dweepa' (sic), the island of the *Dhamma*, the Buddhist concept of what Sri Lanka should be. Even thirty years ago such a statement from Catholic priests would have been unthinkable. In effect it signals the acceptance by the priesthood of the ascendancy of the Sinhalese Buddhists in Sri Lanka. In attempting to come to terms with its own colonial heritage and the resurgence of Sinhalese Buddhism, the Catholic Church in Sri Lanka, or at least the Sinhalese branch of it, has been forced to accept even the language of Buddhism. On one level such statements are signals to the majority community that the Church has given up its separatist stance. On another, the message to the Tamils is that they too should accept the rule of the Sinhalese Buddhists and the ideal of *dhamma dipa.*

If the Sinhalese Catholics and the Sinhalese Catholic priests blamed much of the violence on the Tamils, a further element in the picture was that the Sinhalese priests held the Tamil priests to be particularly responsible. A common claim amongst the Sinhalese priests is that they hold a much less influential position in Sinhalese society than do Catholic priests in Tamil society. Sinhalese priests claim that all Tamils, no matter what their religion, hold priests in peculiar respect, and thus if the Tamil priests had come out strongly enough and early enough against the TULF, the *Eelam* movement and the 'Tigers', then there would have been much less anti-Sinhalese violence and thus the riots of 1983 would not have occurred. What evidence there is for the claims of the Sinhalese priests I cannot judge, but Tamil priests deny it saying that their position in Tamil society is much the same as that of priests in Sinhalese society.

Indeed, what runs through the overall picture of the Sinhalese Catholic response to the riots is a sustained effort to shift responsibility away from the Sinhalese onto the Tamils.[31] For most of the laity and the majority of the priests, this was how they genuinely understood the situation. Their identity as Sinhalese implied that Tamils must be at fault. This in turn related to the idea that the only true citizens of Sri Lanka were Sinhalese and that others who lived in Sri Lanka must accept this. Tamils by not being Sinhalese were, therefore, not true citizens and their demands over language, local autonomy and so on were thus seen as totally unreasonable.[32] For other priests, however, the matter was one of political calculation. They believed that if priests began to condemn the Sinhalese then there would be a real risk of an anti-Catholic backlash.

I have already mentioned the fear amongst certain sections of the Catholic Sinhalese population that they might be the next victims of Sinhalese – Buddhist chauvinism. In a few cases these fears restricted the response of the priests to the riots. In one town, for instance, the senior cleric of the area considered excommunicating those Catholics who had been involved in attacks on Tamils and Tamil-owned property. He was dissuaded from this course of action by his advisers who argued that it could be used to brand the Church as anti-Sinhalese, and that it could alienate a sizeable proportion of the Sinhalese Catholic population who might turn to Buddhism, join one of the Protestant sects, or become secessionist groups of Catholics.

Only a very small minority of Sinhalese priests came out forcefully against the violence committed against the Tamils or indeed, had much sympathy for the Tamils in general. This small minority found itself in an extremely difficult situation under attack from their own congregations and from other priests who branded them as traitors, whilst the hierarchy tried to prevent them from making statements which might be interpreted as 'inflammatory'. These few priests have almost all spent a number of years abroad and in a sense owe their primary allegiance to universal values rather than ethnic bonds. In at least one case a priest's statements from the pulpit and his arguments in private would seem to have ended his chances of promotion within the hierarchy, and after the riots he was considering leaving Sri Lanka since he saw no future for his interpretation of Christ's teaching in the Sri Lankan church today.

For the Tamil Catholics, the most obvious result of the 1983 riots was the reinforcement of their identity as Tamils and the growing distance which they felt between themselves and their Sinhalese co-religionists. In the north and east of Sri Lanka, the activities of the government and the army had already alienated large sections of the Catholic Tamil population, yet as late as the 1982 referendum, sizeable numbers of Catholics in these areas still voted for the Jayewardene government. A number of Tamil priests told me that until the riots many Catholics had seen Jayewardene as the only Sinhalese politician whom they could trust. After the riots this support for Jayewardene dissolved. Many priests who had previously either opposed the separatist movement or had given it only lukewarm support moved to much more extreme positions. They, like their more 'Eelamist' colleagues, began to consider that only solution to the problem of Tamil–Sinhalese relations was the partition of the island. A few high-ranking priests have even begun to talk about a 'war of national liberation' and see this as inevitably involving years of struggle. Priests and laymen who were previously firmly against violence had now become resigned to its necessity.

Linked to the growing demand for separatism was a sense of shock and outrage not just at the scale of the violence but also at the manner in which Tamils had been killed in the riots. A number of Tamil priests when talking to me dwelt at great length on the details of the massacres in Welikade Jail, the brutal murders by the Sinhalese mobs, and the actions of the soldiers in Tamil areas. The thrust of their comments was twofold. First, they contrasted Sinhalese attacks on Tamils as a people with Tamil attacks which they claimed were directed not against the Sinhalese *per se* but against the institutions of state: government officials, the police and army personnel. Secondly, they contrasted the sadistic and gruesome means employed by the Sinhalese to kill Tamils with the 'clean' way, as they put it, in which the 'Tigers' shot representatives of the state.[33] But despite the claims that they were not anti-Sinhalese but rather anti-state, even amongst the most liberal of Tamil priests there was a growing element of anti-Sinhalese feeling. 'Look at them. They won't even kill a fly but they will cut Tamils up in pieces' was a comment made by more than one priest.

The riots of 1983 are only the most recent of a series of incidents which have made Tamil Catholics and their priests more aware of their identity as Tamils. The riots forced all Tamils including Catholic Tamils into a more extreme position. As a result, Tamil Catholics have begun to take a renewed interest in Tamil culture. One of the striking features of the comments made by Tamil priests after the riots was their contrast between 'Tamil culture and civilisation', with 'Sinhalese barbarism'.[34] The cultural revival of the late nineteenth century which was directed against the British barbarians has re-emerged, but now the oppressing culture is that of the Sinhalese.

Not surprisingly, one of the most marked foci for the anger of the Tamil priests was the Sinhalese priesthood. In general, Tamil priests criticised the Sinhalese priests for what they saw as their cowardice during the riots. Whilst recognising that there were a few notable exceptions, Tamil priests branded the Sinhalese priests as racists or as having sold out to the Sinhalese – Buddhist majority. Tamil priests claim that Sinhalese priests have no understanding of what it means to be a second-class Tamil citizen living in an occupied country and overestimate the status of priests in Tamil society. Their most bitter comments were reserved for the Sinhalese-dominated hierarchy who, in the opinion of many Tamil priests, had done nothing to control the Sinhalese Catholic laity nor put pressure on the government to protect the Tamil community. A small minority of the priesthood are even talking about a completely separate ecclesiastical hierarchy for the Tamil areas of Sri Lanka whilst a larger minority now believe that Tamil priests would be better trained in Indian seminaries than in the national seminary at Ampitiya which they see as Sinhalese-dominated.

In sum, then, the Catholic community in Sri Lanka is in disarray. What was once a self-confident unified body led by an aggressive hierarchy is today hopelessly split between the Sinhalese and the Tamil wings of the Church. Where once Catholics formed a unified entity in contrast to the Buddhists and the Hindus, today religion counts for much less and ethnicity for much more.

As Sinhalese Buddhists rose to their present position of dominance in Sri Lanka, the Catholics were the first of the minority groups to come into conflict with the majority community. To a certain extent, the accusations made against the Catholics in the years leading up to the 1960s were similar to those against the Tamils: that both groups had benefited unfairly under colonial rule, that they were over-represented in the universities, the civil service and the professions, that both ran 'Mafias' to look after their own, and so on. In the 1960s the Catholics lost their battle, one of the reasons being the ethnic split within the Catholic community. Unlike the Tamils there was no ethnic basis to being Catholic; no 'primordial loyalty' on which to base a more convincing defence against the Sinhalese Buddhists. In the long run of course the Catholics would still have had to give way, but there is an interesting comparison here between the Catholic and the Muslim communities in Sri Lanka. Whilst the universal Catholic Church has had to accept the fact of racial and ethnic differences, Muslims in Sri Lanka have created for themselves an ethnic identity as 'Moors', the supposed descendants of Arabian traders. This has allowed the Muslims to avoid the ethnic clashes of recent years by being neither Sinhalese nor Tamil, but how long this can last is another matter. With the rapid rise in the last few years of the Muslims in terms of wealth and economic power, increasing numbers of Sinhalese — both Buddhist and Catholic — are today voicing anti-Muslim sentiments. There is a real danger that the next Sri Lankan community to face attack by the Sinhalese will be the Muslims.[35]

But to return to the Catholics, any chance there might have been for the Church to act as a bridge between the Sinhalese and the

Tamils in Sri Lanka has now disappeared. If the Church attempts a mediating role, then it throws itself open to attack from the Sinhalese Buddhists. If it continues its present policy of accommodation with the government, then the split between Sinhalese and Tamil Catholics will only become more extreme. Racism recognises no religious frontiers.

Notes

1. This paper is based on data obtained during a long-term study of Roman Catholicism in Sri Lanka which started in 1976, although I have been involved in research in Sri Lanka since 1969. I was in Sri Lanka during the earlier riots of 1977 and 1981 as well as those of 1982. Immediately after the 1983 riots I visited some Tamil areas as well as the Sinhalese coastal area where the Sinhalese Catholics are concentrated. It should be added that most of my knowledge of the Catholic community in Sri Lanka comes from Sinhalese sources, and that I am not a Roman Catholic.

2. See *The Kotahena Riots, Sessional Paper IV of 1883.*

3. A long list of these outbreaks of violence between religiously defined groups is given in A.C. Dep, *A History of the Ceylon Police, Vol. 2 (1866–1913)* (Colombo, 1969).

4. *The Kotahena Riots*, p. 5.

5. *The Catholic Messenger*, 7 October 1899.

6. Ibid., 10 September 1909.

7. Today, Roman Catholics in Sri Lanka number just over one million, of whom roughly 200,000 are Tamils, mainly Sri Lanka Tamils. Catholics therefore comprise over 10 per cent of Sri Lanka Tamils, and just under 8 per cent of all Sinhalese.

8. See K. Malalgoda, *Buddhism in Sinhalese Society 1750–1950* (Berkeley, 1970); G. Obeyesekere, 'The Vicissitudes of the Sinhala Buddhist Identity Through Time and Change' in M. Roberts (ed.), *Collective Identities, Nationalisms and Protest in Modern Sri Lanka* (Colombo, 1979).

9. See A. Guruge (ed.), *Return to Righteousness* (Colombo, 1965); G. Obeyesekere, 'Religious Symbolism and Political Change in Ceylon', *Modern Ceylon Studies*, i (1970), pp. 43–63.

10. J. Russell, *Communal Politics under the Donoughmore Constitution: 1931–1947* (Dehiwala, 1982); R.N. Kearney, *Communalism and Language in the Politics of Ceylon* (Durham, NC, 1967).

11. See K.N.O. Dharmadasa, 'Language Planning and Identity Planning in Modern Sinhalese Diglossia', *Ceylon Studies Seminar*, series 6, serial 90 (1980).

12. *The Catholic Messenger*, 27 January 1931.

13. This was particularly true for the Catholic fishing villages, but more generally the priests often acted as unofficial government officers.

14. *The Catholic Messenger*, 16 March 1957.

15. The non-Catholic churches, especially the Anglicans, avoided making such claims and made a much more successful adaptation to independence.

16. See W.H. Wriggins, *Ceylon, Dilemmas of a New Nation* (Princeton, 1960); H. Bechert, 'S.W.R.D. Bandaranaike and the Legitimation of Power through Buddhist Ideals' in B.L. Smith (ed.), *Religion and the Legitimation of Power in Sri Lanka* (Chambersburg, 1978); Kearney, *Communalism and Language.*

17. These attacks were orchestrated by the All Ceylon Buddhist Congress through such publications as *The Betrayal of Buddhism* (Balangoda, 1956). *The Tribune* was

also outspoken in its attacks on the Church. The Catholic response came through its periodicals such as *The Catholic Messenger* and *Gnanartha Pradeepaya*, through pamphlets, and through the publication of the *Companion to the Buddhist Commission Report* (Colombo, 1957). See also S.U. Kodikara, 'Communism and Political Modernisation in Ceylon', *Modern Ceylon Studies*, i (1970), pp. 94–114.

18. *The Catholic Messenger*, 7 January 1961.

19. Ibid., 21 January 1961.

20. See D.L. Horowitz, *Coup Theories and Officers' Motives* (Princeton, 1982).

21. *Daily News*, 24 March 1983.

22. Some of the more radical priests became associated with the journal, *Pavidi Handa*, which brought together clerics from different religions in opposition to the government.

23. During the period of Dutch rule in coastal Sri Lanka, Catholics were liable to varying degrees of persecution and priests were frequently banned. Missionaries who worked during this period are now treated as heroes by many Catholics because of their work for the faith against the Dutch authorities.

24. Unlike Colombo, it seems that there was little pre-planning of the riots in these areas although the situation may have been different in Wattala.

25. *Daily News*, 12 August 1983.

26. *Sun*, 12 August 1983.

27. Ibid.

28. See the speech made by Anandatissa de Alwis and published in the *Daily News* on 1 August 1983. This speech is discussed by Elizabeth Nissan elsewhere in this volume.

29. *Daily News*, 6 August 1983.

30. *Sun*, 19 September 1983.

31. Elsewhere in this volume, Jonathan Spencer has remarked on the 'collective conscience' of the Sinhalese and the attempt to deal with their guilt over the violence and destruction through blaming it all on the Tamils.

32. See the paper by Elizabeth Nissan in this volume.

33. The contrast in the styles of violence would make an interesting, if rather gruesom, study.

34. Note the parallels between the Tamil comments on the Sinhalese reported here, and the Sinhalese comments on the Tamils reported by Nissan and Spencer elsewhere in this volume.

35. There have already been a number of minor outbreaks of violence between Buddhists and Muslims such as that in Puttalam in 1976 and another in Galle in 1982.

12 HILL COUNTRY TAMILS IN THE AFTERMATH OF THE VIOLENCE

R.P. Slater

Within a couple of months of the disturbances of mid-1983 in Sri Lanka, the casual observer could see that much of the physical damage which occurred during the violence had been patched up. A sense of calm had been created that might have encouraged one to dismiss the violence. Predicted shortages of some consumer items and disruption to many public services did not materialise for any length of time. In the industrial and commercial sectors, although the damage was known to be extensive, many felt that innate competitiveness would assist a speedy recovery. These signs were very welcome to the government which was well aware of the importance of restoring confidence and a sense of normality, so that vital investment from foreign firms and governments would not be jeopardised.

An important measure of such a restoration of normality would have been a return to 'business as usual' by all ethnic groups, most especially the Tamils. This paper will assess some of the implications of the violence of mid-1983 by looking at the experience of Tamils living in the predominantly Sinhalese hill country. It will focus upon three groups: public employees, the small business community and estate labourers.

First of all, how do they perceive the disturbances? Tamils in the hill country towns tend to disbelieve claims of both the government and many of its critics that the violence was mainly the work of a nationwide organisation. They view the violence which they experienced as organised but *locally* organised, a phenomenon perpetrated by what eyewitnesses often describe as groups of local 'thugs' and 'shanty people'. Local Sinhalese racketeers and local people thought to be possible charismatic leaders of the mobs of midsummer have shown inordinate sensitivity to examinations of evidence concerning the events of July and August. And many consumer items looted from Tamil premises have since been recovered from shanty areas. These developments lend credence to the view that pre-existing groups of urban thugs capitalised on the deteriorating situation for criminal purposes. Hill country Tamils' disbelief in a nationwide organisation does not, however, make them feel any less vulnerable since local attackers were far more likely than outsiders to be able to identify and target local Tamils.

How many have returned to normal working? Most Tamil public servants in the hill country have continued in their posts. Those who fled to the north and east appear to have felt the need to return rather quickly in the absence of any real possibility of obtaining a transfer in the already oversubscribed public sector. Many Tamils in this part of Sri Lanka have only weak links or no links at all with those apparently safe areas. People in public employment recognise that they cannot throw away the jobs that they have often fought hard to obtain, if for no other reason than sheer economic necessity. A number of senior professionals with recognisable skills in the medical and academic fields have either secured posts overseas or are seeking them with renewed urgency. But most Tamils in this sector have had to resign themselves to the need to return to normal work. There has as yet been no direct sabotage of their positions.

Tamils in the small business sector, consisting mainly of shopkeepers, have responded in a complex way. With a partially or totally destroyed business, there is little incentive to resume work. By successful claiming on insurance, a shopkeeper can convert his assets into liquid form and move away. But in the less badly hit provincial towns, where many Tamil retailers escaped major damage, the situation is not that simple. Here the businessman often feels as tied to his fixed assets as the public servant does to his job. He remains aware of the continuing demand in the particular market in which he has expertise. A commonly expressed sentiment is that a move to a Tamil area would not be sensible because of the existing competition in those areas.

Within this sector two quite extreme and opposed reactions were detected. In Kandy, for example, a number of the more successful retailers who were badly hit have taken advantage of the situation and decided not only to open up again, but to expand their operations. Where they once operated from a two-storeyed building they now claim that they will build a four-storeyed complex. A small group of traders have decided that they will expand their former operations by buying out not only their own premises which they held on lease, but also their neighbours' destroyed premises. They will also protect themselves for the future by striking up a partnership with a Sinhalese businessman. This sort of reaction is confined to the particularly successful merchants. At the other extreme, and perhaps more obvious in the smaller towns than in Kandy, is the retailer who has simply closed his shop and left, perhaps never to return.

Between these extremes stand many small businessmen, including both those who were hit and those who escaped, whose response has been tentative and ambiguous. Although ostensibly back at work as normal, they are operating scaled-down businesses with minimum overheads. Initially some of these businesses were not even re-stocking. Now that a number of months have passed since the violence, they have been forced to re-stock to stay in business. Whereas they would formerly buy in bulk, they are now stocking only about half a dozen of any one item. With stocks kept so low, they are suffering restrictions on suppliers' credits over and above the general credit squeeze that has been in existence in the country since the disturbances. This has resulted in a severe cash-flow problem for many of these Tamil small businesses. They are now operating on a severely reduced turnover, often as much as 50 per cent down on pre-July trading, with corresponding falls in profitability. Events during the months immediately following the violence indicate that any vacuum created by the departure or contraction of Tamil businesses will quickly be filled by Sinhalese and Muslim traders without any obvious shortages or inadequacies in service. What has partially occurred, and what could gather momentum, is a shift in small business activity in the hill country in favour of non-Tamil groups.

Many of the Tamil public employees who felt compelled to return to work find themselves unable to tackle their jobs with the same enthusiasm and vigour as before. Like many other Tamils in pre-dominantly Sinhalese areas, they have decided to split up their families, sending out wives and children to relatives in 'safe areas'. This has obviously led to a fairly unstable and unsatisfying state of affairs for the husbands who suffer all of the anxieties of separation and a lack of domestic security. These *de facto* bachelors no longer run a home but simply live in a home, taking their meals from local cafés and restaurants whenever possible. Many are anxious about their future which seems highly uncertain.

Estate labourers live grouped together on plantation lines, which means that they are less vulnerable than other members of the Tamil community, but also much less affluent — a more isolated and homogeneous group that is not well integrated into society. Since the violence, these estate labourers have been vociferous in demanding effective protection and security. As a result of the flight of many urban Tamils from neighbouring towns, they feel much more exposed. In an attempt to control and channel this emotion, many are now lobbying to be moved to higher elevation estates.

The estate labourers' response has, more than that of the others, been determined by a lack of reasonable alternatives. None the less, there exists among Indian Tamil estate workers a degree of out-migration such as has taken place after every incident of anti-Tamil violence since 1977. This now threatens to grow considerably. The patterns of migration are varied, ranging from a shift to estates further up country, to sectoral transfers to farming with estate workers ending up as wage labourers in the mainly Tamil north, to emigration to India or, increasingly, to the Middle East.

A major psychological change has occurred in all sectors of the Tamil community in the hill country since the violence. The terrible fear of midsummer has given way to a feeling of substantial depression and uncertainty. This has caused many people to feel less free in the way they live and work. Many seek to maintain a low profile and exhibit introverted tendencies without any desire to establish new friends or contacts. Businessmen, for example, claim to have severely cut marketing activities such as advertising, public relations, demonstrations and displays. Many Tamils admit to serious morale problems since the violence, to a considerable loss of interest in their work, and to high absenteeism. Many no longer have much hope of a minimal integration with the majority of the population. This has led to attempts by many to foster social and domestic links with the Tamil areas of the country. A certain amount of savings and profits are being converted into liquid form in the hill country and invested in property in the north, east and abroad. The tendency for Tamil labourers on estates to cluster in the higher elevations will similarly lead to a more isolated Indian Tamil plantation community. Increasingly Sinhalese labour will fill gaps left by Tamils, a trend which has already been observable for some time. In some mid-country estates, the Sinhalese element comprises more than 50 per cent of the labour force.

Many hill country Tamils see these recent changes as fundamental. The violence of mid-1983 has made them a weaker community. Their intensified isolation may arouse future antagonism, since any group that is perceived to be exclusive is a potential target. Far from bouncing back, most of them are cautiously and tentatively monitoring the situation. Many of them were quick to resurface and thereby created a sense of normality, but in reality they remain deeply uncertain and confused about the future. For the Tamils of the hill country, 'business as usual' can only be resumed if a lasting settlement is soon achieved.

NOTES ON CONTRIBUTORS

Lalith Athulathmudali is a barrister, and until recently Minister of Trade and Shipping in the Sri Lankan government. He is now Minister of National Security and Deputy Minister of Defence.

C.R. de Silva is Dean of Arts and Associate Professor of History at the University of Peradeniya.

James Manor is lecturer in Politics at the University of Leicester and Editor of the *Journal of Commonwealth and Comparative Politics*.

Eric Meyer is Director of the Centre d'Études de l'Inde et de l'Asie du Sud in Paris.

M.P. Moore is a Fellow of the Institute of Development Studies, University of Sussex.

Elizabeth Nissan is a doctoral candidate in anthropology at the London School of Economics.

Robert Oberst is Assistant Professor of Political Science at Nebraska Wesleyan University.

Gananath Obeyesekere is Professor of Anthropology at Princeton University.

'Priya Samarakone' is an established scholar in Sri Lanka who has convinced the Editor that there are compelling reasons for the use of a pseudonym.

R.P. Slater is a doctoral candidate in anthropology at the School of Oriental and African Studies, University of London.

Jonathan Spencer is a doctoral candidate at the Institute of Anthropology, University of Oxford.

R.L. Stirrat is Lecturer in Anthropology in the School of African and Asian Studies, University of Sussex.

219

INDEX

Compiled by Paul Nash